Beiträge zum Strafrecht –
Contributions to Criminal Law

edited by

Volume 7

Jörg Eisele (ed.)

Past and Future

Transitional Justice versus Traditional Criminal Justice?
Ways of Dealing with Past Conflicts and Past Autocracies

Nomos

This publication was printed with the financial support of the Elisabeth-Käsemann-Foundation gGmbH.

The Deutsche Nationalbibliothek lists this publication in the Deutsche Nationalbibliografie; detailed bibliographic data are available on the Internet at http://dnb.d-nb.de

ISBN 978-3-8487-6818-9 (Print)
978-3-7489-0918-7 (ePDF)

British Library Cataloguing-in-Publication Data
A catalogue record for this book is available from the British Library.

ISBN 978-3-8487-6818-9 (Print)
978-3-7489-0918-7 (ePDF)

Library of Congress Cataloging-in-Publication Data
Eisele, Jörg
Past and Future
Transitional Justice versus Traditional Criminal Justice? Ways of Dealing with Past Conflicts and Past Autocracies
Jörg Eisele (ed.)
216 pp.
Includes bibliographic references.

ISBN 978-3-8487-6818-9 (Print)
978-3-7489-0918-7 (ePDF)

Onlineversion
Nomos eLibrary

1st Edition 2020

3rd Elisabeth Käsemann Symposium, Buenos Aires 2019 Past andFuture

New Ways of Dealing with Conflicts and Autocracies Versus Traditional Criminal Prosecution

From 30 September until 2 October 2019, federal judges, lawyers and academics from Argentina, Germany and Columbia met at the University of Buenos Aires to discuss ways of dealing with past autocracies and violent conflicts. The conference focused on the opportunities and limits of traditional legal instruments and concepts of transitional justice. Based on specific national approaches, which are closely linked to the respective nation's administration of justice, the articles in this conference transcript offer not only insights into the respective legal systems but also important findings on the social context of the different ways of coming to terms with an adversarial and authoritarian past.

The three-day conference, held by the Elisabeth Käsemann Foundation in cooperation with the Criminal Law and Criminology Department of the Law Faculty of the University of Buenos Aires and its director Mario Villar, and the Chair of the German and European Criminal Law and Criminal Procedural Law, Commercial Criminal Law and Cyber Law at the Eberhard Karls University of Tübingen under Jörg Eisele, made a relevant contribution to the intercontinental transfer of knowledge on dealing with crimes against humanity, and deepened personal relations between the German and Latin American participants.

We would like to thank all the contributors for sharing their outstanding expertise at the symposium, and for providing their articles for this publication.

Especially, I would like to thank Mario Villar for the generous hospitality, Jörg Eisele for the expert conference concept, and Daniel Rafecas for his willingness to support the idea for this symposium and its realisation.

We are deeply grateful to Silvina Alonso for her professional arrangement of the conference at the Universidad Buenos Aires, and to Ramiro Vera-Fluixa for discreetly looking after the logistics during the conference.

A great many thanks go to Scott Stelle for the English edit, and to Kristine Böhm for her meticulous final edit.

Dorothee Weitbrecht, managing director of the Elisabeth Käsemann Foundation

Stuttgart, August 2020

Content

International Dialogue as a tool for truth and accountability: shared experiences in the third Elisabeth Käsemann Symposium

Fabián Martínez, LL.M.

I. Introduction

For the third time the Elisabeth Käsemann Foundation organised its symposium in order to foster cooperation and international dialogue about coming to terms with the past and creating a commemorative culture. This year's theme revolved around the issues of traditional prosecution and alternative ways of dealing with crimes in scenarios of large-scale human rights violations, with the examples of Germany, Argentina and Colombia.

As a trilateral academic exchange of ideas and experiences the event provided the opportunity to present the different approaches of recovering from violent conflict which these three countries have pursued in the face of a somewhat similar problem: systemic human rights violations due to autocratic regimes or armed conflict.

The German approach in dealing with the crimes of the Nazi regime showed a focus on the prosecution of the perpetrators through traditional legal instruments and a commitment between the State and society for memory and non-repetition. The Argentinian approach moved between early efforts to prosecute the senior leaders of the dictatorship followed by amnesty laws, the reaction of the civil society and a struggle for justice, truth and dignity for the victims. For its part Colombia has taken a different approach to transitional justice in order to put an end to a 60 year long armed conflict and recently implemented an "Integrated System of Truth, Justice, Reparation and Non-Repetition" departing from the path of traditional criminal prosecution in exchange for recognition of individual responsibility and reparations for victims.

II. The Panels

The first panel took on the traditional legal instruments used to bring justice to the societies that have experienced autocratic regimes. In Argentina it has been necessary to reform the legal system for taking into account crimes enshrined in international criminal law. The aim should be to transform the previous jurisprudence into an adjudicated right that is accepted by society. An arduous and hard-fought process has led to the use of international law to prosecute crimes committed during the military dictatorship.

In Germany the jurisprudence which initially allowed prosecuting lower-ranking perpetrators who had participated in the Holocaust changed around the nineteen-sixties, making it more difficult to obtain a judgement without evidence of direct participation of the crimes. Only until 2014 the Federal Court of Justice returned to the criteria that allowed a broader take on participation, paving the way for the trials of the last surviving perpetrators.

The second panel touched on the leniency programs in Germany and Colombia, but not in Argentina where the legal system has not considered such programs in cases of crimes related to the dictatorship. In Germany the legislation has provided for leniency programs to uncover conspiratorial backgrounds of crimes, mostly to tackle terrorism and organized crime, but also in the case of state-organized crimes committed by police, military or paramilitary units. Practitioners tend to support the leniency programs. Academia, on the opposite side, takes a sceptical view of leniency programs, criticising the conflicts of them with other legal principles characteristic of the German legal system.

In Colombia the leniency programs had traditionally been used to face organized crime and politically motivated acts of violence but without considering the interests of victims, turning them as a general legal remedy to shorten or suspend proceedings, in order to avoid the risk of overburdening the courts. With the signing of the peace agreement between the Colombian guerrilla organization and the national government, a new approach to transitional justice was enshrined into an innovative form of mixed transitional justice, consisting of judicial (the Special Jurisdiction for Peace) and extrajudicial (a truth commission and unit for the search for missing persons). In contrast, Argentina has been sceptical of amnesties and other forms of leniency mechanisms in matters related to the crimes of the dictatorship. Today, on the basis of international law, and in particular since the Rome Statute came into force, a reduction in punishment, but never impunity, could be offered.

The third panel discussed the role of truth commissions in the reconciliation processes not only in the three countries but also with an overview of different African experiences. An important outcome of these discussions is that what reconciliation means and how it is achieved varies according to the specificities of each society. Thus, the supposedly contradictory approaches of truth commissions and criminal trials should be reconsidered. The models of truth commission and traditional criminal justice should not be understood as closed and incompatible systems. Moreover, a combination of measures from both models could be constructive. For instance, the Argentinian experience shows that thanks to the work of the civil society organizations in Argentina, the "right to truth" has become a pillar of the international jurisprudence in human rights.

III. Conclusions

Germany, Argentina and Colombia have lived through troubled times, each country had to endure atrocities that shaped their core values. Those kinds of challenges cannot be compared in scale nor in gravity, but the endeavours undertaken to come to terms with the past, to satisfy the right of the victims for truth and justice and to give the society a chance to overcome autocracy and violence should be studied and serve as guidance for other countries in similar situations.

There are idiosyncrasies of the legal systems that lead to seemingly opposing solutions: Germany had to reconcile with itself for the evils of the Nazi regime, and for that it built an admirable constitutional system with fundamental rights and the democratic rule of law at its core. In Argentina, there was no place for leniency programs for perpetrators of human rights violations, not least thanks to the engagement of the civil society against a system that favoured impunity. In Colombia, after many legal reforms only a less punitive approach to criminal liability served as a way out of the armed conflict, but the sacrifices in terms of retribution should be compensated with truth, reparations and guarantees of non-repetition.

However individual the paths chosen for each country, there is a common ground between them. Impunity is unacceptable for accountability is the best deterrent; truth is a right not only for the victims but also for the society as a whole. Finally, the international community is a strategic ally that accompanies, supports and, when needed, gives voice to the claims of victims.

The platform offered by the Elisabeth Käsemann Foundation to discuss matters of justice, memory and reconciliation is as important today as it has ever been. For these questions should always be present, to honour those who suffered injustice and restore the dignity once taken away by the arbitrariness of violence

I. Traditional legal Instruments

The Argentine Criminal Code Reform

Prof. Dr. Mariano Borinsky[*]

I. Introduction

The criminal justice system considers war crimes, crimes against humanity, genocide and the crime of aggression, directly as fundamental crimes, because they are the most serious for the international community. This affirmation demands that the maximum efforts be made in the field of the administration of justice, for which it is essential to have substantive and adjective normative instruments that can rise to the challenge.

In Argentina, the coming to power of the last military government, starting on March 24, 1976, resulted in the existence and organization of the state power that, based on a systematic criminal plan based on a doctrine of action, used the public force of the State as a whole for the achievement of the ideological and political purposes that inspired it.

The recovery of Democracy in 1983 led to the possibility of subjecting to a constitutionally valid trial the deployment of those behaviours that were the result of State terrorism. There was a first stage of judgements, marked by selectivity in terms of authors and based on some principle of efficiency, with substantiation of criminal proceedings and convictions to military and civilians.

However, with the sanction of the laws "due obedience" and "end point" a large number of criminal cases aimed at investigating the acts committed during the last military dictatorship were paralysed; situation chart that was drastically modified with the realization of the “truth trials”, in compliance with the recommendations of the Inter-American Commission on Human Rights so that the Argentine State could guarantee the truth claims (Report 28/92). Then a second stage took place, in which the mere "clarification" of the facts as a way of fulfilling the duties (and powers) of the Argentine State in that direction was considered sufficient.

---

* Federal judge, professor at the law faculty, University of Buenos Aires, president of the Comisión para la reforma del Código Penal, federal judge at the Cámara Federal de Casación Pena.

The third stage – which we can consider contemporary – began with the issuance of the "Arancibia Clavel" ruling[1], which determined the retroactive application of the imprescriptibility of criminal action for such crimes against humanity; in addition to the issuance of the "Simón" ruling[2], which declared the unconstitutionality of laws 23.492 (final point) and 23.521 (due obedience), denying those norms any effect that could oppose the progress of the processes or to the trial and eventual conviction of those responsible, or hinder ongoing investigations. Thus, we returned to a criminal process but expanding the basis of facts and authors.

These decisions (to which others were added, by which the right to the truth about the facts involving serious human rights violations[3]) recognized the victim a leading role in this type of process[4] – and replaced the reach of the guarantee "res judicata", compatible with the crimes investigated[5] – and also produced the opening and advancement of a large number of causes throughout the country.

It is paradigmatic that such efforts to raise any risk of impunity in the face of events of such great significance for our history will develop without having a correlation with the adequacy of repressive legislation. As well as that after thirty-six years of the return of the constitutional order the repressive legislation on the matter has not been updated in accordance with the parameters that force our country internationally.

II. The Criminal Code Reform Commission

The Project prepared by the Criminal Code Reform Commission[6] seeks to pay off that fundamental debt of Argentine legislation, by proposing to incorporate in the Criminal Code the criminal figures accepted by the Argentine State after ratification of international instruments such as the Convention on the Prevention and Punishment of the Crime of Genocide and the Convention on the Non-Applicability of Statutory Limitations to War Crimes and Crimes Against Humanity. Numerous legislative projects attempted to engrave such crimes into our repressive substantive legislation. However, none of these initiatives managed to have legislative treat-

1 Judgements: 327: 2312.
2 Judgements: 328: 2056.
3 "Urteaga", Judgements: 321: 2767.
4 "Hagelin", Judgements: 326: 3268.
5 "Videla", Judgements: 326: 2805.
6 Created by Decree 103/17.

ment by the full Chamber. That is why this Project constitutes a renewed and fundamental opportunity to settle that debt, a commitment not only political and legal but also moral, as a way of recognizing the peculiar harmfulness of practices such as genocide and crimes against humanity for the whole of the Argentine population

It should be noted at this point that the National Criminal Code currently in force in the Republic of Argentina is from 1921 and has suffered numerous modifications – around 900 – that caused it to lose its organic and systematic character.

Given this scenario, on March 1, 2017, the Commission for the Reform of the National Criminal Code[7] was established, with the main objective of preparing a draft reform law and comprehensive update of the National Criminal Code that concentrates all criminal legislation in a single regulatory body.

The Commission worked on the basis of the current Criminal Code, trying to maintain its original structure, also worked with the National Constitution as a supreme law, as well as international conventions ratified by the Argentine Republic, integrated special criminal laws, systematizing them in a single system, assessed the projects of criminal reform with parliamentary status and considered the work done by the previous 17 Commissions of Reform of the Criminal Code. Especially the Preliminary Draft Criminal Code presented in 2006 by the members of the "Commission for the Preparation of the Draft Law on the Reform and Comprehensive Update of the Criminal Code"[8], the Draft Criminal Code presented in 2014 by the "Commission for the Preparation of the Draft Law on the Reform, Update and Integration of the National Criminal Code"[9] and the text proposed by the Renewal Front[10].

The Commission also analysed the comparative law, the jurisprudence of the Supreme Court of Justice of the Argentine Nation and the lower courts, the doctrine and the advances in the area of regional integration of the country, in order to favour the harmonization of legislation in its fundamental aspects, to promote and facilitate cooperation between States and the implementation of coordinated strategies, these elements of ut-

7 Decree of the National Executive Power № 103/17.

8 Draft 2006- (created by Resolution of the Ministry of Justice and Human Rights N ° 303, of December 14, 2004).

9 Draft 2012- (created by National Executive Power Decree No. 678/12, of May 7, 2012).

10 File number 3518-D2015 of 06/19/15 before the Honourable Chamber of Deputies of the Nation.

most importance in the face of certain criminal modalities such as transnational organized crime (terrorism, drug trafficking and corruption).

Also, in order to ensure federal and pluralistic representation of society, requesting the protection and promotion of human rights, the Commission received and took into account the opinion of Non-Governmental Organizations, associations that bring together victims or relatives of victims of criminal acts.

Communication channels were opened through the Justice 2020 Program through the Ministry of Justice and Human Rights of the Nation, so that citizens can express their concerns and concerns.

The Commission met with governors, deputies and senators from across the national territory and from across the political arch, as well as with ministers, academics and system operators to ensure the federal nature of the Criminal Code, which is applicable throughout the Argentine Republic. It held meetings and exchanges with the National Ministries of Security, Justice and Human Rights, Social Development, Agribusiness, Health and Environment and Sustainable Development, as well as received specialists in related disciplines or related to criminal matters.

On March 25, 2019, the National Executive Power sent the bill to approve this new Penal Code to the National Senate. He entered through the Unicameral Commission of Justice and Criminal Matters. In turn, the Minister of Justice and Human Rights of the Nation, Germán Garavano together with the President of the Unicameral Commission of Justice and Criminal Matters, Pedro Guillermo Ángel Guastavino, made presentations before the Senate of the Nation on June 4, 2019.

The Commission for the Reform of the National Criminal Code is made up of a plurality and heterogeneity of intervenors, men and women, who are in permanent contact with the current practical problems that are manifested in the application of criminal law.

Judges and prosecutors of the Judicial Power of the Nation and of the provinces, members of the Public Prosecutor's Office, the Ministry of Justice and Human Rights of the Nation, the Ministry of National Security and the Ministry of Social Development of the Nation, university professors and lawyers, who are linked to professional practice and the daily problem of the exercise of criminal law.

Within the new modalities contemplated by the Draft Criminal Code we find terrorism and its financing; drug traffic and drug related crimes; tax, customs and exchange crimes; military crimes; the illegal traffic and permanence of migrants; crimes against freedom and dignity of work; organ trafficking, blood and genetic crimes; the crimes against the Environment as well as crimes against Archaeological and Paleontological Heritage; crimes in sport; computer crimes; crimes against intellectual property; and – especially in what is of interest for this exhibition – crimes against the international order (genocide, crimes against humanity, aggression and war crimes).

III. The newest Reform of the Criminal Code

For the first time, a new Book to the Criminal Code is included, proving the importance that has the set of crimes to which we have just made outstanding reference is evident for the Draft Criminal Code.

The decision to include a new Third Book to the Criminal Code, which typifies crimes against humanity, forced disappearance of people, genocide, war crimes and crimes against the administration of justice of the International Criminal Court, is due to the need to contain within the same framework a general part of these crimes, since they have a different nature from the remaining crimes currently provided for in the Criminal Code and the new criminal modalities that are incorporated in the Draft. General rules applicable to the aforementioned international crimes and definitions currently contained in international instruments are established in this new Book, in order to give them autonomy with respect to the remaining crimes of the Criminal Code.

Among the specific general rules that characterize this class of crimes are the imprescriptibility of the criminal action and the penalty imposed, the inapplicability of the pardon or amnesty, the universal jurisdiction, as well as the circumstance that obedience cannot be invoked as a defence due to the orders of the superiors.

However, the applicability of the general rules set forth in the First Book of the Criminal Code is also established, insofar as they are compatible with international jus cogens and the nature of international crimes.

The formulation of the structure of the Third Book took into account international treaties ratified by the Argentine Republic on the subject, such as the Inter-American Convention on the Forced Disappearance of Persons, the Convention on the Prevention and Punishment of the Crime of Genocide and in the Statute of Rome of the International Criminal Court, and national legislation, in particular, Law 26.200, and it was decided to incorporate crimes in different Titles and Chapters, together with the specific international law definitions applicable.

In that direction, the crimes of forced disappearance of persons, genocide, crimes against humanity, war crimes and crimes against the administration of justice of the International Criminal Court were incorporated into the Criminal Code in the new Third Book. Maximum penalties were established in the criminal legal system – maximum sentence of life imprisonment -, revealing the importance of legal assets in guardianship.

In turn, taking into account that through Law 27.318 the Argentine Republic ratified the Amendment to Article 8 of the Rome Statute of the International Criminal Court, adopted at the Review Conference of the Rome Statute, which took place in the city of Kampala – Republic of Uganda – from May 31 to June 11, 2010, approved by resolution 5 of June 10, 2010, the crime of aggression was also incorporated.

With respect to the crime of forced disappearance of a person, it was decided to transfer the typification of the current article 142 ter of the Criminal Code to the Third Book, since by its characteristics it is compatible with the general rules applicable to crimes against the international order, especially taking into account account of what is indicated by the Inter-American Court of Human Rights in the decision "Bulacio vs. Argentina"[11].

In addition, it was decided to eliminate the aggravating circumstance currently provided for in article 142b, when the victim is a person born during the forced disappearance of his mother. This, since, after consulting with experts in international law, it was understood that such a rule would lead to the inconsistency that the perpetrators of this type of crime receive less penalty when they perform abortions on unborn children of mothers who are victims of crime of forced disappearance of a person who when they allow their birth. Therefore, in order to provide proportionality and consistency to the Criminal Code, this aggravating factor was eliminated.

On the other hand, the elimination of this aggravating factor allows the imputation of the forced disappearance of the mother in a real contest with that of the children born in that situation. This reflects the reality of what happened, which is not a single criminal act, particularly aggravated by the birth in these conditions, but two independent acts of forced disappearance of persons, for which their perpetrators must be tried and convicted.

With regard to the crime of genocide, the wording of Art. 6 of the Rome Statute and the Genocide Convention of 1948 is maintained. The penalty of life imprisonment is provided when the death of any person occurs, according to art. 80 of the Second Book that includes aggravated homicides and the criminal code in force, as well as in accordance with Law 26.200.

---

11 Judgement of September 18, 2003, Merits, Reparations and Costs.

In addition, the crime of instigation of genocide is incorporated. French law provides for this figure in art. 211–2 of the French Criminal Code and responds to the provisions of section "e" of the paragraph of art. 25 of the Rome Statute.

The crimes against humanity include the crime of apartheid under the Rome Statute. It is understood that it must be included due to the possibility of judging in the country facts committed outside its territory, in accordance with the rules of the principle of spatial validity of the criminal law, and in addition, in accordance with the Convention on imprescriptibility – Law 24,584 – which includes apartheid.

The crime of illicit recruitment of minors – 18 years of age – is defined as a war crime. Although according to the Rome Statute, the infraction consists in the recruitment of children under fifteen (15) years of age, Law 26,200 established as age 18, in accordance with the International Convention of the Child.

The crimes against the administration of justice of the International Criminal Court are provided for in the Rome Statute and were included in the Third Book with the penalties indicated in Law 26.200.

The impossibility of accessing probation for repeat offenders and for those convicted of malicious crimes committed with violence that have caused serious physical or mental harm or death to the victim is maintained. For example, for crimes against humanity, genocide, war crimes and terrorism until they have completed 35 years in prison or, in case of multiple recidivism, 40 years.

Finally, in the new Criminal Code it is contemplated the possibility of confiscating the assets in advance and in a definitive manner – before the criminal conviction – for all crimes (including crimes against humanity in case certain conditions are verified, whether the subject asset involved a natural or legal person.

IV. Conclusion

Up to this point, we can see that the criminal justice system has dealt with sufficiency, but also at the cost of a big effort, the crimes against humanity committed during the last Argentine military dictatorship, despite the fluctuations derived of the conjunctures that marked each one of the stages of his judgement and even without counting on a positive order that was at the height of such circumstances. We find there a merit related to a traditional way in the persecution of this kind of conflicts linked to the past, within a context of post conflict.

Actually, the recognition and systematic location of these crimes in a new book of the projected Criminal Code, independent of the rest of the crimes of the digest and for the amounts of penalty provided for these cases – of life imprisonment, maximum penalty provided for in the legal order – they reflect the relevance that the Argentine society granted to Human Rights within its value system.

This transformation does not attempt to start over, but to build, order and improve from what we have and know; by the hand of tools that were already implemented, although with significant friction quotas and jurisdictional wear that, we understand, would have been paved to have directly had the appropriate regulatory mechanisms within the Criminal Code (as an example, the paradigmatic figure of the "disappeared" lacked a correlation in the existence of the definition of forced disappearance of persons in the vernacular legislation in the background).

Regardless of any quota of normative fetishism – which we allow ourselves to discard, based on the awareness acquired about such a deep problem over the years during which the issuance of numerous convictions ratified even in the highest judicial instance – we understands that the importance of the proposal towards positive law will have the ability to build an unprecedented communication bridge with society. It is a safe-conduct that will revalidate the path taken by judicial law, with a very clear message about the reaffirmed repudiation towards those forms of crime, although with closer tools – everyday ones – for those who integrate the justice administration service.

Traditional legal instruments: Germany and the Prosecution of National Socialist Crimes

Jens Rommel[*]

I. Introduction

The term transitional justice covers the full range of processes and mechanisms associated with a society's attempt to come to terms with a legacy of large-scale past abuses.[1] When we use this term with regard to national socialist crimes *during* the Second World War, we should take into account that this notion has arisen from the confrontation with dictatorships and armed conflicts (internal or international) *since* the Second World War.[2] Except for truth commissions, over the decades all transitional justice mechanisms have been applied to some extentextend in Germany: criminal prosecution, amnesty[3], restitution[4], and verification of public service[5]. The present text will only deal with the efforts through criminal law in the Federal Republic of Germany.

The hitherto unknown extent of national socialist crimes during the dictatorship in Germany since 1933 and during the Second World War from

---

* Judge at the Federal Court of Justice, Karlsruhe; 2015 – 2020 Chief Public Prosecutor at the Central Office for the Investigation of National Socialist Crimes, Ludwigsburg.

1 Report of the Secretary-General – The rule of law and transitional justice in conflict and post-conflict societies; UN Doc. S/2004/612 of 23rd August 2004, p. 4.

2 Gerhard Werle/Moritz Vormbaum: Transitional Justice – Vergangenheitsbewältigung durch Recht [, Berlin 2018], p. 5.

3 There were two express amnesty settlements in 1949 and 1954; Gesetz über die Gewährung von Straffreiheit vom 31. Dezember 1949; Federal Law Gazette (Bundesgesetzblatt) I, p. 37 and Gesetz über den Erlass von Strafen und Geldbußen und die Niederschlagung von Strafverfahren und Bußgeldverfahren (Straffreiheitsgesetz 1954) vom 17. Juli 1954; Federal Law Gazette (Bundesgesetzblatt) I, p. 203.

4 The so-called indemnity includes measures from the first Federal Compensation Act 1953 to the establishment of the Foundation "Remembrance, Responsibility, Future" in the year 2000.

5 In the public service review, one can point to the very broad Allied approach to denazification, which was not limited to civil service – on the other hand, the provisions of the Act on Article 131 of the Basic Law are in the opposite direction.

1939 to 1945 has led to different answers: by the Allies in the International Military Tribunal at Nuremberg[6], by numerous foreign states that have punished the crimes committed on their territory, by the four occupying powers in Germany[7], and finally by the Federal Republic of Germany and the (former) German Democratic Republic. The international approach may be characterized by three attributes:

(1) After the end of the war, special penal provisions wereare laid down retroactively, specifically tailored to state mass crimes, especially crimes against humanity.
(2) Only for these procedures, a special tribunal is set up, whose staff comes from the victorious powers.
(3) The process is based on a specially created procedural code partially restricting the rights of the defence.

There are considerable reservations about this approach in Germany. The argument of "victors' justice" was rather political – meaning an unfair procedure by the winners of WW II against the losers. A legal objection is relevant: The Allied laws apply with retroactive effect to crimes committed before the rules were passed. In Germany, therefore, the accusation is raised loudly that this approach violated itself the elementary legal principle "*nulla poena sine lege*". As a reaction to "Nuremberg" – but also to the experiences with the abuse of criminal law during Hitler's dictatorship – the German constitution upholds a strict prohibition of retroactive penal law.[8] In addition, there was a political motto: "„No special law for Nazi perpetrators".". This led to a solution that deviated in all three points from that of the Allies:

- the applicable law (II.)
- the competence of the general law enforcement authorities (III.)
- the general procedure and rules of evidence (IV).

---

6 Agreement for the prosecution and punishment of the major war criminals of the European Axis, Signed at London, on 8 August 1945; https://www.un.org/en/genocideprevention/documents/atrocity-crimes/Doc.2_Charter%20of%20IMT%201945.pdf.

7 Control Council Law No. 10; Punishment of persons guilty of war crimes, crimes against peace and against humanity, 20 December 1945; www.legal-tools.org/doc/ffda62/pdf/.

8 Article 103, Paragraph 2 of the Basic Law for the Federal Republic of Germany.

II. Difficulties with the prosecution of the crime of genocide and crimes against humanity committed by a state on the base of traditional offencesoffenses

1. Legal basis in the criminal code

In (Western) Germany, no special legal basis has been established retroactively for dealing with national socialist (NS) crimes. The crime of genocide was incorporated in the Criminal Code in 1954.[9] Crimes against peace are stipulated in the Constitution and since 1968 the Criminal Code[10]. The offenceoffense "Crimes against humanity" washas been introduced only in 2002[11]. Consequently, German courts can only pass judgements in accordance with the provisions of the German criminal code – applicable already during the "Third Reich"[12].

2. Mass murders

The "mass murders by state authority [were] an unprecedented novelty in history [...] to which the penal code was not tailored"[13]. This raises the problem that usually a perpetrator acts against the state order – and criminal law tries to establish his individual guilt. When it comes to Nazi murders, the state itself tolerated or even organized the crimes on various levels through its administration, police and military or party organizations.

9 Section 220a – now section 6 of the German International Criminal Code – Völkerstrafgesetzbuch vom 26. Juni 2002, Federal Law Gazette (Bundesgesetzblatt) I, p. 2254; www.gesetze-im-internet.de/vstgb.

10 Article 26 of the Basic Law for the Federal Republic of Germany; Section 80 – Vorbereitung eines Angriffskriegs; today Section 13 of the German International Criminal Code: Crime of Aggression.

11 Section 7 of the German International Criminal Code; When the general powers in the former British and French Occupational Occupationals Zones were cancelled the application of Control Council Law No. 10 was terminated on 31st August 1951, which had been the basis for judgements on crimes against humanity by German courts; Edith Raim, Nazi Crimes against Jews and German post-war justice [Berlin 2017].

12 (German) Criminal Code, 15th May 1871 – in the version promulgated on 13 November 1998, Federal Law Gazette (Bundesgesetzblatt) I p. 3322; www.gesetze-im-internet.de/englisch_stgb; Some argue that the mass murders had been committed in accordance of the German law of the time; e. g. Gerhard Werle/Thomas Wandres, Auschwitz vor Gericht [Munich 1995], p. 38.

13 Federal Court of Justice (Bundesgerichtshof), 24th May 1968 – 5 StR 704/68; juris.

Our criminal law and procedural law are based on individual acts, i.e. the behaviour of a perpetrator as far as it can be seen as a uniform event from a natural point of view. When it comes to mass crimes, many killings have to be qualified as a unity: On the one hand, this helps to preserve the meaning of an individual's acts as part of the extermination program. On the other hand, the crimes must also be manageable by means of criminal law. There was no clear line in the German practice: Largely, the indictments and verdicts focus on the victims of a given deportation train to a concentration camp.[14] Regarding the extermination camps Sobibor, Treblinka and Belzec, the entire camp activity was considered to be one crime.[15] In recent trials on Auschwitz, the "Hungary action" was seen as such a unity: several weeks of deportation with more than 300.000 victims in Auschwitz-Birkenau.[16] However, the Federal Court of Justice (Bundesgerichtshof) has explicitly refused to see all murders in Auschwitz as one crime.[17]

3. *Offences*

We have to deal with the definitions in the code, established for individual acts with individual motives: distinguishing for example between different offences of killing. Almost all offences are statute barred since May 1960: Manslaughter, bodily harm with fatal consequences and unlawful detention with fatal consequences as well as petty and grand larceny were typical offence during deportation and in concentration camps.

Only murder (Section 211 of the Criminal Code) was liable at the time of commission to the death penalty but since the coming into force of the Basic Law for the Federal Republic of Germany to (mandatory) life-long imprisonment. Murder in the understanding of German criminal law is not any premeditated killing but defined by special circumstances or mo-

14 Federal Court of Justice (Bundesgerichtshof), 20th February 1969 – 2 StR 280/67, NJW 1969, 2056 = Justiz und NS-Verbrechen, vol. XXI, p. 838 ff. (Verfahren Nr. 595b), Auschwitz case.

15 Federal Court of Justice (Bundesgerichtshof): Treblinka – 3 StR 17/68, Justiz und NS-Verbrechen, vol. XXII, p. 221; Sobibór – 4 StR 47–48/69, Justiz und NS-Verbrechen vol. XXV, p. 234; Belzec – 1 StR 464/65, juris.

16 Federal Court of Justice (Bundesgerichtshof), 20th September 2016 – 3 StR 49/16; juris, Gröning case; see Nestler infra p. 40 f.

17 Federal Court of Justice (Bundesgerichthof), 20th February 1969 – 2 StR 280/67, NJW 1969, 2056 = Justiz und NS-Verbrechen, vol. XXI, p. 838 ff. (No. 595b), Auschwitz case.

tives: A murderer is a person who kills another person "from thirst of blood, for sexual gratification, out of greed or otherwise base motives, by stealth or cruelly or by means that pose a danger to the public or in order to facilitate or to cover up another offence". An example for stealth would be the killing in gas chambers, where the victims were unaware of what was coming. A (recent) verdict qualifies as "cruel killing" the forced labour of prisoners without any or adequate housing, nourishment or medical support and the following painful dying due to lack diseases.[18]

4. *Individual responsibility*

There is no room in criminal legislation for the concept that mere membership in an agency or unit participating in a crime provides *prima facie* evidence of culpable conduct.[19]

The early years of criminal investigation were marked by the demarcation between perpetrator and accessory – with some problematic results: By accenting the subjective element, many accused were only regarded as accessories, which led to extremely mild penalties.[20]

The most difficult legal question is: Where does personal responsibility begin in a criminal regime? For a long time, the jurisdiction was prevalent: Not everyone who was *somehow* integrated into Auschwitz concentration camp is responsible for *everything* that happened in the context of the extermination program. Rather, it must be demonstrated how the individual's behaviour *concretely* supported the murders.[21] Only in 2016, the Federal Court of Justice (Bundesgerichtshof) has clarified where to draw the line: Today, it is sufficient for someone to have kept the murder machine

18 Regional Court (Landgericht) Detmold, 17th June 2016 – 4 Ks 45 Js 3/13- 9/15, juris.

19 Article 2 paragraph 1 lit d of Control Council Law No. 10 (Membership in categories of a criminal group or organization declared criminal by the International Military Tribunal) or nowadays sections 129 and 129a/b of the Criminal Code (forming criminal/terrorist organizations).

20 Federal Court of Justice (Bundesgerichtshof), 19th October 1962 – 9 StE 4/62; NJW 1963, 355 – Staschynskij case; see Nestler infra p 34.

21 Federal Court of Justice (Bundesgerichthof), 20th February 1969 – 2 StR 280/67, NJW 1969, 2056 = Justiz und NS-Verbrechen, vol. XXI, p. 838 ff. (Verfahren Nr. 595b), Auschwitz case.

running by performing his general duties in a certain function (e. g. as a guard).[22]

5. *The plea of "superior orders"*

An important role in the defence put forward by the accused in Nazi trials is the frequent invoking of the plea of "superior orders". According to the Military Penal Code[23], where the execution of an order in respect of official duties infringes a penal law, the sole responsibility for this shall be borne by the superior officer issuing the order. His subordinate carrying out the order shall however be deemed to be an accessory

(1) if he exceeded the bounds of the order issued.
(2) if he was aware that the order issued by his superior concerned an act designed to bring about a general offence or crime.

6. *Duress*

Since the days of the trials in Nuremberg, defendants have argued time and again that they only committed the alleged crimes in the face of an otherwise inevitable threat to their own life and limb. Indeed, according the Criminal Code a "person who, faced with an imminent danger to life, limb or freedom which cannot otherwise be averted, commits an unlawful act to avert the danger from himself, a relative or person close to him, acts without guilt."[24] The Central Office has looked into every case in which it was firmly alleged that refusal to carry out a criminal order would have resulted in injury to their life and limb: There was no single instance where the allegation was substantiated.[25]

Much greater practical significance attaches to "putative duress". As the results of judicial investigations have shown, there is no denying the conviction held by many subordinates or deliberately induced in them by

22 Federal Court of Justice (Bundesgerichtshof), 20th September 2016 – 3 StR 49/16; juris, Gröning case; see Nestler infra 40 f.
23 Section 47 of the Military Penal Code of 10th October 1940 – Law Gazette (Reichsgesetzblatt) I, p. 1347.
24 Section 35 of the Criminal Code (current version).
25 Rückerl, The Investigation of Nazi Crimes 1945–1978 – A Documentation, Heidelberg [1979], p. 81.

their former superiors that refusal to carry out even manifestly criminal orders would put their life and limb in jeopardy. Such an emergency situation sincerely believed to exist on the strength of false assumptions counts, pursuant to the court rulings, as excluding guilt and frees the person concerned from prosecution.[26] In Western Germany, many proceedings have been terminated on these grounds, especially against lower-ranking defendants.

7. *Statutory limitations*

Recourse to the general criminal law led to the application of the usual statutory limitations. Only NS crimes defined as murder can be prosecuted already since May 1960. This is the result of a broad discussion in German Parliament in 1965, 1969, and 1979 that also reflected the international development: the non-prescription of genocide and crimes against humanity. Here again, the German solution is not limited to Nazi crimes but applicable to any murder case.

When it comes to accessories, the situation is more complicated.[27] Due to a clandestine legislative change in 1968, prove of intent is no longer sufficient regarding murder out of base motives. Here, we have to prove that the accessory himself acted out of racial hatred or antisemitism as his personal motive. This is particularly difficult for "armchair culprits" such as the bureaucrats in the Reichssicherheitshauptamt (RSHA) where the deportation and extinction of Jews was planned and organized.

III. *The advantage of a centralized prosecutorial office in such cases*

1. *Problems with the traditional decentralized approach*

In addition to these material problems there are no special provisions concerning the procedure or jurisdiction. The judicial power is exercised mainly by the courts of the *Länder* – meaning a decentralized system.[28] The

26 Rückerl, (fn. 25), p. 82.

27 Section 50 paragraph 2 of the Criminal Code (now Section 28 paragraph 1); Adalbert Rückerl, (fn. 25), p. 62.

28 Unlike acts of terrorism, there is no competence for federal institutions when it comes to Nazi crimes (Article 96 paragraph 5 Basic Law).

local public prosecutor's offices and criminal courts are primarily responsible only for crimes conducted in their district or for defendants resided in the respective area. However, most of the crimes had been committed outside Western Germany. Often, the victims did not know the names of the suspects or their whereabouts. Thus, in the beginning no institution seemed to have jurisdiction to deal e.g. with Auschwitz.

In addition to these legal restrictions, in the early years there were de-facto-limitations on the prosecution of Nazi criminals due to shortage of manpower in the judiciary and police, and registration documents getting lost. The division into zones of occupation also made supra-local communication difficult and showed already the lack of coordination of public prosecution. In the 50s50ies, staff in administration and police, prosecutor's offices and courts were re-employed, who had exercised their offices during the dictatorship. Even if obstruction is difficult to determine on a case-by-case basis, these people should not have had any particular interest in effective prosecution.[29]

2. *Creation of the Central Office*

Just as the number of procedures had decreased sharply in the mid-fifties, the approach in the Federal Republic changed. By mere coincidence, there was the so called "task force trial" *(Einsatzgruppen-Prozess)* in Ulm[30]. Two things became clear to the public and politicians: Not all crimes had been investigated. And, we can no longer leave it to chance to determine whether a crime is prosecuted.

That is why the Ministers of Justice have founded the Central Office for the Investigation of National Socialist Crimes in Ludwigsburg in 1958[31]. An authority was and still is needed filling the considerable gap within the areas of judicial competence, an authority that would do some preparatory

29 Rückerl, (fn. 25), p. 127.

30 Regional Court (Landgericht) Ulm, 29th August 1958 – Ks 2/57, Justiz und NS-Verbrechen, vol. XV, p. 1 (No. 465).

31 Administrative Agreement – Verwaltungsvereinbarung über die Errichtung einer Zentralen Stelle der Landesjustizverwaltungen zur Aufklärung nationalsozialistischer Verbrechen of 6th November 1958, amended by agreement of 24th January 1967; sl.juris.de/sl/gesamt/NSUnrZtrStEVwVbg_SL.htm.

work in advance, push and bundle investigations of the public prosecutor's offices and provide support for them.[32]

3. *Task and ways of working*

The task of the Central Office is to collect, to scrutinise and to evaluate the whole accessible material on NS crimes worldwide. The Central Office was initially restricted to investigating crimes that occurred *outside* of Western Germany and only those related to wartime operations (but committed beyond such operations) against civilians. In 1964, this competence of the Central Office was extended to NS crimes committed *in* Western Germany, which also led to preliminary investigations against members of the highest Reich administration[33]. The main principle of investigating only NS crimes against civilians was insofar changed that since then the Central Office has also been investigating (certain) crimes against prisoners of war.

Our main aim is searching for acts limited in space and time and committed by a certain group of culprits in order to determine which persons involved into these atrocities can still be prosecuted. Unfortunately, the Central Office can neither obtain court decisions nor impose coercive measures – like a house search. Instead, we rely on the voluntary participation of witnesses, on publicly available sources and on the support of the police or from abroad by means of legal assistance. Therefore, the decisive disadvantage is the complicated structure of a provisional authority, which has neither been assigned the powers of public prosecution nor the power to bring charges.

As soon as the Central Office has found the group of the perpetrators who are to be prosecuted, the preliminary investigations are closed and the files are transferred to the prosecutor's office in charge. Furthermore, the Central Office renders investigative assistance based on the expertise in Ludwigsburg concerning historical facts, military organization or legal aspects. With the exception of Baden-Württemberg and North Rhine-Westphalia, there is no institutional specialisation of public prosecutor's offices.

---

32 The Central Office is constructed as a judicial institution – but its task is very similar to a fact-finding body – only limited to murder crimes and without any mandate to awareness programs.

33 New Section IIa (zur erweiterten Zuständigkeit in der geänderten Verwaltungsvereinbarung).

IV. Collecting evidence for the prosecution of NS-crimes

The requirements in Nazi trials as the regards the furnishing of proof are the same standards as those stipulated in any other criminal trial conducted along constitutional lines in order to produce enough evidence to convict someone. Our main difficulty is the passage of time since the deeds. In more than two generations, the evidence has deteriorated in every way. The accused have also aged or died in the meantime. Nowadays, the defendants are between 92 and 99 years of age. The CentralCentrals Office's task is not to collect historical knowledge but to further criminal investigation. Proceedings are only possible if the accused is still alive and as long as he is fit to stand trial.[34]

1. Confessions

In some of the early Nazi trials, the courts were able to base their verdicts on a confession by the accused. Since the 60ies, this has played no role at all until the recent trials of our days. The defendants in the various criminal proceedings have maintained contact with each other and enjoyed the opportunity of exchanging notes on the experience gained in their trials. Of course, it is the right of every defendant to remain silent. According to our experience, the investigating officials and judges have come up against a wall of silence or subterfuge – at least, they have found no sign of regret for the victims.

2. Judicial inspection

Another form of evidence usually lacking in Nazi trials – unlike other legal proceedings against crimes of violence – is the local taking of evidence by a judge visiting the scene of the crime. In the overwhelming bulk of cases, a local inspection was not possible during the Cold War – a fact that is even more important when we take into account that most crimes have been committed on the territory of Poland or the former Soviet Union. Nowadays, most scenes of the crimes are accessible – but can no longer help to

34 Federal Court of Justice (Bundesgerichtshof), 17th June, 2004, 5 StR 115/03, juris, Engel case; Berlin Constitutional Court, 12th January 1993 – VerfGH 55/92, juris, Honecker case.

ascertain the true facts because of changes in property and vegetation. Moreover, of course, most of today's means of evidence are not available, such as DNA analysis, wiretapping, control of accounts etc. Sometimes, modern techniques are used: The conditions in a camp can be illustrated with a modern 3D-virtual reality-model of Auschwitz; thus, it can also be clarified, what a defendant could see from his position.

3. *Witnesses*

Courts are compelled to base their verdicts to a large extent on the testimony of witnesses and on documentary proof.

The armchair culprit, making his decisions on life or death for hundreds or thousands of people far away from the actual scene of the crime, remained unknown in name and appearance to the victims. The only witnesses whose evidence may be taken into account in such a case were usually those people who worked close to the "mastermind" in question and knew of the relevant responsibilities and chains of command. Such persons mostly display great reluctance to come forward because they fear possible implication among the accused or criminal prosecution.[35]

The second group comprising the actual perpetrators of the crimes and their accomplices may be described as the "physically involved culprits": the members of the firing squads, the guards and personnel at the concentration and extermination camps, the drivers of the gas vans – all those who actually looked into the eyes of their victims. The "physically involved culprits" were hardly ever individually named on documents relating to the crime because of their mostly subordinate duties and low rank; as a rule they could only be convicted on the strength of witnesses' testimony.[36]

Compared with other criminal trials, the obstacles encountered in Nazi cases are much greater because of the almost complete absence of "neutral" witnesses. The number of witnesses available for the Nazi trials has been decreasing since WW II. To the losses from death and illness must be added the reluctance and exhaustion of witnesses from among the victims – especially those who have emigrated to North America or Israel.[37]

---

35 Rückerl, (fn. 25), p. 86.
36 Rückerl, (fn. 25), p. 86.
37 See Nestler infra p. 34 ff.

4. Experts

Experts have largely taken their place. Historians or military historians, in particular, are teaching us about the state of research, general events, chains of command, or constraints in the dictatorship. Interestingly enough, the branch of contemporary history only got underway through the criminal proceedings of the 50ies and 60ies.

5. Documents

Documents have been the most important evidence, especially in the past for “armchair culprits”. Today, they also have gained significance for the aiders on the crime scene, because each piece of the puzzle can give an indication to the general service, for example, of a guard in a concentration camp.

Many documents have been deliberately destroyed by the SS (*Schutzstaffel*); others have been lost by the effects of the war or have been inaccessible for decades in foreign archives. Staff members of the Central Office who until 1964 were forbidden by the federal government making trips to Eastern Europe, received permits during the Cold War in the second half of the 60ies.[38] After the changes in the former Eastern bloc, the Central Office has gained access to large parts of the archive material. Soon after German reunification, the Central Office looked through the NS-Archive in the “Ministry of State Security”, access to which had been denied by the authorities of the German Democratic Republic. Since many years, the Central Office has been cooperating with similar authorities from abroad, which also deal with NS crimes, especially with the United States Department of Justice and with the Commission for the Prosecution of the Crimes against the Polish Nation.

6. Main Focus

The preliminary investigations focus on sources in Germany and abroad, which help us to locate still living staff members of concentration camps, task forces or other units. Available evidence rarely proves concrete aiding and abetting of a particular murder, but it can prove participation in the

38 Rückerl, (fn. 25), p. 86.

system of mass murder. This wide approach has built the basis for the investigations concerning Auschwitz and Lublin-Majdanek. In 2018, five alleged perpetrators were indicted before courts in Germany. The Central Offices has transferred proceedings concerning the concentration camps of Stutthof (near Danzig), Buchenwald, Sachsenhausen and the women's camp Ravensbrück to the public prosecutor's offices. Recent investigations deal with further camps, e. g. Flossenbürg, Groß-Rosen, Mittelbau-Dora, and Natzweiler.

V. *Mixed results*

The balance sheet after decades of investigations is ambivalent. "Too few, too mild, too late" might be a way of putting it. There were proceedings against more than 170,000 defendants. Only against 17,000 of whom were brought charges, which ledlead to the conviction of 6,700 defendants (1,100 of whom were convicted of homicides).[39] Often, the punishments were very lenient. Courts regarded life imprisonment (the mandatory punishment for murder) as inappropriate since the defendants had committed the act only in the special circumstances under the dictatorship and the war. In addition, many procedures just came too late. The reasons are both legal difficulties caused by national criminal law, which was not tailored to state crimes, and factual limitations – but also a widespread unwillingness among the population, which is also reflected in the lack of competence of the Central Office.

On the other hand, the Federal Republic strives for clarification up to this day. Through trials since the 1960ies, individuals have been repeatedly held responsible for their acts. The proceedings have informed the public, which has contributed to the painful debate in the post-war society. There was also a learning process within the judiciary – demonstrated in dealing with the crimes of communism in the GDR in the 90ies. Possibly, the factual findings are what will remain: be it the irrefutable proof of what has happened in Auschwitz, be it the view on the perpetrators (Were they really just "ordinary men"?).

39 Andreas Eichmüller, Die Strafverfolgung von NS-Verbrechen durch westdeutsche Justizbehörden seit 1945 – Eine Zahlenbilanz, in: Vierteljahreshefte für Zeitgeschichte 2008, p. 621 (626); In addition, there were about 78.000 verdicts against Germans and Austrians by foreign courts, see Norbert Frei, Einführung und Bilanz; in: Norbert Frei (ed.), Transnationale Vergangenheitspolitik [, 2006], p. 31/32.

In October 2018, a trial in Hamburg has begun against a 92-year-old man. As a guard at the German concentration camp Stutthof, in 1944, he allegedly has contributed to more than 5,000 systematic killings of Jewish deportees.[40] For survivors or members of family, it is often very important and it remains a remembrance that such acts will be prosecuted until the end. This gives both sides the opportunity to tell their stories: both the defendant and the victims (or their relatives) are heard by the current German state. We have to accept the fact, that the mass crimes of the former German state were only possible with the participation of thousands in the Nazi death machine and that they should therefore share responsibility. The Central Office will continue its efforts to investigate murder crimes of the Nazi-regime for some more years. It is *only* an attempt – but *at least*, an attempt.

40 Press release, Regional Court Hamburg 30 August 2019; justiz.hamburg.de/presse mitteilungen/12869044/pressemitteilung-2019–08–30-olg-01.

Crimes committed by a state and culpability – can the perpetrators "at the bottom" of the organization be held culpable?

Prof. Dr. Cornelius Nestler[*]

I. Who were the principal perpetrators, who were (only) the accessories?

This distinction is of crucial importance for my topic: "How did the German criminal justice system deal with the Shoa and especially with the mass murder of the Jews in the extermination camps of the SS?". Because, according to German criminal law, the perpetrator of a murder is (mandatorily) sentenced to life imprisonment, whereas the one who was only involved in the murder as an accessory can only be sentenced to up to 15 years fixed-term imprisonment.

The systematic prosecution of the perpetrators of the Shoa began – only after far more than a decade after the Shoa – with the establishment of the central office in Ludwigsburg in 1958. Soon thereafter, the first criminal investigations were carried out against members of the SS of the extermination camps of Chelmno, Belzec, Sobibor, Majdanek-Lublin and of course, Auschwitz. By then, also the first major criminal trial was foreseeable – the famous Frankfurt Auschwitz trial. It is precisely during this period that the German Federal Court of Justice, by judgement of October 19th, 1962, used the "Staschinski Case"[1] (an Ukrainian citizen, recruited as an agent by the KGB and hired to murder politicians in exile in Munich) for fundamental reflections on questions of injustice and guilt in crimes committed upon state command.

First of all, the Federal Court of Justice presents its criminological understanding of such crimes: "Recently, however, certain modern states – under the influence of radical political views, in Germany under National Socialism – have begun to plan political murders or mass murders and to command the execution of such bloody acts. The mere recipients of the commands are not committing these officially ordered crimes on personal

* Chair of Criminal Law, University of Cologne, prosecutor.

1 BGHSt 18, 87, citations from the verdict, loc. cit., p. 93 ff.

impulses that already have been researched by criminologists or on such impulses that are in any case similar. Rather, they find themselves in the morally confusing, sometimes hopeless situation of being commissioned by their own state, which, with clever mass propaganda, tends to appear to many people to be the undoubted authority, to commit the most reprehensible crimes. They follow the orders under the influence of political propaganda or under the influence of the authority of command or under similar influences of their own state, from which, quite on the contrary, they are actually entitled to expect the upholding of law and order. This means that these dangerous criminal impulses emanate, under blatant abuse of power, from the bearer of state power itself rather than from the recipients of commands. (...)"

With regard to the legal consequences, the Federal Court finds that: "By no means these special circumstances of state-ordered crimes exonerate those participating from criminal guilt. (...)". That is to say, even within the sphere of influence of criminal regimes, people are still capable of deciding for the right and against the wrong. What follows, is a wording that provides the template for all the criminal proceedings against the Nazis in the following decades: "Under special circumstances, however, acting on state orders when committing crimes may provide grounds for mitigating punishment." In concrete terms, the mitigation of punishment will be granted to those who have disapproved of the criminal state commands and to those who were reluctant to carry out the orders, but who, however, at the same time did succumb to the orders due to human weakness as they could not withstand the superiority of the state authority.

What we all know from the academic world of German criminal law scholars as the leading decision for the subjective theory in the delimitation of perpetration and participation, means in the period of the year 1962: Whoever has *not* adopted or embraced Hitler's criminal will, will *not* be sanctioned – regardless of how substantial his contribution to the crime in fact was – with the *mandatory* life imprisonment for murder, but he will only be sanctioned with a *fixed-term* imprisonment for accessory to murder.

What a successful trick: This setting of the course, which turns the Nazi perpetrators into mere accessories, is not outlined using the example of a perpetrator in the SS who himself shot hundreds of Jews at the pit, but using the rather exotic case of the KGB agent Staschinski. And, of course, all of the perpetrators have later "disapproved of the crime orders and executed them only reluctantly" – *one* perpetrator (Hitler) and a *nation* of recipients of commands.

Therefore, the legal reasoning in the verdicts of the 1960s began – with a virtually stereotypical wording – as, for example, in the grounds for the verdict in the Frankfurt Auschwitz trial: "The main perpetrators were Hitler [as the author of the order on the so-called "final solution"], Himmler [as Reichsführer SS], Göring, Heydrich, and others" – hence (only) the leadership elite of the SS state.[2]

But what about all those who carried out the mass murder? This is exemplified by the verdict against Mulka, who was initially one of the company commanders of the "SS-Totenkopfwachsturmbann" in Auschwitz, and then a representative of Rudolf Höß for almost a year and thus responsible for the mass murder of hundreds of thousands of victims. The Frankfurt District Court accepted his statement that he had only acted on orders, that he had *not* adopted Hitler's criminal will: He was only convicted for accessory to murder.[3]

Even the most important organizer of the extermination of the Jews, Adolf Eichmann – as he presented himself in Jerusalem[4] –, would have had a good chance before a German court of only being convicted for accessory to murder.

II. What has to be proven – certain acts or just the function in the system?

This question was answered quite simply from the courts in the beginning – the participation in the mass murder by fulfilling a function in the system was sufficient for a conviction as accessory.

For example, some of the defendants, who were accused by the Bonn District Court of accessory to murder of more than 150,000 Jews killed in gas vans of the Chelmno extermination camp, argued before the court of appeal, that they had only served as guards within the scope of ordinary duties of the SS police.

The answer of the 2nd Senate of the Federal Court of Justice was unequivocal: The defendants "helped to kill the victims solely by their membership of the special unit, which had been formed specifically for the extermination of the Jewish population of Poland. The nature of the tasks

2 Gross/Renz, Der Frankfurter Auschwitz Prozeß (1963–1965), p. 674.
3 Loc cit., p. 685.
4 Arendt, Eichmann in: Jerusalem: A report on the Banality of Evil, [1963]. On the Eichmann as he presents himself in the so-called Sassen Protocols, which were produced in Buenos Aires, as a fanatical strategist of the "final solution", see the great study by Stangneth, Eichmann before Jerusalem, 2nd edition 2018.

they had to perform while carrying out the individual operation is therefore (...) of no importance".[5]

And also the question of what exactly the act of the crime was, the defendants had helped to commit as accessories, is clarified in this decision on the basis of the so-called "natural unity of action": The act of the crime was the murder *of all victims* during an extermination period that was spatially and temporally coherent. Therefore, the defendants were convicted of accessory to the murder of all victims during one of the two spatially and temporally coherent extermination period in the Chelmno camp. And this was also completely *irrespective* of whether it could be proven that the accused had fulfilled his function at all times when the murder took place, i.e. that he had specifically facilitated every single murder.

The verdict in the Frankfurt Auschwitz trial (1963 to 1965) chose a completely different path and did not adopt this very concept, according to which everyone of the camp personnel – simply by just belonging to the camp personnel – had participated in this one act of crime, i.e. in the murder of all people who were killed in the camp. Rather, the Frankfurt Regional Court, even in the case of systematically organized and carried out mass murders, looked for individual acts and their facilitation by the defendant by means of a specific and individual act of accessory. This procedure was not only historically wrong but it only worked by describing the facts in a rather absurd manner and by assessing the facts in a legally wrong way.

The trial of Mulka, the main defendant and deputy camp commander, serves as a striking example of this method and of the implications of this limited perspective. As it is comprehensively described in the indictment[6], in the oral reasoning by the presiding judge Hofmeyer[7] as well as in the written grounds[8], Mulka was responsible for the proper functioning, especially of the extermination of people in the gas chambers. Due to this func-

---

5 Verdict, 11/25/1964 – 2 StR 71/64 -, JuNSV Nr. 594c, p. 352.

6 "With regard to the special functions of the Auschwitz concentration camp as an extermination camp and as a mass extermination institution, it follows from the established and unambiguous scope of the adjutant's duties that the accused Mulka had to work very broadly and comprehensively towards the trouble-free extermination of inmates during his employment as an adjutant next to the commander." in: Gross/Renz, loc. cit., Vol. I, p. 296, 300.

7 Copy of the tape recording of the 182nd day of the trial, 19.8.1965, at: www.auschwitz-prozess.de.

8 For the assessment of evidence in the case of Mulka as well as for the sentencing in the case of Mulka see pages 664 et seq. and 690 et seq. in Gross/Renz, loc.cit. [Fn 14], vol. II = JuNSV, pages 435 et seq. and 454 et seq.

tion that he fulfilled, he should have been convicted of accessory to murder of all victims who were killed in the gas chambers immediately after their arrival in Auschwitz during the period of his deployment in Auschwitz. But the court found that this function alone was not sufficient. Instead, it looked for the concrete individual act and found it in the forwarding of three operational orders after the announcement of the so-called *Judentransporte* [trains with Jews who were deported],[9] in the supervision at the ramp in two cases, and in the orders for the procurement of Cyclone B and of gas-tight doors for the new crematoria.

Since the forwarding of the orders and the supervision of the ramp could theoretically have concerned the same transports, the court assumes ultimately only three acts of accessory. Furthermore, the court then summarizes the use of Cyclone B and the use of the gas-tight door to one act of accessory to the murder of the victims from at least one (of many) transports. Finally, Mulka was convicted for at least these four cases.[10] One does wonder how the court would have decided if it hadn't come across the three operational orders and the documents on the orders for Cyclone B and the doors during the taking of evidence – perhaps say, only one conviction in two cases of the supervision at the ramp? And then, what if no witness had remembered seeing Mulka at the ramp – would that mean an acquittal for the adjutant of the camp commander of Auschwitz?

But why does the court, which in general does not misjudge the important role of the adjutant of the commander for the extermination process,[11] focus in such a way on the concrete contribution to the crime, and thereby dismantles the collaborative and factory-like mass murder into small individual pieces, almost atomizing it, as the famous public prosecutor Fritz Bauer called it?[12] This is because the court always considers one act of extermination as a separate crime. For example, in the case of the so-called Judentransporte, the crime is the murder of the people from only *one* of the several hundred transports that arrived at the ramps in Auschwitz.

---

9 The transports of Jews, after whose arrival the selection took place at the ramp, were announced beforehand by telegraphs from the Reich Security Main Office in Berlin.

10 In: Gross/Renz, loc. cit., p. 672 f. = JuNSV, p. 441f.

11 The court writes with regard to the sentencing: "As an adjutant he participated in an important and responsible position in the realization of the extermination program of the Nazi rulers," ibid., p. 690 = p. 454.

12 Bauer, "In the Name of the People (1965)", in: The Humanity of the Legal System, Ed. v. Perels/ Wojak, [1998], p. 84.

But there was a set of facts in the Shoa, which means the murder of the six million Jews, to which the criteria of one act of crime in the sense of the natural unity of action (consistent planning, spatial limitation, uniform procedure[13]) clearly applied, namely (besides the extermination of the Jews in the other camps of the operation "Reinhard"[14]) the extermination of the Jews who were selected at the ramp after their arrival at Auschwitz for being killed in the gas chambers.

The decisive sentences with which the District Court of Frankfurt avoided this consequence in its verdict are the following: "The individual acts of extermination were each carried out by the SS members, who were assigned to ramp duty, by expressing their will on each occasion. And every time, meaning with every new action, the SS members also had to express their will anew. (...)."[15] At this point, the verdict becomes downright grotesque:

Every morning when waking up, or at least every time they were ordered to do the ramp duty, the doctors who selected, the adjutant who was responsible for the procedure at the ramp, the guards and other SS members at the ramp – they all should have decided to join in again every time anew? How should one imagine this daily decision, for example like this – "I'll do it again today, but maybe not tomorrow"? That is – to say the least – absurd. After everything we know about the perpetrators in Auschwitz, they decided at the beginning of their deployment to join in and they did not decide every day anew whether they would fulfil their tasks or not.

In its appellate decision of 1969, the 2nd Senate of the Federal Court of Justice confirmed this verdict of the Frankfurt District Court. And this leads to the assumption that because of this jurisprudence, for over almost half a century no further convictions were handed down against the well over a thousand SS members who had kept the Auschwitz murder machine going. According to this jurisprudence, it was now necessary to prove that a suspect had contributed with a precisely ascertainable act to a very narrowly defined (in terms of space and time) act of murder.

---

13 See Fischer, StGB, 65. Vol. 2018, section 52, recital 3.

14 Aside from Auschwitz-Birkenau, these were the extermination camps Belzec, Sobibor und Treblinka.

15 In: Gross/Renz, loc.cit., p. 679 = JuNSV, loc.cit., p. 448.

However, the practice of the Frankfurt public prosecution, which had special jurisdiction for the investigation of the mass murder in Auschwitz, shows a different picture.[16]

On the one hand, the knowledge, that a suspect was assigned a certain function – often the fact that he belonged to one of the companies of the "SS-Totenkopfsturmbann" – was not used as an opportunity to further investigate the matter. In those cases, the charges were often dropped due to a lack of reasonable suspicion in accordance with § 170, para. 2 of the Code of Criminal Procedure.[17] But in all the other cases in which the public prosecution assumed, for example, on the basis of a confession or on the basis of witness testimony that the suspect was an accessory to murder, the charges were also dropped – because of "minor guilt" in accordance with § 153b of the Code of Criminal Procedure[18] in conjunction with § 47 exp. 2 MStGB[19].

The first of the criminal proceedings with which this practice was established serves as a paradigmatic example.[20] The case was brought against members of the so-called "drivers on duty-call division" in Auschwitz. During their interrogations, the accused had described that they often had driven the Jewish victims who were no longer able to walk from the ramp to the gas chambers with the trucks. Thus, also according to the standards of the Frankfurt Auschwitz verdict of 1965, there was sufficient evidence of concrete participation in the act of murder. But the standards that the Auschwitz verdict had set continued to have an effect – only other than expected. At the end of the prosecutorial decision to dismiss the charges, it says: "In the overall assessment of what happened in the Auschwitz concentration camp, the members of the drivers division appear as small 'henchmen'. (...) Their contribution to the crime was much smaller than

16 There are 51 orders of suspension from the years 1972 to 1984, with a recognizable emphasis on the years 1976 and 1977, taken from BA-No. 162/ (each) 2687; 2689; 2693 to 2698; 2700 to 2703; 27487; 30750.

17 Exemplarily: "The accused served later at the 1st SS-Totenkopf-Sturmbann. In the course of 1942, he was promoted to the position of a SS-Rottenführer and, after a training course in 1943, to the position of a SS-Unterscharführer," order of suspension of August 27, 1976, Federal Archives, B 162/ 2693, pp. 002685 ff.

18 According to the old version of the statute, meanwhile the numbering has changed.

19 In the event that a subordinate had realized that the order he had been given involved an act that was a crime, the 1944 version of § 47 (2) MstGB, which had to be taken as the basis, stipulated: "If the subordinate's guilt is low, his punishment may be waived."

20 Public prosecution at the Frankfurt District Court, 4 JS 1031/61 and 4 JS 798/64.

that of a selecting SS officer or a member of the SS who was directly involved in the process."

The prosecution then takes a closer look at the sentences imposed by the Frankfurt District Court in the Auschwitz verdict: "The SS physician Dr. Frank, who decided on life and death of the people arriving at the ramp in Auschwitz-Birkenau, was sentenced to five years' imprisonment (...) because of the selection of at least 1,000 persons for death by gas." Thereupon, the head of the Frankfurt prosecution then draws the conclusion: "The sentences of guilt and punishment against this group of people has set standards. The guilt of the members of the drivers division may be measured against these guilty verdicts. Their guilt seems to be minor".[21] According to this pattern, a practice was established by the public prosecution in the 1970s, which de facto put an end to prosecuting lower ranks of the SS for participation in the mass murder in the extermination camps.

III. More recent criminal proceedings

The beginning of the investigations against John Demjanjuk in 2008 in Ludwigsburg marked the turning point. The only fact known about his contribution to the mass murder in the Sobibor extermination camp was, that in 1943 he was deployed to Sobibor for several months as a guard. That the activities of a security guard in the extermination camp legally qualify as an accessory to murder was rather self-evident for both the public prosecutor and the Munich District Court. With regard to the legal term of the crime, the court decided not to assume one act of accessory to murder of the people from the 16 transports during the period concerned; instead, it decided to follow the jurisprudence of the decisions in the Frankfurt–Auschwitz trial and assumed 16 acts of accessory to murder. Thus it had to be proven that Demjanjuk had fulfilled his duty on each day of the murder of the victims from each of these transports. The court solved this problem simply by making the factual assumption that Demjanjuk had been deployed as a security guard on the arrival of each of these transports.[22]

---

21 Injunction of 30. August, loc. cit., under 9. This decision was issued on the base of § 153a German procedural code in the version valid until 1975; after the introduction of the new § 153a, the former § 153a became § 153b.

22 It says: "The Chamber is convinced that the defendant served in his function as guard (...) during the arrival of the 15 deportation trains and during the deporta-

In a next step, the public prosecutor in the case against Oskar Gröning in 2014 based his indictment on the legal grounds that had been common before the verdict in the Auschwitz Trial in Frankfurt from 1965. He decided that the killing of at least 300,000 Hungarian Jews between May 16th and July 11th 1944 who were brought to Auschwitz in 147 trains in the so-called "Hungaria Operation" must be seen as *one* crime in the legal sense.

Gröning was accused of committing accessory to murder because he at least made a subordinate contribution to clearing the railway ramp at the Auschwitz-Birkenau camp from the considerable quantities of luggage so that there was no evidence of the preceding selection process left and so that the inmates from the next transport at arrival would not get suspicious right away about what was planned for them. For this act Gröning was accused and convicted "of having knowingly provided assistance to others in deliberate, collective murder, committed by another person, by means of malicious and atrocious killing in coincidence of at least 300,000 offences."

Up until to this point, the public prosecution had only focused their attention on the factory-like murder of the victims in the extermination camps who were murdered in the gas chambers immediately after their arrival and selection at the ramp. But in 2016, for the first time, the Dortmund public prosecutor took Auschwitz for what it was beginning with the year of 1942 – a institution of organized mass murder for all the Jewish inmates. The Prosecutor charged Reinhold Hanning, a sergeant in one of the companies of the SS-Totenkopfwachsturmbann in Auschwitz, also with accessory to the systematic murder of the prisoners who died due to the living conditions in the camp. And in a further step, the Dortmund public prosecution then also accused SS personnel who were members of the guarding division not in Auschwitz, but in the Stuffhof concentration camp.

The following excerpts of the indictment in the (most likely) last case against a former SS-guard in Stutthof which will commence at the district court of Hamburg in October, gives an example of the recent concept of the prosecution of NS crimes:

"The defendant is charged with having, as a juvenile and young adult at Stutthof concentration camp on today's national territory of the Republic of Poland during the time from 09/08/1944 to 26/04/1945 in at least 5,230

---

tion transport from Izbica and was not deployed elsewhere or remaining elsewhere," ibid. comm. p. 355.

nominally coincidental cases willfully provided assistance to others to commit insidious and cruel murder.

1. *The accused is charged with the following:*

His duties as an SS guard included guarding the camp, especially preventing escape, revolts and the freeing of inmates. This work was performed by him as part of a continuously changing general guard duty, always armed with a gun, on the watchtowers established around the concentration camp, on sentry positions around the camp (minor and major cordon) and by accompanying and guarding work details. The working time of all guards was continuous on all seven days of the week, ten to twelve hours a day or at night, in each case interrupted by short standby periods.

During the accused's work as a member oft he SS guards at Stutthof concentration camp the so-called "final solution of the Jewish question" started to develop by direction of the government (…) for the systematic killing of the camp's Jewish inmates. The accused who as a result of his guard duty assisted the execution of the state-ordered mass murder, on account of his personal perception in part had detailed knowledge of the methods of killing performed or was informed so credibly by his comrades about the procedures that he had no doubts about them.

2. *Killing by causing and maintaining conditions hostile to life*

No later than from October 1944 onwards, apart from the subcamps the main camp at Stutthof was also overcrowded several times over its existing constructional capacity in consequence of the imminent breakdown of the military situation on the entire eastern front due to the numerous arriving prisoner transports. To comply with the extermination order mentioned, the systematic killing of the inmates subject to anti-Semitic persecution by means of the direct killing methods no longer appeared to be efficient enough, and besides not required any more either. The object of killing was now achieved in such a way that the inmates who were completely exhausted due to the regular compulsion to perform very harsh labour at Stutthof or the inmates subject to anti-Semitic persecution, who had reached the camp in transports already completely exhausted from other camps, as a result of systematic denial of sufficient food, denial of minimal sanitary conditions and any medical help following exhaustion or disease were selected, watched by the guards and taken to the so-called "death block (block 29 and 30 in the so-called "Jews camp"), where they, without any help, especially also without water, died within a short time in the straw soaked with excrement and pus.

After the outbreak oft he typhus epidemic in November 1944, which continued until the liquidation oft he camp in April 1945 and against which nothing was done with the exception of appropriate vaccinations of the camp personnel and certain inmates who had been in contact with the camp personnel, at least 5,000 people lost their lives in great pain. The completely emaciated corpses were thereafter "pulled out" of the barracks by fellow inmates and "flung" onto hand-carts which, until they were covered with several layers of corpses, were pulled or pushed to the crematorium or in most of the cases – because the capacities of the crematorium were exhausted – to the so-called "pyre". In the crematorium, the corpses were burnt in the two ovens. In the case of the "pyre", the corpses were piled up in a pit, doused with fire accelerant and lit."

Summary: Fulfilling duties that provide assistance to others to commit crimes is known as punishable accessory in most legal systems. The German criminal justice system has finally, after more than half a century, applied this concept also to the Nazi crimes that were committed as part of the mass murder of the Jews of Europe.

IV. Participation of victims in trials against former SS-personal

The following is a press release I made together with two colleagues in February 2016, right before the beginning of the trial against the former Auschwitz guard Hanning in behalf of our clients, most of them survivors from Auschwitz. It kind of summarizes the aspects that were important for our clients.

„Trial against Reinhold Hanning before the Detmold District Court

We are the legal counsels of more than 25 Jewish co-plaintiffs. Their next of kin were murdered in Auschwitz between January 1943 and June 1944. Almost all of our clients were selected for labour on the ramp and survived Auschwitz, death marches and other camps of the SS.

It is the hope for justice that brings the co-plaintiffs to these proceedings.

The accused Hanning will be tried for his participation in the murder of our clients' parents and siblings as well as the extermination of their families. Seventy years have passed since then. Pain and loss, decades of despairing nightmares surrounding the hell of Auschwitz will be heard before the

Detmold District Court in the voices of those of our clients who will give testimony in the trial.

The co-plaintiffs wish to bear witness, and thereby also make evident to the broader public, what the "Holocaust" has brought upon them individually as well as their families. The co-plaintiffs place great emphasis on having the opportunity to describe to the court the consequences that any participation in these murderous deeds produced for their own individual lives. Justice will be granted to the co-plaintiffs only if the trial does not stop at presenting numbers of murdered victims but also grants a voice to parents and siblings, bringing an image of these persons to life. In the courtroom, robbed human dignity can be restituted by way of respect for the co-plaintiffs.

The co-plaintiffs have decided to participate in these proceedings fully aware of the great strain this will put on them individually. They have taken this burden upon themselves, even in old age, because they believe they owe it to their murdered families to be recognized in a German court case.

After the trial against Oskar Groening, these proceedings against Hanning are one further step to bring an end to a failure of justice that has lasted for almost 50 years. Also in these proceedings, the standards for culpable behavior are applied that were and are valid in any "normal" criminal proceeding 50 years ago as well as now.

And finally, the prosecution in the criminal proceedings against Hanning is taking the right path. The indictment against Hanning does not only include the murder of those victims who where taken to the gas chambers right after their arrival on the ramp, but the indictment also includes the systematic annihilation of those, who were selected for slave labour, due to the living conditions and particular the cruel death from starvation. The trial promises justice, albeit far too late."

The legal definition of genocide in the Argentine case

Prof. Dr. Daniel Eduardo Rafecas[*]

I. Introduction

In the Argentine Republic, since the reopening of criminal cases henceforth in 2005 throughout the country related to the investigation of illegal detentions, torture and murders during the last military dictatorship (1976–1983), various procedural actors have been advocating the introduction of the legal qualification of genocide in resolutions and sentences related to these cases, to connote the framework in which those crimes against freedom, dignity and life were committed.

This initiative was promoted mainly by those who represent the victims of these crimes, but also by some representatives of the Public Prosecutor's Office. Certainly, based on abroad social consensus that the frequent reference to the Argentine genocide seems to have, to refer to the dire consequences of the State terrorism that has prevailed in Argentina since March 24, 1976, or the designation as *génocidaires* of those accused in this type of process, by broad sectors of the political class, by not few mass media, and even by certain academic and cultural circles.

Now, for these petitioners, it would be a question of translating the reference to the *Argentine genocide* into judicial sentences, that is to say, into the communicational circuit proper to the judicial sphere, as it already seems to be notably consolidated politically and in the media. This is without prejudice to the fact that the condition of *crimes against humanity* that must be assigned to each of the crimes that are usually considered proven in this type of judicial case is beyond any doubt, a condition that ensures the non-applicability of statutory limitations to such crimes, as well as the other consequences that the legal system foresees in this respect. Even so, there are quite a few accusers who also claim that the crimes under investigation should be classified as having been committed *in the context of genocide*. In order to deal with this issue, I must begin the analysis from a *factu-*

* PhD in Criminal Law and Criminal Law Professor (University of Buenos Aires). Federal Judge, in charge of the investigation of crimes against humanity committed during the last dictatorship in Argentina.

al perspective – based on the elements of judgement gathered so far in judicial investigations, but without ignoring other sources – and then move on to deal with the *legal perspective*, both at the level of international and domestic law, through the analysis of doctrine, jurisprudence and comparative legislation, after which I will give my conclusions.

II. The Facts

In view of the particular requirements of the subject of *genocide*, it is appropriate to pronounce first on whether the apparatus of state power employed was systematically guided by some particular motive for the purpose of carrying out the crimes that have been proven in these trials. In this sense, there is increasing evidence, based on historical and judicial investigations, including those carried out in the framework of the case related to the acts committed by the First Army Corps, that the military dictatorship that assumed power on March 24th, 1976, led by Lt. General Jorge Rafael Videla, carried out a systematic methodology of State terror, especially through clandestine centres, made up of thousands of kidnappings, tortures, forced disappearances and murders, guided eminently by *political considerations* in order to determine who were the recipients of the illegal punitive power deployed.

In fact, today we know, the intelligence information machinery, fed basically from the systematic torture of captives, which activated the operations of the *task forces*, aimed to dismantle the circuits of political militancy and economic support of the armed organizations, and of what the military considered their organizations cover or material or discursive support: teachers, students, intellectuals, politicians, trade unionists and other representatives: in short, all kinds of real or potential *political dissidents*.

Following the path traced by other right-wing military dictatorships in the region, aligned under the *National Security Doctrine* that sought to stop the *communist advance* in the South American continent after the Cuban Revolution, the dominant ideology separated from the *Western and Christian community* under the aegis of the Army and the Catholic Church, those who were considered *stateless*, or *foreign to the community*, basically the holders of ideologies contrary to what power considered as *the Argentine soul*, especially those who commonly identify with socialism and communism in their different strands. This machinery developed as a part of a bigger, regional framework, as a result of the impact of the *cold war* in South America. On this basis, the dominant ideology stated that all groups considered as enemies of the western and Christian way of life (such as communists and socialists) must be obliterated, because those strange ideologies are incompatible with "Argentine nationalism", sculpted by the Military and the Catholic Church. So, the persecution under the rules of the 1976 Dictatorship was clearly linked with these, political motives (other ones, such as the fact of belong to an ethnical, religious or racial group, were meaningless).

There is nothing to be said from the factual point of view regarding national, ethnic or racial considerations, since it is evident and certainly indisputable the homogeneity in this sense between perpetrators and victims, or if you like between *deviant and not deviant* according to the particular logic of the authoritarian model under study. If there was an objective motive that guided the persecution of the victims, it was anti-Communism. People were not persecuted because of their nationality (Argentine, or foreign in hundreds of cases), and less because they belonged to a particular ethnic group or because they had been assigned specific racial attributes. With regard to the reference to the *national group*, those arguments that seek to invoke a kind of strategy of replacement of one national being by another, new, delineated by the ideological demands of authoritarian power (thus, for example, "[a]*ll integrated* [a single] *national group, all were Argentineans and all were eliminated according to their dispensability -decided by the repressors- for the 'new Argentine nation'*") are not convincing[1]. It is that in these speculations, at all times reference is being made to ideological questions of a purely political nature, certainly far removed from the question of *nationality*, which was never questioned or persecuted in itself, which is – at least from this first perspective – what is of interest, and without prejudice to what may be added in the second part of this analysis, in relation to eminently legal questions about what should be considered a *national group*.

And with respect to the last constellation, that of persecution for reasons of *religion*, the over-representation of the Jewish collective among the regime's detainees, of between five and ten percent, when they represented no more than 1 % of the population, is basically explained by the fact that the repression was directed to a greater extent against the large urban centres, where the great majority of Jewish *Argentineans lived.* And who were overly represented in activities (e.g., university students), professions (psychologists, lawyers, etc.) and sectors of political militancy (of the left) during the period immediately prior to the coup of 1976 than average Argen-

1 Cfr. Words by Juez Baltasar Garzón, in: Raffin: La experiencia del horror, [2006] p. 221.

tine citizens. For all these reasons, it is necessary to refer once again to the eminently political motivations that led to the detention of Argentinean Jews.

Moreover, many of the judicial investigations of those episodes, recently reopened after the declaration of unconstitutionality of the impunity laws that had been dictated in the mid-1980s, have allowed us to see that in the majority of cases, the repressive machinery only recently revealed its anti-Semitic matrix when it "discovered" that this captive for political reasons that was now at its mercy for torture, was also Jewish, generally due to the verification of his real name and surname, or because objects or books related to Judaism were found in his home, or because they already had this information extracted under torture from another captive, among other possibilities. It was from this moment on that an overt anti-Semitism was put into practice, in a more or less institutionalized manner, within the clandestine detention and torture centres (CCDT), of a racial or political nature, although sometimes also of religious origin, but which in no way calls into question the political motives or qualifies to allow the framework within the scope of the Convention and its restricted definition of *genocide*. Apart from these specific cases, the possibility of justifying, in a more diffuse way, the persecution of the victims of the dictatorship due to their belonging to a *religious group*, encompassing the presumably *atheistic* or anti-religious aspect on the part of the victims, as a consequence of defending the Marxist ideology, identified as contrary to the cultural project that was intended to be imposed from the dictatorial power, is an argument of little convincing weight (so..., Spanish Judge Baltasar Garzón, inasmuch as he held that "[t]o destroy a group because of its atheism or its common non-acceptance of Christian religious ideology is also the destruction of a religious group [...] It is genocide of a religious group the systematic and organized destruction, in whole or in part, of a group because of its atheistic or non-Christian ideology, that is, because of the imposition of a Christian religious ideology"[2]).

Thus, from the moment that this characteristic -which at this point wants to be brought to the foreground-, is nothing more than another facet of a long list of postings, characteristic of a spectrum of political ideologies (of the left) that had assumed their positions in all aspects of social life, including among many other institutions and *superstructures*, the question of religion. But this does not move the certainty that it was political motivations that guided the designs of the perpetrators, and that they

2 See Raffin, ob. cit., p. 221.

imposed themselves over religious motives there when one and the other interfered with each other.

The support of a religious motive to support the repression unleashed by the perpetrators, moreover, is contradicted not only by the fact that none of the institutional representatives of the other confessions -and even less, their cults and practices-, including Protestant Christianity, Orthodox Christianity, Jewry and Islam, among others, have been persecuted in that period, but also, in a forceful way, in the face of the statistically proven fact that the great majority of the victims professed exactly the same religion -Catholic- as the one officially defended by the dictatorship. In fact, hundreds of priests, seminarians, nuns and other persons actively linked to the Catholic Church throughout the country were persecuted during this period. Many of them were murdered or are still missing. It should also be added that a few Christian groups were persecuted and dismantled, not because of their religious belief, but because of the suspicion that behind their outward religious appearance was some kind of social and political militancy, which was considered an enemy of the authoritarian State.

III. International law

In this regard, I must first point out that the plain or social meaning of the word *genocide* is indeed broad and encompassing, and coincides in this sense with the accusatory pretensions analysed here, because just by going to the Dictionary of the Real Academia Española, we notice that there it is defined as "[e]extermination or systematic elimination of a social group for reasons of race, religion or politics". In addition, as already mentioned in the introduction, we are witnessing a generalization of the reference to the *Argentine genocide* by the mass media as well as by referents of the political or legislative agencies of the national State, without a doubt based on the influence that the works of prestigious sociologists such as Daniel Feierstein[3] or Marcelo Raffin[4], among others, all of them defenders -in the field of sociology- of a definition of *genocide* that reaches the events that occurred in Argentina during the last military dictatorship.

---

3 Cfr. El genocidio como práctica social [2007] and more recently, "La Argentina: genocidio y/o crimen contra la humanidad? Sobre el rol del derecho en la construcción de la memoria colectiva", at Nueva Doctrina Penal, [2008] pp. 211–230.

4 La experiencia del horror, [2006].

However, the introduction of the term *genocide* in the *legal* language requires a more detailed analysis of the issue, since it is about the incorporation into the jurisdictional circuit of a *normative* term and for this, every definition, every concept, must necessarily have a *formal source* of a legislative nature, be it in Criminal Law or in Civil Law, be it in International Law or in Domestic Law, in order to be able to be received and, from there, to generate the consequences that this same legal system foresees for its use. What is required, then, specifically, for the purposes intended by many of the private prosecutors in these processes, in the first place, is that we have some legal rule in force that has introduced *genocide* into our system. And secondly, that this legal definition of *genocide* allows the episodes that are discussed in these processes to be framed in this definition, in order to accede to what has been petitioned and thus project the legal consequences -material, symbolic- that are legitimately intended.

The first question is absolutely beyond doubt, since Argentina, on April 9, 1956, ratified the text of the *Convention on the Prevention and Punishment of the Crime of Genocide*, approved by the United Nations on December 9, 1948, and whose entry into force took place on January 12, 1951. International Charter which, since the constitutional reform of 1994, acquired constitutional rank due to its express provision in article 75, sub-paragraph 22, N.C. In this international instrument, which is constitutional letter in Argentine domestic law, we then have the first *legal* definition of *genocide*, namely:

> "In the present Convention, genocide means any of the following acts committed with intent to destroy, in whole or in part, a national, ethnical, racial or religious group, as such:
>
> (a) Killing members of the group;
> (b) Causing serious bodily or mental harm to members of the group;
> (c) Deliberately inflicting on the group conditions of life calculated to bring about its physical destruction in whole or in part;
> (d) Imposing measures intended to prevent births within the group;
> (e) Forcibly transferring children of the group to another group".

This definition has been ratified more recently in the international concert of nations, through article 6 of the so-called *Rome Statute* of July 17, 1998 -which provided for the creation of the International Criminal Court-, to which Argentina adhered on February 8, 2001. As a corollary of this initiative, on 9 January 2007 Law 26,200 was published in the Official Gazette of the Argentine Republic, which implements the treaty that gave rise to the International Criminal Court in the domestic legal order. Well, in its article 6, the Rome Statute defines genocide in legal terms of international law as follows:

> "For the purpose of this Statute, "genocide" means any of the following acts committed with intent to destroy, in whole or in part, a national, ethnical, racial or religious group, as such:
>
> (a) Killing members of the group;
> (b) Causing serious bodily or mental harm to members of the group;
> (c) Deliberately inflicting on the group conditions of life calculated to bring about its physical destruction in whole or in part;
> (d) Imposing measures intended to prevent births within the group;
> (e) Forcibly transferring children of the group to another group".

Sitting then that the first question about whether we have in Argentine law any existing legal norm that allows the introduction of the normative concept of *genocide* in a hypothetical jurisdictional pronouncement, must be answered in the affirmative. As we can see, we effectively have in Argentine a legal norm (coming from International Law) that allows the introduction of the normative concept of *genocide*, to be eventually used in a domestic, judiciary sentence.

Let us now analyse the second question, which consists of determining whether this *legal* concept of *genocide* allows the facts established in judicial investigations to be included in this definition. And here, in order not to distract us from the matter, I will have to dispense with the analysis of other discussions regarding the legal definition of *genocide* in order to concentrate on the central point of the question posed, which is the deliberate exclusion, on the part of the conventional international legislator of 1948, as well as that of 1998, of *genocide* for *political reasons*, also called *politicide*, from the list of possible motivations reached both by the Convention and by the Statute. As we´ll see, the first steps in developing the concept of *genocide* were certainly auspicious for those who maintained the idea of building a definition which included a broad scope in terms of targeted groups. In this sense, it should first be noted that the term *genocide* was coined in 1944 by the Polish professor of Jewish origin Raphael Lemkin (1900–1959) in his work "Axis Rule in Occupied Europe"[5], and defines it as “a coordinated plan of different actions oriented to the destruction of the essential grounds of the life of national groups, with the intention to

5 Carnegie, Endowment for Internacional Peace, [1944]. Same author, Genocide, a New International Crime [1946], p. 360, and Genocide as a Crime in International Law, at American Journal of International Law, № 41, 1947, p. 172.

eliminate them [...]. Genocide is directed against the national group as an entity and its actions are directed against individuals as members of the national group". The work within the United Nations, referring to the elaboration of a document related to the prevention and punishment of *genocide*, began on November 2, 1946, when the delegations of Cuba, India and Panama requested the Secretary General of the United Nations to include the issue in the agenda of issues to be dealt with.

Thus, on 12 November of that year, the issue was discussed and the issue began to be studied in specialized committees, which submitted a *first draft resolution on genocide*, which was dealt with by the General Assembly on 11 December 1946, in which the draft was adopted unanimously and without debate, thus becoming General Assembly resolution 96 (I). In that resolution, which can be considered the first relevant document on the subject, and on which work would later be done in order to achieve a definitive text, *genocide* was defined in a way that was certainly broad in point to the motivations that should guide the perpetrator, and it is worth reproducing it here[6]:

> "Genocide is the denial of the right of existence of human groups, just as homicide is the denial of the right to live of individual human beings; such denial of the right of existence follows great losses to humanity by the deprivation of the cultural and other contributions represented by those human groups, and is contrary to moral law and to the spirit and purposes of the United Nations."

Many cases of such crimes of genocide have occurred when racial, religious, political and other groups have been wholly or partially destroyed. In resolution 96 (I), the General Assembly mandated the UN Economic and Social Council to draft a convention on the crime of *genocide* for its consideration. However, the Economic and Social Council, around April 1947, instructed the Secretary General to undertake, with the collaboration of jurists, such a project. Thus, the preliminary draft was considered by three experts invited by the Secretary General, one of whom was Raphael Lemkin himself (the other two were Professors Donnedieu de Vabres and Vespasiano Pella, the latter president of the influential International Criminal Law Association, AIDP). Well then, in May 1947 the first draft of the Convention, known as the "*Draft Convention prepared by the Secretariat*", came into being, stating in Articles 1 and 2 that:

---

6 See complete text in Robinson/Nehemiah: La convención sobre Genocidio, [1960], p. 111.

I. "The purpose of this Convention is to prevent the destruction of racial, national, linguistic, religious or political groups of human beings.
II. "In this Convention, the word "genocide" means a criminal act directed against any of the above-mentioned groups of human beings, with the purpose of destroying them in whole or in part...".

This first project, as of July 7, 1947, was submitted to the survey of the States Parties, and at the same time, it began to revolve around the different commissions of the Organism, especially the one dedicated to legal matters (Sixth Commission), to which it was formally sent on September 23 of that year. Numerous amendments were proposed. Faced with the complexity of the matter under discussion, an Ad Hoc Commission was set up which inaugurated its work on 10 May 1948 and reformulated a new draft Convention, which even went beyond the previous ones in terms of foreseeing possible motivations, since its Article II reads:

> "In this Convention genocide means any of the following deliberate acts, committed with the intent to destroy a national, racial, religious or political group, for reasons of national or racial origin, religious belief or political opinion of its members...".

This draft, which was discussed on 26 and 27 August 1948 by the Economic and Social Council, was referred without change to the General Assembly, which dealt with it at its 142nd plenary session, at which it was decided to refer it to the Sixth Committee (on Legal Affairs). The Commission held 43 arduous working meetings between September and November 1948, at the end of which a final text was adopted within the Commission by 30 votes to 0, but with the abstention of the USSR and five other countries of the Eastern European Communist bloc, plus South Africa and the United Kingdom. It was this draft that was finally adopted unanimously and without abstentions by the General Assembly on 9 December 1948 (albeit with the absence of South Africa and its *apartheid* regime).

Let us recall once again that, as far as this topic is concerned, the Convention adopted does not define *genocide* as such (despite a proposal to that effect by France), but through the enumeration of the acts that are considered as such for the purposes of the Convention, its main characteristic being that the act must be directed towards the intentional destruction of a *group*. And here I quote Robinson: "[but] not all groups are protected by the Convention. Political groups, as well as economic or similar groups are specifically excluded. The exclusion of political groups is, as noted above, a deviation from General Assembly Resolution 96 (I). It is worth noting that initially [on 15 October 1948], the Sixth Committee had decided to keep political groups among those protected by the Convention [...] The main reason was the argument that political groups are not stable enough; that their inclusion would be a serious obstacle to the ratification of the Convention by a large number of States and that the inclusion of political groups could allow some international authority to intervene in a country's domestic disputes and introduce the United Nations into a country's internal political struggles. Instead, the Sixth Committee added "ethnic" groups to "national" and "racial" groups in order to avoid a possible interpretation of "national" as equivalent to "political"[7]. In order to complete this reference, it should be added that the proposal to remove the *political groups* from the scope of the Convention, during the sessions of the Sixth Committee, was based on the one formulated jointly by Iran, Egypt and Uruguay, and was adopted by 22 votes to 6 with 12 abstentions (including the pro-Soviet bloc).

In addition to having transferred this restricted definition of genocide to the Rome Statute in 1998, already mentioned, it must be added that, both article 4 (2) of the Statute for the Former Yugoslavia of 1993 (ICTY or International Tribunal for the Prosecution of Persons Responsible for Serious Violations of International Humanitarian Law Committed in the Territory of the Former Yugoslavia, Resolution 808), as well as Article 2(2) of the 1994 Statute for Rwanda (ICTR, Resolution 995), followed the same path, and this is also very clearly reflected in the jurisprudence of both instances of the respective tribunals. For its part, the specialized doctrine on international human rights law is practically unanimous in recognizing this genealogy[8] and in resigning the inclusion of political groups within the framework of the Convention -and therefore, of the Rome Statute-, generally with a critical imprint against such exclusion, which is judged arbitrary and regrettable, motivated by political reasons related more than anything to ensuring the rapid endorsement of the Convention, which by

7 Ob. cit., p. 56. In the same line, expert Natan Lerner, from the University of Tel Aviv: "There were promises to include the political groups, but they were rejected at the Sixth Commission of the General Assembly which considered that such groups were not permanent and their inclusion in the text could bring adverse consequences in the process of ratification" (cfr. "De Auschwitz y Nuremberg a Srebrenice y Darfur: la sexagenaria Convención contra Genocidio", published at Persona y Derecho, № 58, pp. 45–70).

8 See, for example, the analysis by William Schabas in respect of the process and negotiations that ended with the adoption of the Convention, which took him to conclude that political groups were initially included, within the groups to be protected, and later excluded in order to gain a fast ratification (Genocide in International Law. The crime of crimes, Cambridge University Press [2000]).

the way was widely achieved[9]. The main cost of reaching such a universal consensus has undoubtedly been the exclusion of *political genocide* or *politicide* from the targeted groups under protection of the Convention, and with it, the impossibility of legally defining *genocide* as around three quarters of the mass crimes that have taken place in the world since then (because all of them have been politically motivated), which, as I said, has been the subject of harsh criticism, particularly in the field of international criminal law, by jurists such as Albin Eser, Kai Ambos or Hans-Heinrich Jescheck among others[10].

For example, Prof. Natan Lerner recently stated in this regard that "it is clear that the Convention must be updated and, in the opinion of some, extended to also protect other groups than those currently covered by Article 2 of the text. Serious cases of mass extermination against populations defined by their social extraction or political orientation have taken place and a strict application of the Convention does not authorize its extension to such situations..."[11]. Allow me also to quote the renowned expert Barbara Harff – who coined the suggestive term *politicide* to denote *political genocide* – who in a recent paper argued in this regard:

> "In the first place, the Convention [against Genocide] does not include groups of victims defined by their political position or their actions in that sense. Raphael Lemkin (1944) coined the term genocide and then sought the support of as many states as possible for the elaboration of a legal document prohibiting collective killings and establishing sanctions against potential perpetrators. Since the first version of the Convention, which included political groups, was rejected by the USSR and its allies, the final version omitted any reference to political

9 See positions in favour and against this exclusion in Lozada, Martín: El crimen de genocidio. Su renovada dimensión a 60 años de su construcción conceptual, published at Revista de Derecho Penal y Procesal Penal, Nº 6, junio 2009, pp. 996–997.

10 See footnotes in Feijóo Sánchez: “El Genocidio en el Derecho Penal Español (art. 607)”, publ. at Cuadernos de Doctrina y Jurisprudencia Penal, Año V, Nº 8-c, p. 561.

11 Cfr. ob cit. The mentioned author adds that the Convention, in this sense, responded basically to the teaching of the Second World War, especially, the Holocaust.

killings. The concept of *politicide* is used here to encompass cases with politically defined victims..."[12].

In this work, Harff crystalized a profound investigative work in which he identified either as *genocide* or as *politicide*, or as both jointly, all acts carried out that met such characteristics, between 1955 and 2001. In *genocides*, victim groups are defined by their perpetrators primarily on the basis of their communal characteristics. In *politicides*, on the other hand, the groups are defined primarily in terms of their political opposition to the regime and the dominant groups. Both have in common that killings are neither by accident nor do they result from individual acts, "but are carried out under the explicit or tacit direction of the State authorities, or of those who claim the authority of the State"[13]. Well, following Harff, it turns out that during that period of almost half a century (1955–2001), 25 *politicides* were committed against only 5 *genocides*, while in 7 other cases both occurred simultaneously. Among the cases of *politicide*, Harff records the Argentine case, between March 1976 and December 1980, with a rank of murdered victims of up to 20,000 people. Lawrence Le Blanc is also blunt in considering political groups excluded from the scope of the Convention[14]. In the same vein, Harvard University Professor David Nersessian has recently said, in the framework of a comparative analysis between the legal concepts of *genocide* and *persecution* (which refers to the notion of crime against humanity), the following:

> "Because they constitute separate crimes that can be cumulative, both genocide and persecution can describe the purpose of crimes committed against members of racial, national, religious and ethnic groups. But this is not the case for members of political groups because there is no analogous crime of political genocide in international criminal law", the aforementioned jurist concludes that "...the absence of a parallel crime of political genocide demonstrates that political groups are afforded less protection [at the international level]".

---

12 Harff: ¿No se aprendieron las lecciones del Holocausto? Evaluando los riesgos de genocidio y matanzas políticas desde 1955", in: Feierstein, Genocidio. La administración de la muerte en la modernidad. [2005] pp. 172–173.

13 Ob. cit., p. 174.

14 In: "La Convención de Naciones Unidas y los grupos políticos: ¿deben los EEUU proponer una enmienda?" (título traducido), publ. at Yale Journal of Internacional Law Nº 13, pp. 268–294, mentioned by Harff, ob. cit., p. 172.

And regarding this absence in the international context of a crime of political genocide, he cites the following example, which has led, in his opinion, to "an unusual and meaningless application of international law":

> "During the 1994 atrocities in Rwanda for example, the Hutus were massacred along with the Tutsis. The Tutsis were targeted for destruction by the ethnic factor, while the so-called "moderate Hutus" were targeted for their political beliefs (they opposed the genocide of the Tutsis). However, in the face of mass killings committed at the same time and in the same place by the same perpetrators and as part of the same scheme to create a Tutsis-free Rwanda, the dead Tutsi on the floor of a church is classified as a victim of the genocide and the dead Hutu lying next to him as a victim of persecution...".

And Nersessian concludes with the following recommendation to the international community: "It is reasonable that international lawyers and politicians continue to revisit, after sixty years, the decision to exclude political groups from the protections of the Convention"[15]. To the same conclusion arrives Lerner: "[u]ndoubtedly, the genocides committed in the decades following the adoption of the Convention demand [...] the broadening of the definition. The cases of Cambodia, Russia under Stalin, massive crimes against political opposition, as in Argentina or Chile [...] are weighty considerations and a reform of the Convention or the adoption of an optional protocol seem to be the needs of the hour"[16]. In the same sense, Lozada pronounces himself when, after invoking the principle of progressivity, he maintains that the question "deserves to be reconsidered and updated. Especially when the persecution, destruction and death of dissidents and political opponents in the last decades is so evident"[17].

Let us now turn to the analysis of jurisprudence. The decision in 1997 of the Magistrate of the Central Court No. 5 of the National Court, Baltasar Garzón, in the case of Adolfo Scilingo, to decide to open the trial in that court against the accused, defining -in the *legal* sense of the term- as *genocide* what happened in Argentina during the last military dictatorship, has had singular significance. However, what happened with that jurisdictional decision at the time of the passing of the respective sentence by the Na-

---

15 Cfr. Nersessian: "Comparative Approaches to Punishing Hate: The intersection of Genocide and Crimes Against Humanity", en Stanford Journal of Internacional Law, Stanford, University School of Law, 2007, vol. 43, nº 2, pp. 221–264, same note as above.

16 Cfr. ob. cit., pp. 69–70.

17 Op. cit., p. 997.

tional Court, Criminal Chamber (Third Section) on April 19, 2005, and two years later, on October 1, 2007, when the Second Criminal Chamber of the Spanish Supreme Court intervened on appeal: in both instances, the decision of the examining magistrate was revoked in full. There, the SC in its cassation sentence, and in relation to the crime of genocide, clearly identified the problem to be dealt with, relating "...to the identification of protected groups, especially in relation to the possibility of including political or ideological groups" in the scope of the Convention against genocide, especially from the reference to the *national group*. Further on, he argued:

> "A group can be understood as a relevant number of people related to each other by common characteristics that differentiate them from other members of the population. The national group has been understood as a group of people with a common national origin. More profoundly, the ICTR [International Criminal Tribunal of Rwanda], in the Akayesu case, defined the national group as "composed of those individuals who share a legal bond based on common citizenship that grants them reciprocal rights and obligations" [...] In any case, the identifying mark of the group in order to establish the object of the destructive purpose in the author must necessarily be one of those provided for in the legal definition, i.e., national, ethnical, racial or religious [...] The question has been raised primarily in relation to political groups".

Coinciding with what has been affirmed so far, the Supreme Court agrees that "[t]he doctrine is practically unanimous in the sense of accepting that those who drafted the Convention agreed not to expressly include political groups. They also seem to agree to a critical vision of such a limitation to the scope of the Convention, when stating in the sentence that "…the exclusion of political groups has sometimes been based on their lack of stability and on the fact that the reasons for belonging are variable and are left to the will of the subject, which, as one author has emphasized, is barely consistent if religious groups are accepted as protected groups, in respect of which such characteristics are to some extent equally predictable". In any case, this deleterious view of the international legislation in force on the matter does not move the obligation of judges to interpret the rules applicable to the case:

> "However, it is the literal text of the precept that prevents the protected group from identifying itself without taking into account one of the typical aspects. The absence of a closing clause or similar expres-

sion is a strong indication that they are not listed by way of illustration [...] Thus, a national group could not be divided into two or more national groups differentiated from each other on the basis of criteria alien to the legal definition. This way of interpreting the rule would lead to the irrelevance of the inclusion of one or other groups, contrary to what results from the text, giving rise to an analogical extension of the definition to the detriment of the defendant, and therefore prohibited...". "In other words, if two national groups share the same nationality, that element will not be useful in identifying the group to be destroyed. Genocide of a national religious, national ethnic or national racial group is possible, since the purpose of the destruction of the group is generally confined to a certain geographical area, normally delimited by the borders of the country. On the contrary, it would not be the destruction of a national group, part in turn of the same national group, only distinguishable from each other by another different criterion". "In the case, it is not possible to identify the group formed by the victims of the facts as a national group, since its members share nationality with the group of the perpetrators, which prevents it from being taken as an identifying and distinctive element. On the other hand, although in the proven fact some references are made to elements of a religious nature, alone or together with others, as characteristic of some members of the group of principals, they are insufficient to consider that the distinctive element of that group was precisely religion".

In a note to this ruling, the expert jurist Alicia Gil Gil, Criminal Law Professor of the University of Zaragoza and the UNED, author of several works in this matter, maintained in support of the decision of the plenary judges of the National Court, that "...the international concept of genocide is and has always been strict [...] The crime of genocide has not changed an apex since its definition in 1948 until today and it is not for the judge to question its, on the other hand, very clear wording [...] The partial destruction of a national group is not equivalent and should not cover "autogenocide", i.e. the partial destruction of the national group itself, although there may be "subgroups" differentiated by ideology"[18].

This jurisprudential path had already been somewhat open from what the Supreme Court decided in its ruling on Spanish jurisdiction in the "Guatemala case", since there, to the detriment of a broad interpretation of

18 Cfr. "La Sentencia de la Audiencia Nacional en el caso Scilingo", publ. at "Revista de Derecho Penal", № 2005–1, p. 532.

the crime of genocide that had been suggested in the background of the case, the SC limited itself to opening the Jurisdiction to the possibility that the facts denounced "...could constitute a crime of genocide insofar as they affect the Mayan people as an ethnic group", discarding the possible political motivations as constituting the crime[19]. Thus, Spanish jurisprudence at the highest level – the Spanish Supreme Court – left behind some precedents of the lower court, which had been favourable to the position imposed by the complaints, specifically, the two judgements (which endorsed what was decided by the Examining Judge) of the Plenum of the Criminal Chamber of the National High Court, both of November 5, 1998, in the "Pinochet case" and in the "Argentine case". This Court, which, as we saw, also reviewed its position on the matter, adopting in the Scilingo case, in its ruling of April 19, 2005, the restrictive thesis, later confirmed by the Supreme Court.

With respect to those first two simultaneous judgements of 1998 of the National Court that included the *political groups* within the figure of genocide, the sharpest criticism that had opportunely been directed from the doctrine, emphasized the overlap in which the Court incurred, between the social or plain concept of genocide and its legal meaning, giving preeminence to the first at the expense of the second. The critique pointed out that the National Court, in its foundations, "...affirms that the "social" concept of genocide includes the destruction of any human group, in a surprising argumentation that disregards the "juridical" concept and the literal tenor of the law. In order to demonstrate the existence of this pretended social concept, he refers to texts prior to the legal definition of the crime of genocide [...] And he affirms by incurring in an evident analogy in malam partem that "national group" does not mean "group formed by persons belonging to the same nation", but simply "national human group, differentiated human group, characterized by something, integrated in a greater collectivity"..."[20]. In the same vein, Bernardo Feijóo Sánchez, a Criminal Law Professor at the Autonomous University of Madrid, after referring to the plain concept of genocide that arises, for example, from the dictionary of the Real Academia Española, argues that "...it does not appear that from a criminal-legal point of view this definition corresponds to the historical

19 Cfr. Sentence of the Spanish Supreme Tribunal N° 327 of 25 February, 2003, publ. at Repertorio de Jurisprudencia Aranzadi, 2147/2003.

20 Cfr. Gil Gil, ob. cit., p. 533 and more specifically in her work Derecho Penal Internacional, Tecnos, Madrid, 1999, p. 181; besides, against the idea of autogenocide, Schabas, William A.: Genocide in internacional law, Cambridge University Press [2000], mentioned there.

meaning of the 1948 Convention which has led to the emergence of this crime against the international community [...] the preliminary work of the Convention included "political genocide", but this was removed from the final wording of the Convention..." and adds in the footnote that "[i]n art. 6 of the Statute of the ICC adopted in Rome on 17 July 1998, this exclusion is maintained..."[21].

So far, however, we have dealt with the definitions of genocide that exist at the international level. But what is certain is that, in order to channel the attempts to define the Argentine case as *genocide*, we could perfectly well have referred to local criminal legislation to deal with this crime. For, without prejudice to the full force of the Convention, nothing ever prevented States parties from criminalizing *genocide* in their respective criminal codifications, even going beyond the scope assigned by the International Charter, so as to cover, for example, *political genocide* or *politicide* within their territories.

Moreover, the coinage of criminal figures that repress genocide in the domestic legislation of States parties was expressly encouraged by the United Nations in its resolution 96 (I) of 11 December 1946, in which, "the General Assembly affirmed that genocide was a crime under international law and invited States members of the United Nations to enact the necessary legislation for the prevention and punishment of this crime"[22]. And indeed, there are quite a few States that provide in their penal codes for the crime of genocide.

Although the majority of local legislators respected the scope assigned by the Convention with respect to the persecuted groups (race, ethnicity, religion or nation), as it is the case with art. 607 of the Spanish Criminal Code of 1995, art. 220 of the German Criminal Code or Italian law 962 of 1967, there are not few examples of criminal definitions of genocide that went beyond this standard, and in all cases, in this way, projected criminal protection also to the *political group*.

In this line, we find art. 211-1 of the French Criminal Code, which, after mentioning the four constellations referred to in the 1948 Convention, then adds "...or any other group determined on the basis of an arbitrary criterion...", and points especially to political motivations on the part of those who seek the total or partial destruction of a group, in execution of a preconceived plan. On the other hand, it is interesting to refer to the Spanish case, given that some of the positions in favour of amplifying the scope

---

21 Cfr. ob. cit., p. 561.
22 Cfr. Robinson, cit., p. 17.

of the figure of genocide are explained by the fact that this crime was introduced into Spanish law by a law of 15 November 1971, with express references in its *explanatory statement* to the need to bring the Spanish Criminal Code (SCC) into line with the content of the Convention against Genocide of 1948, to which that country had acceded in 1968. This was translated into article 137 bis of the 1971 version of the Code, which defined genocide as the commission of certain acts, carried out with the purpose of destroying, in whole or in part, "a national ethnic, social or religious group". It was not until 1983 that Spain adapted its criminal definition of genocide, literally, to the text of the Convention, a formula that was maintained in the current article 607, SCC.

In our continent, we can cite the case of Bolivia, which in article 138 of its Criminal Code, after defining the crime of genocide and determining national, ethnic and religious groups as protected groups, establishes: "The same sanction shall be imposed to the perpetrator or perpetrators, or other direct or indirect persons responsible of bloody massacres in the country". This reference is so broad that it undoubtedly allows the planned acts of group destruction due to political motivations to be reached. References that also refer to the protection of *political groups* can also be found in article 319 of the Paraguayan Criminal Code (which lists the national, ethnic, religious or *social* group); article 101 of the Colombian Criminal Code (which, in addition to the four groups of the Convention, also mentions the *political group*, although it limits it to the group "acting within the framework of the law"); and article 319 of the Peruvian Criminal Code, which also reaches *social groups* in its definition of genocide. Finally, mention may also be made of article 375 of the Costa Rican Criminal Code, which protects groups of persons on the grounds of "nationality, race or religious or political belief".

In Argentina, as early as 1951, that is, a few years after that UN appeal to the international community, it was planned to incorporate into the Criminal Code an article similar to those referred to in the previous paragraph, under the name of genocide. It was a project drafted by the Institute of Criminal Law and Criminology of the University of Buenos Aires (UBA) – composed of Francisco Laplaza and Alfredo Molinario, among other jurists – which punished with a prison term of 20 to 30 years or life imprisonment "anyone who, with the purpose of destroying, totally or partially, national communities or communities of a religious, racial or political nature, perpetrated, by any means, crimes against the life of members of that community...". Unfortunately, this bill was never made into law. If the fate of this bill had been different, and if such a regulation had remained in force until the time of the events investigated here, the situation would have been very different in terms of the subject we are analysing.

There were other projects at different times in our institutional history, including the one recently carried out by a committee of jurists appointed by the National Ministry of Justice, who in 2006 presented their Draft Bill for the reform and comprehensive updating of the Criminal Code, article 70 of which provides for the crime of genocide, respecting the 1948 Convention and the 1998 Statute as to the scope of persecuted groups, that is, excluding the *political group*[23]. In short, in spite of the UN recommendation of more than fifty years ago; in spite of the generalized definition in comparative legislations -even in our region-; in spite of the very serious acts of State terrorism experienced in our country, it is regrettable that even so we do not have in our criminal legal system a criminal figure that reaches genocide. In order to be able to base the scope of the *political groups* on the definition of genocide, it is necessary in a very elementary way, at least, of a legal definition in Criminal Law that contemplates this crime, and on this basis, that this penal conduct reaches among the persecuted groups, the political one. In Argentina, we have neither the one nor the other.

IV. Argentine case law

For the most part, the courts responsible for investigating and prosecuting crimes committed during the period of State terrorism in Argentina have classified them as crimes against humanity, and have rejected, with arguments similar to those presented here, the attempts to introduce the reference to genocide in indictments and convictions[24]. On the other hand, some trial courts have admitted this frame in the operative part of their

23 The possible reasons for this point of view are explained in Filippini: "El Derecho Internacional en el Anteproyecto", at NDP, [2006-B], pp. 689–691.

24 Among others, Tribunal Oral en lo Criminal Federal (TOCF) N° 2, Bs. As., in "Godoy", 15/6/2012 (fs. 405–406); TOCF 4 Bs. As., "Zeolitti", 23/9/2011 (fs. 1145–1153); and with a different composition, "Cacivio", 26/3/2015 (fs. 333–339); TOCF 5 Bs. As., "Vergez, Héctor", case N° 1461, 13/2/2013 (fs. 115–127); TOCF ad hoc Mar del Plata -by majority-, "Duret, Alejandro y otro", case N° 2200, 7/8/2009 (fs. 208–218); TOCF Posadas, "Herrero", 16/10/2010 (fs. 380–401); TOCF 1 Córdoba, "Menéndez", 11/12/2009 (from fs. 273), TOCF Santa Fe, "Brusa", 15/2/2010 (from fs. 122); TOCF Formosa, "Colombo, Juan C.", case N° 2333, 26/11/2009 (from fs. 449) and TOCF Neuquén, "Reinhold", 18/12/2008 (fs. 651–661). In the same line, the context is considered to be crimes against humani-

sentences, with the intention of giving a context to the crimes against humanity that were considered proven to have been committed "within the framework of the genocide suffered by our country during the last civil-military dictatorship"[25].

In this regard, it is worth noting the rejection by the Federal Court of Cassation, Chamber III, of the attempt to frame the crime of genocide in the Argentine case, by confirming the provisions of the Federal Trial Court of Formosa, in the conviction handed down against the then de facto Governor of that province. The country's highest criminal court stated that "political beliefs contrary to that of the regime prevailing at the time, which as a link could be predicted with respect to the victims of State terrorism begun in 1976 in our country, have been excluded from the definition of the crime of genocide and, therefore, from the scope of protection of the [UN] Convention [against Genocide of 1948]". He especially stressed that the Argentine case does not fall under the label "national group", since "the objective pursued at the time was not intended to suppress Argentine nationality, even if only partially... but to eliminate those subjects who were considered "subversives" by the de facto regime. This "qualifier" constituted the element that characterized the victims, grouping them into a group against which the attack conceived in the dictatorship's plan was directed". He pointed out that the classification as a crime against humanity is "the maximum limit to which one can aspire in a State

---

ty with excellent arguments by TOCF 2 Mendoza, in re: "Ruiz Soppe", 15/12/2010 (fs. 350–369 and fs. 397–399). We should also add here TOCF Tucumán, which classified in 2014 the facts as crimes against humanity, but mentioning, in one paragraph, that "the crimes committed constitute genocidal practices within a definition of genocide that is not a legal one" (cfr. "Varela", fs. 2018–2026); and TOCF Salta that stated "the responsibility of the crimes committed against the victims is equal to that of the international crime of genocide… and in this sense the facts constitute genocidal practices but… we understand that the victims cannot be included in none of the groups protected by such crime" (in re: "Mulhall", 28/10/2014, fs. 465–472), published at www.cij.gov.ar.

25 A pioneer in this sense was the sentence by TOCF 1 La Plata, PBA, in re: "Etchecolatz, Miguel O.", case N° NE 2251, 19/9/2006, with footnotes -among others- by Daniel Feierstein and of the sentence by Judge Garzón, invoking an extensive interpretation of what should be understood by "national group" since art. 2 of the CONUG (cfr. fs. 97–106), with which lately, with the same arguments, some tribunals agreed -at least- TOCF San Luis, in re: "Fernández Gez, Miguel y otros", case N° 344, 12/3/2009 (from fs. 453), TOCF N° 1, Mendoza, "Menéndez, Luciano y otros", case N° 1326, 6/10/2011 (from fs. 512) and TOCF Bahía Blanca, in re: "Bayón", majority vote (cfr. fs. 541), all publ. at www.cij.gov.a r.

governed by the rule of law in which the principle of legality operates not only as a limit of *ius puniendi*, but as a guarantee for all citizens"[26]. They added that to consider events as genocide "implies the application of the law outside the framework of legal regulation", beyond the scope of the precept, although they clarified "without this meaning ignoring the plausibility of sociological and political definitions -some broader than the legal notion- around this concept in their respective areas of operation"[27].

In the same sense, the same high court, Chamber I, pronounced itself in the preceding case "Albornoz" of Tucumán, in which it held, among other concepts, that "[c]orresponds to reject the motion... tending to qualify the facts as genocide if the crimes committed in the framework of a generalized attack against the population, fit into the category of *lesa humanidad*"[28].

This claim was also rejected by Chamber IV of the aforementioned federal cassation court, which held that "[t]he treatment of the grievance relating to the declaration that the facts of the case were committed in the context of the international crime of genocide is pointless if such circumstance does not produce concrete legal effects with respect to the situation of the convicted"[29].

26 This argument was also accepted in 2014 by TOCF Tucumán in the sentence in the case "Arsenales/Jefatura de policía", reaffirming "the exclusion of political groups from the scope of the CONUG in the legal definition of genocide". It was said: "It is not a fetishist commitment with the mentioned definition, but it has to do with the circumstance that including political groups in the definition affects the strict limits of the principle of legality in a criminal procedure" (in re: "Varela", fs. 2024).

27 Cfr. Federal Criminal Court of Cassation (CFCP), Chamber III, "Colombo". This Chamber got to the same conclusion in relation with crimes linked to the appropriation of children, as in such cases, precisely, "we do not see in these crimes… a subjective element that could be adapted to the crime of genocide" (in re: "Manacorda, Nora y otra", case N° 366/2013, 16/6/2014).

28 Cfr. CFCP, Chamber I, "Albornoz, Roberto H.", case N° 14.763, 22/12/2012.

29 Cfr. CFCP, Chamber IV, in re: "Migno Pipaon, Dardo y otros", case N° 15.314, 31/10/2012, publ. at CIJ.

V. Conclusions

Thus, and as a sort of final survey of what has been reviewed so far, we can draw the following conclusions:

First: Argentina suffered during the last military dictatorship in which State terrorism systematically persecuted its victims for politically motivated reasons.

Second: Argentina has never in its history approved a legal definition that punishes genocide; therefore, this lack of a legal, internal definition deprived so far of a domestic discussion regarding the matter of the targeted groups.

Third, however, it is by resorting to the international normative production to which Argentina adhered that we have a legal definition of genocide, a definition that arises, harmoniously, both from article 75, paragraph 22, of the National Constitution -UN Convention against Genocide-, and from Law No. 26,200 -ratification of the Rome Statute and Creation of the ICC-.

Fourth: this legal definition of genocide, coming from International Law, the only formal source of application to the case – given the historical omission in its treatment at the local level – does not allow *political groups* to be defined as possible victims of this kind of crime.

It is from the logical chaining of these conclusions that a negative response to this type of question is arrived at, because although it has been proven that the facts under investigation undoubtedly constitute *political genocide* or *politicide*, since these types of cases have been excluded from the scope of the international texts already dealt with, in addition to the legal orphanhood prevailing in the local order, it is forbidden for the judge to modify this situation, no matter how commendable the reasons are for doing so. To do otherwise would not only violate the principle of legality enshrined in article 18 of the Constitution; it would also be a clear example of the appropriation of legislative powers by the jurisdictional body, which would violate the republican scheme that governs us and would undermine a fundamental procedural guarantee such as the right of every accused person to due process of law. In political terms, it is a matter of resigning certain punitive desires that are prohibited due to the full and effective enforcement of criminal and constitutional procedural guarantees in favour of all accused, including those involved in these processes.

If it is true that in the rectitude of these trials the ethical superiority of the Rule of Law over the authoritarian State is at stake, then we must be careful, within the framework of the administration of criminal justice, not to incur in situations that put in suspension the frontal and categorical devaluation of the latter, especially of its arbitrariness and unpredictability.

Trials for crimes against humanity in Argentina: *Contributions of criminal proceedings to constructing Memory and Truth.*

PhD Valeria Thus[*]

I. Introduction

It is well known that the process of judging those responsible for crimes against humanity committed during Argentina's last military dictatorship (1976–1983) has been unique in Latin America's long history of human rights abuses.[1] At the same time, there are different ways of accounting for this process, based on different approaches or perspectives. This paper will focus on the *interaction between civil society and State institutions* – an approach that is far from straightforward. On the contrary, it is often marked by tensions, conflicts, disputes, complications and divergences.

This presentation has four main objectives. Firstly, it analyses how civil society, and specifically the human rights movement, *acts upon and is, in turn, acted upon* by institutions, particularly by the 'justice system' or, as we will see, the legal system in a broader sense. Secondly, it explores the model proposed by the human rights movement to resolve our (violent) past, and how it can be supported by the instruments in the Transitional Justice 'tool box.' Thirdly, it examines the way in which Memory, Truth, and Justice are interrelated. It will argue that in Argentina, we would do better to speak of *'Justice, Truth, and Memory.'* given that the courts have become a *battleground for the political ownership of the past*. Finally, it shows that this type of justice is unique because of its special relationship to *time* and its purpose of *compensating* the victims (anamnestic and messianic justice).

---

* Doctor in Criminal Law and Master in International Human Rights Law (University of Buenos Aires); Coordinator of the Program 'Justice and Memory', Faculty of Law, University of Buenos Aires.

1 By March 2019, 226 sentences had been handed down, 611 cases were pending, of the 3,161 persons investigated 901 had been convicted and 142 acquitted for crimes against humanity; of the 977 persons detained 650 were under house arrest. (Cf. information relating to the trial process at the national level updated on March 15, 2019 by the Crimes against Humanity Prosecutor's Office of the Public Prosecutor's Office: www.fiscales.gob.ar).

II. The Trial Proceedings and their stages.

1. The role of the human rights movement.

The assumption of this presentation is that the only *consistent* attempts to resolve or deal with the State terror of the 1970s have come from the human rights movement. These NGOs have fought for decades to bring to trial the perpetrators of the genocidal social practices to which our country was subjected by the (latest) civic-military dictatorship.[2]

To understand the importance of these NGOs, we need first to consider briefly the different stages our country went through in judging those responsible for crimes against humanity: 1) the Trial of the Juntas; 2) the so-called impunity laws; and 3) the reopening of trials. There is no room here to discuss these stages in any great detail. Rather, what I propose to do is highlight the main contributions of the human rights movement at each of these stages.

In the *first stage,* before and during the Trial of the Juntas, the human rights organisations achieved the following:

a) They reported crimes both at national and international levels. These reports motivated the visit of the Inter-American Commission on Human Rights (IACHR) at the height of the dictatorship in 1979.
b) They opposed the simplified explanations of the time, which aimed at publicizing what was happening through simple depoliticized messages in order to gain international protection. In particular, Augusto Conte and Emilio Mignone's analysis of the crimes as *genocide*, published in 1981, was ground-breaking in raising our understanding of these events to a more complex level.
c) The human rights organisations unambiguously rejected the 'due obedience' clause written into the legislation establishing the judicial procedures for the trial. Here it should be pointed out that President Alfonsín had already proposed three levels of responsibility for human rights violations: those who gave the orders, those who followed them,

2 By genocidal social practice I mean 'a technology of power—a way of managing people as a group—that aims (1) to destroy social relationships based on autonomy and cooperation by annihilating a significant part of the population (significant in terms of either numbers or practices), and (2) to use the terror of annihilation to establish new models of identity and social relationships among the survivors'. (Feierstein, *Genocide as social practice: reorganizing society under the Nazis and Argentina's military juntas* [2014], p.14).

and those who exceeded the orders for personal gain or gratification. Most importantly is Alfonsín's proposal during the 1983 election campaign, which excluded from investigation those who 'simply' followed orders, giving them the right to participate in the democratic process. He proposed a modification of the Military Penal Code to establish that all defendants below the rank of colonel had acted under superior orders and duress. This proposal was rejected by Congress due to pressure from the human rights movement. Instead, Law 23,049 created a rebuttable presumption of due obedience which could be overcome by evidence that the orders were illegal. This defence was not allowed for aberrant or atrocious acts.[3]

d) The human rights organisations won the right to appeal sentences in civilian courts. This right was included in Law No. 23,049, which also allowed a case to be transferred to civilian jurisdiction at any stage of the proceedings if the military delayed the trials unjustifiably.[4]

e) Although at first reluctant to do so, some human rights organisations participated in the CONADEP and in the Trial of the Juntas.[5] In fact, what they really wanted was a bicameral commission of investigation in Congress that would include representatives of the victims' families to ensure political condemnation of the crimes. For this reason, they were sceptical at first when Alfonsín set up the CONADEP instead. Later some organizations chose to participate actively, while other groups remained on the side-lines.[6]

In the *second stage*, the human rights organisations filed complaints with international bodies in order to prevent impunity. Tappatá de Valdez has analysed their trajectory and their achievement as follows:

---

3 For an exhaustive analysis in Spanish see: Nino, *Juicio al mal absoluto* [2006], p. 122 et seq.

4 Tapatta de Valdez, in: *Verdad, Justicia y Reparación. Desafíos para la democracia y la convivencia social*, IIDH [2005] p. 85.

5 The National Commission on the Disappearance of Persons (CONADEP) was an advisory commission created by President Alfonsín (presidential commission) on December 15, 1983 and made up of prestigious and independent citizens who had the power and independence to investigate human rights violations perpetrated by the latest civic-military dictatorship in Argentina.

6 For a detailed analysis in Spanish of how the human rights organizations participated in CONADEP see: Crenzel, *La historia política del Nunca Más. La memoria de las desapariciones en la Argentina* [2008].

Beginning in 1989, human rights organizations under the leadership of the Centre for Legal and Social Studies (CELS) increased pressure on international bodies because they were denied justice in Argentina.

a) Petitions before the IACHR: The human rights organizations insisted that the IACHR review the behaviour of the Argentine government, which had violated constitutional mandates and ignored the imprescriptibility of crimes against humanity by sanctioning the Full Stop and Due Obedience laws. In 1992, the IACHR concluded in Report № 28/92 that the Government had violated the American Convention on Human Rights.
b) Truth Trials: In 1997, the Commission once again played an important role in revitalizing domestic criminal proceedings. The 'right to truth and mourning' gained international recognition and became the driving force behind what is now known as the 'Truth Trials'. These trials have been carried out with the active participation of the victims and their families since 1999, in different federal courts in Argentina (La Plata, Buenos Aires, Bahía Blanca, Mar del Plata, Córdoba and Rosario).
(c) Criminal proceedings in other countries according to the principle of 'universal jurisdiction': these include cases brought in Spain, Italy, France, Germany and Israel, in which several human rights abusers (Suárez Mason, Riveros, and Astiz) received sentences.

The *third stage*, since the reopening of the trials, has been played out in the legal field. Without prejudice to other actions, human rights organisations have achieved the following:

1) The application of strategies for speeding up both individual, isolated trials and so-called mega-trials (with large numbers of victims and accused, depending on the size of the detention centres where atrocities were committed).
2) Avoidance of revictimization, in that the victims have not been forced to testify repeatedly about their experiences. This achievement later gave rise to Decision 1/12 of the National Chamber of Criminal Cassation.
3) Participation in the Commission for the Coordination and Expediting of Cases for Crimes against Humanity created by Argentina's Supreme Court.
4) Repudiation of the decision by Argentina's Supreme Court to allow for reduced sentences for dictatorship-era crimes (Muiña case). A mass

demonstration in the Plaza de Mayo quickly led to the passing of Law 26,732 and changes in subsequent jurisprudence (Batalla case).

It is clear then that various NGOs within the 'human rights movement' have played a key role in the evolution and development of the trial process itself, and have even managed to bring about changes in public trial procedures.

In my view, the role of political *governance* that typified this third stage is problematic. Nevertheless, whatever one's views on the interventions of the human rights movement outlined above – and some of these are open to criticism -, their impact on developing a policy for judging crimes against humanity from the last dictatorship is undeniable.

2. *Process of 'Memory, Truth and Justice' or why do we punish?*

Now that I have highlighted the leading role of the human rights movement in what is known as the 'Memory, Truth and Justice' process in Argentina, I will move on to consider the objectives pursued in prosecuting State crimes.

1) Some consider that human rights organizations advocate a model of retroactive justice focused on retributive punishment. To put it simply, they seek to punish each and every one of those responsible, through a model of Justice and Truth (in that order) by making them serve the maximum penalty for their crimes in common prisons. That is to say, neither more nor less than what is implied in the political slogan 'Trial and Punishment'.[7]
2) At the same time, some see the human rights organizations as rejecting the models of Transitional Justice proposed at a global level, or rather, as rejecting the idea of the 'tool box' that this model proposes, which includes forgiveness and reconciliation as legitimate ways to deal with a violent past. As Tappatá de Valdez points out, the Transitional Justice model is seen as a process of replacing the memory of what happened with *forgetting*.[8] This is due to the fact that in the Argentine case the appeals for reconciliation and forgiveness emanate in general from sectors

7 Carlos Nino's early reflections on this topic are very enlightening. See: Nino, op. cit.

8 Tapattá de Valdez, op. cit., p. 91.

that participated in the dictatorship (the hegemonic media, the Catholic Church, etc.).

A second core argument is that in order to be 'forgiven' one must repent: something that has not happened in Argentina. On the contrary, the perpetrators have not provided any information regarding the fate of the disappeared or the stolen grandchildren, and continue to deny the existence of archives in their possession.[9] Here, it is interesting to note that even during the 'Truth Trials' (comparable – with certain differences – to the truth commissions of the Transitional Justice model) the accused did not provide any information; all the evidence – the truth – was provided exclusively by the victims.

Now, I perfectly understand that the choice of an *exclusive* model of Justice – one that *excludes* other possible provisions- may cause concern. It not only seems at odds with abolitionist models of criminal law (as a possible epistemological horizon for the penal system in general), but also contradicts sentencing guidelines in our country, which aim at social reintegration.[10]

However, I am inclined to think that what is at stake is something *much more complex* than whether Argentina has adopted a retributive model of justice or has reintroduced an authoritarian Natural Law Theory (or, even worse, penal coercion in the form of 'Neopunitivism').[11] It is worth remembering that Argentine democracy has been under threat for decades, with successive dictatorships from the 1930s onwards. Perhaps most seriously, at least one forced disappearance has occurred in this century.[12] So the efforts of the justice system to resolve our past can be seen as a necessary tool to strengthen democracy.

---

9 Tapattá de Valdez, op. cit., p. 85.

10 Cf. resocialization model: Argentina's Constitution, Art. 18 and Law 24,660.

11 For a critical look at the trial process, see Daniel Pastor's classic work. Pastor considers that the trial process is the result of a Neopunitivist drift embodied in human rights organizations and activists and that this has brought the trials into disrepute. (Pastor, 'La deriva neopunitivista de organismos y activistas como causa del desprestigio actual de los derechos humanos,' in: *Nueva Doctrina Penal*, [2005], p. 73/114).

12 I refer specifically to the case of Jorge Julio López. López disappeared without trace on September 18, 2006, shortly after testifying as a victim and witness in the trial of Miguel Etchecolatz in the Federal Court of La Plata for crimes against humanity. This happened the day before the sentence was handed down.

III. The contributions of the trials forty years later

To summarise what has been said so far, the human rights movement has played an active role in the demand for justice at each of the stages mentioned earlier. At the same time, it has opted for the use of traditional legal systems to punish crimes committed during the dictatorship. This demand for (criminal) justice has remained unchanged over the last forty years, and this leads us to reflect on the benefits of having resorted to the criminal courts instead of seeking other ways to resolve our (violent) past such as those proposed at the global level by Transitional Justice.

I will now explain the motives behind and reasons for this choice and I will attempt to evaluate what these trials have contributed to the construction of Memory and Truth.

Here are some of the general features of these trials:

1) They reinforce the rule of law. Choosing the ordinary rule of law (impartial tribunals, guarantee of a full and fair hearing, etc.) has reduced the desire for private revenge and has helped indirectly to consolidate democracy.[13]
2) The accused are confronted, something that did not happen in the Truth Trials of the 1990s.
3) The State plays an active role. Unlike models of peace and reconciliation, which promote dialogue between individuals (victim and perpetrator), state prosecutions provide a better understanding of the logic behind these crimes. This is important because crimes against humanity affect society as a whole.
4) Public trials reinforce the symbolic weight of the human rights movement's initial demand for Trial and Punishment and send a message to society as a whole.
5) The ongoing nature of the trials (for more than a decade) has encouraged victims to come forward with more denunciations and the opening of new cases. At the same time, the decision to hold the trials in common courts nationwide has meant that people from all over the

---

13 There are no recorded cases of private revenge by family members and victims against any of the perpetrators. In fact, many of those convicted of stealing children have already been released without any protest from the victims. Public protests have been held outside perpetrators' homes, workplaces, etc. only when access to justice has been denied (for example, by the impunity laws of the 1990s) or when perpetrators under house arrest (on medical grounds, etc.) have violated the terms of their supervision.

country have been able to attend them, including neighbours of the victims and the accused.

6) Victims perceive that their suffering is heard and is officially recognised.
7) The publicity generated by public hearings leads to greater public discussion and collective awareness, as well as allowing middle school and university students to become involved as part of a human rights education.

Having pointed out these general aspects, I would now like to consider the *particular* contributions made by these trials to the process of Memory and Truth:

The distinctive and distinguishing feature of these trials is that they have not only punished those responsible for human rights abuses (the coercive dimension); they have also contributed to the *construction of truth*. Nowadays we know much more than we were able to learn in 1985 from the Trial of the Juntas and through the information gathered by CONADEP. Among other things:

a) These trials question the notion, presented in the 'Never Again' report and popularised in the 1980s, that most of the *disappeared* were university students, professionals or qualified middle class workers. Since the reopening of the trials and the passing of laws to compensate the victims, other victims have come to light that were not previously identified, namely, lower class workers from the informal economy.[14]
b) More than 760 Clandestine Detention, Torture and Extermination Centres have been uncovered – not just the 380 initially counted by CONADEP.[15]
c) *New cases* have come to light (more victims have filed criminal complaints for the crimes they suffered).[16]

---

14 Izaguirre, *Lucha de clases, guerra civil y genocidio en Argentina 1973–1983: antecedentes, desarrollo, complicidades* [2009].

15 Cf. The Investigation report of the Unified Registry of Victims of State Terrorism of the Secretariat for Human Rights and Cultural Pluralism of Argentina, Annex V 'List of clandestine detention centres and other places of illegal detention of State terrorism in Argentina between 1974 and 1983' (available in Spanish only as: *Informe de investigación del Registro Unificado de Víctimas de Terrorismo Estado de la Secretaría de Derechos Humanos y Pluralismo cultural de la Nación. Anexo V 'Listado de centros clandestinos de detención y otros lugares de reclusión ilegal del terrorismo de Estado en la Argentina entre 1974 y 1983*).

16 See: Feierstein, 'Los números del genocidio argentino', opinion article, *Página 12*, 11 October 2016.

d) We have a better understanding of how the concentration camp system worked and interaction between the open and clandestine work of State terrorism (strictly speaking, of the terrorist State) to which Duhalde referred.[17]
e) We have access to documentation, files and internal regulations of the Armed Forces and intelligence archives (DIPBA), and declassified information from other countries, which have allowed us to better understand how the different concentration camp circuits worked and their links to those of other Latin American regimes. Today, we can also provide a detailed account of civilian involvement (both companies and the judiciary) in State terror, the system of kidnapping of minors, and sexual violence in the camps.
f) Based on eyewitness inspections, *new* places in the concentration camp circuit have been identified, which in turn has led to public ownership of these spaces by the local community.[18]

In short, the judicial reasoning that makes it necessary to identify the places where crimes were committed, to know who did what, in short, the 'construction of the evidence', has contributed to the process of Truth and Memory. Conversely, the information gathered by CONADEP and in the Truth Trials, forms part of the evidence presented in the current trials.

As already mentioned, the two basic models proposed by Transitional Justice are usually thought of as incompatible. Implicitly, they pose the need to choose between two possible paths: Justice, or Truth-and-Memory. In my opinion, this is a false dichotomy. It is not necessary to choose between the two. The Argentine experience proves this. Although the path chosen was criminal trials, the fact is that these trials have, in turn, made it possible to consolidate Truth and Memory.

Even more importantly, 'Truth-and-Memory' and 'Justice' turn out to be two sides of the same coin. They reinforce one another because Truth-and-Memory does not try to displace the concept of Justice, but rather to fill it with meaning. Conversely, Truth-and-Memory can only be established through a trial process. That is why we speak of an anamnestic justice, which also implies understanding Memory as 'presence', as 'recognition of the reality of the injustices caused to the victims'.

---

17 Cf. Duhalde, *El Estado terrorista argentino* [2013].

18 This is the case of the memorial site 'Escuelita de Famaillá' in Famaillá, province of Tucumán.

IV. *The dispute over the meaning of the past*

Law is *also* seen as an *arena* to resolve disputes over *the political ownership of the past*. It allows us to formulate disputes over the *meanings that shape collective memory*, and in this way, it behaves as an arbiter of truth in the face of denialist discourses and provides compensation for the victims. In other words, law becomes a political tool.

Now, before we question *whether the relationship between law and politics is desirable*, I will ask you to ignore the classic approach and reconsider how the relationship between crime and criminal law came about.[19]

I propose we start from Ferrajoli's later work, which extends his criminal guarantee theory to include the serious violations to the human rights committed during the last century. Ferrajoli proposes a drastic epistemological revision of criminology by separating it from the criminal law and making it an independent and external science. This allows us to investigate categories that come from other disciplines (global Critical Criminology, Genocide Studies, among others), which in turn allows us to think about or rethink these problems beyond narrow legal definitions. This epistemological approach allows us to understand what is really in dispute and what tools we need to dismantle genocidal social practices.

Along these lines, we can highlight theorists like Morrison, Álvarez, Woolford, who consider genocide to be a complex social process that does not merely aim at physically annihilating the victims.[20] The ways in which we narrate and represent their deaths are shaped by the terror we have experienced. For this reason, Feierstein claims that this final stage of genocide – symbolic annihilation – is the most important.

The purpose of symbolic annihilation is to reorganise society by making it impossible to remember a society based on freely chosen social arrangements. Terror is used to encourage denouncement of family, friends and neighbours. And betrayal and fear of betrayal break the bonds of trust on

---

19 Some authors have made severe criticisms of *the intertwining of law and politics* in the face of crimes against humanity committed during the dictatorship. This question has been critically analysed in the sanctioning of Law 27.362 in response to the Muiña ruling and the subsequent modification of the Supreme Court's jurisprudence in the Batalla case. See: Rosler, *'El Estado de Derecho caído en 'Batalla'*, in Letra, Derecho Penal, Año IV, número 7, pp. 20/34 and *'Si Ud. quiere una garantía, compre una tostadora: Acerca del punitivismo de lesa humanidad'*, in: Letra, Derecho Penal, Año III, número 5 [2017] pp. 62/102.

20 See: Álvarez, *Genocidal crimes* [2010[]; Morrison, *Criminology, Civilization and the New World Order* [2006]; Woolford, *'The Next Generation: Criminology, Genocide Studies, and Settler Colonialism.'* 5 September 2013, pp. 138/162.

which society is built. That is why the challenge in post-genocidal societies like Argentina is to discover to what extent this symbolic realization has been achieved or not. That is what is really in dispute.

The problem, then, is not to choose between conflicting models: *memory* (judgements or Truth commissions) or *forgetting* (amnesties, reconciliation and forgiveness). Sadly, it is much *more complicated* than that. If Lemkin was right, and I believe that he was, the targets of genocide are not the dead but us, the *living*.[21] Genocide is not something that happened to others in the past – an attempt to destroy a way of life that once existed – but something that *continues to affect us*. This is apparent in the way we relate to one another and explain to both ourselves and others the reality in which we are immersed. That is why the way of telling what happened to us, of representing it symbolically, is not innocent. On the contrary, it indicates how successful genocide has been. That is why the law, as an eminently discursive phenomenon, gives us a privileged insight into the events of the past and the meanings that shape collective memory.

Let us return now to the role of the human rights movement as a central actor in the policy of prosecution. In recent years the victims have not only testified about *what was done to them (the crimes they suffered), but who they were and why they were activists*. And they have done so in open court. This has brought about a key shift in the dispute over symbolic realisation. Today, the trial process is about recovering social practices embodied in social ties, the historical memory, 'their failed hopes, their untrodden paths, and unfulfilled dreams' -to quote Seyla Benhabib-, rather than describing the horror and condemning the culprits.[22]

---

21 Lemkin argued that genocide has two stages: one is the destruction of the national identity of the oppressed group; the other is the imposition of the national identity of the oppressor. He resorts to two very powerful and disruptive concepts to explain the true nature of genocide, the oppressed-oppressor antagonism, something especially uncommon for a 'jurist'. That is the richness of Lemkin's vision, the one that intuits that the real purpose of genocide is to destroy the identity of a people, not only to annihilate individuals; and that this process of destruction is linked to policies of oppression. (Lemkin, *Axis Rule in Occupied Europe: Laws of Occupation, Analysis of Government, Proposals for Redress*, D.C.: Carnegie, *Endowment for International Peace* [1944].).

22 Benhabib, '*Hannah Arendt and the Redemptive Power of Narrative*', Social Research 57, (1990), p. 196.

V. Conclusion: In defence of anamnestic and messianic justice

The model of justice developed during the trials for crimes against humanity in Argentina is unique, not only because of the large numbers of victims and accused, with numerous cases and convictions; it is also closer to an anamnestic view of law, one which theorises the meaning of suffering as a condition of truth.[23] The function of the trials has not been simply to meet the demand of civil society (represented by the human rights movement) for 'Trial and Punishment'. *During the third stage* – that is, from the reopening of criminal proceedings in 2005 to the present day -, the legal system has been assigned a function *just as, or more important,* than punishment, namely, *compensating the victims.* In this way, the law becomes a way to reorganise the devastated psyche and restructure the social field in such a way as to offer the psyche a chance to heal.

At the same time, this model of justice also establishes *a unique conception of time*: forty years that – in Walter Benjamin's phrase – 'blast a specific era out of the homogeneous course of history'.[24] A time of unaltered strength and vitality. Only those who have attended the 24th March demonstrations, which are held every year, or have participated in the trials, can understand the dimension of this time without *chronos*. But at the same time it is a time full of fragility, of upsets, of dark moments and of setbacks, which also attest to its 'weak messianic strength'. In recovering the tradition of the *Jetztzeit*, perhaps we should not lose sight of the fact that it is not only a question of escaping from, but of putting an end to, the concentration camp as logos of our time. Hence the demand for a new time: a time that recovers a past that is missing from the present. We must pay attention not only to what happened, but to what did *not* happen because a way of life was denigrated, defeated, and ultimately annihilated – a way of life that could not be. There can be no justice in the present without accounting for what was left undone. Perhaps the Argentine case is worth exploring simply because it materializes this disruptive, messianic desire 'to brush history against the grain'.[25]

---

23 Adorno, *Minima Moralia – Reflections on a Damaged Life* [2006].

24 Benjamin, "Theses on the philosophy of history", in: Illuminations, trans [1968], p. 263.

25 Benjamin, *Illuminations*. 1st. ed, [1968], p.256.

II. Leniency Programs

Leniency Programs – A Model to cope with the Past?

*Prof. Dr. Jörg Eisele**

I. Introduction

One instrument which might gain importance when dealing with crimes committed under the rule of authoritarian regimes and during civil wars are leniency programs, for example provisions relating to principal or key witnesses. These are witnesses who give evidence about accomplices in order to gain a reduction or discharge of sentence regarding their own involvement in the respective crime. Another term sometimes used is crown witness, which originates in criminal proceedings in England, where the phrase "to give evidence for the Crown" means that in British Monarchy the public prosecutor represents the Crown.

Coming to the subject of our conference, a perpetrator's testimony, which leads to the detection of accomplices, not only contributes to his punishment but also serves to achieve material justice. Furthermore, disclosure of offender's knowledge promotes dealing with the injustice itself. This holds especially true for cases in which due to the incentives of such leniency programs perpetrators belonging to a closed organization reveal inside knowledge.

German criminal law knows various leniency programs[1] which can lead to mitigation of a sentence or even a discharge in return for a contribution to discovering or averting an offence. Section 46b of the German Criminal Code[2], which was inserted in 2009, contains a universal leniency program regarding sentencing[3]. This provision allows for the sentence of the offender to be reduced or, subject to certain conditions, to be discharged. From a historic point of view, a leniency program didn't exist in German criminal law for a very long time. Only in 1981 a specific provision applicable to

---

* Chair of German and European Criminal Law and Law of Criminal Procedure, Criminal Business Law and Criminal Computer Law, University of Tübingen.

1 See in particular section 129 (7), section 261 (9) of the German Criminal Code, section 31 of the German Narcotics Law.

2 Introduced by the 43rd Criminal Law Amendment Act of 29.7.2009.

3 See only Kinzig, in: Schönke/Schröder, 30th ed. 2019, section 46b recital 4; Streng, in: NK, 5th ed. 2017, section 46b recital 1.

drug offences was introduced. In 1989 a leniency program with respect to terrorist offences was passed, which was later extended to Organized Crime. My colleague Professor Heinrich will subsequently elaborate on the developments in this area. My intention is – starting from the aforementioned general provision of the German Criminal Law – to discuss fundamental questions as to the design of leniency programs to cope with cases of conflict including severe human rights violations.

II. Objective of the Section

Section 46b: Contributing to the discovery or prevention of serious offences

(1) If the perpetrator of an offence punishable by an increased minimum sentence of imprisonment or a sentence of life imprisonment,

1. *has substantially contributed to the discovery of an offence under section 100a(2) of the Code of Criminal Procedure which is related to his own offence by voluntarily disclosing his knowledge, or*
2. *voluntarily discloses his knowledge to an official authority in time for the completion of an offence under section 100a(2) of the Code of Criminal Procedure related to his own offence, the planning of which he is aware of, to be averted,*

   the court may mitigate the sentence under section 49(1); a sentence of life imprisonment shall be replaced with a term of imprisonment of no less than ten years. In order to determine whether an offence is punishable by an increased minimum sentence of imprisonment, only aggravations for especially serious cases but no mitigations shall be taken into account. If the offender participated in the offence, his contribution to its discovery under the 1st sentence No. 1 above must exceed his own contribution. Instead of a reduction in sentence the court may order a discharge if the offence is punishable by a fixed-term sentence of imprisonment only and the offender would not be sentenced to a term exceeding three years.

(2) In arriving at its decision under subsection (1) above the court shall have particular regard to:

1. *he nature and scope of the disclosed facts and their relevance to the discovery or prevention of the offence, the time of disclosure, the degree of support given to the prosecuting authorities by the offender and the gravity of the offence to which his disclosure relates, as well as*

> 2. *the relationship of the circumstances mentioned in No. 1 above to the gravity of the offence committed by and the degree of guilt of the offender.*
>
> *(3) A mitigation of sentence or a discharge under subsection (1) above shall be excluded if the offender discloses his knowledge only after the indictment against him has been admitted by the trial court (section 207 of the Code of Criminal Procedure).*

Section 46b of the German Criminal Code entails two objectives, namely privileging contributions to the discovery of an offence as well as contributions to averting an offence[4]. The aspect of crime prevention can be neglected for the purposes of my lecture, even though it might seem promising at first glance. For averting an offence as meant by section 46b doesn't entail preventing certain crimes in general, such as state or terrorist acts. Instead, the perpetrator has to disclose his knowledge so timely that the completion of a specific offence, which is related to his own offence and planning of which he is aware, can be averted[5]. This is, however, not tailored to cases of state crime, because the issue of a principal witness's testimony arises only with substantial delay in the course of coming to terms with the injustice.

Focus will thus rest on offence discovery, although I shall not discuss whether section 46b of the German Criminal Code could serve as an example for a regulation regarding crimes committed under the rule of authoritarian regimes and during civil wars. I will rather look at the essential ideas underlying this provision.

1. *Incentive for Cooperative Perpetrators*

From the legislature's point of view, leniency programs can become relevant in those areas of crime that are characterized by conspiracy[6]. This surely applies to acts in the context of terrorism and organized crime. But it holds true all the same for governmentally organized crimes within police and military as well as paramilitary units, for they commonly appear as

---

4 See only Maier, in: MK, 3rd ed. 2016, section 46b recitals 1 et seq.

5 To the prerequisites Kinzig, in: Schönke/Schröder, 28th ed. 2010, section 46b recital 15.

6 German Bundestag document 16/6268, p. 1; Maier, in: MK, 3rd ed. 2016, section 46b recital 3; Streng, in: NK, 5th ed. 2017, section 46b recital 1.

hierarchically organized entities of esprit de corps which need to be broken by investigating authorities.

Therefore, the objective pursued by the German provision is certainly applicable and can be generalized. Lawmakers intended to make it easier for investigating authorities to discover unknown or clear up unsolved crimes and to infiltrate and break open closed circles[7]. Thus enhancing the probability that criminality will be detected. The instrument shall be deployed especially with regards to severe crimes, as demonstrated by the field of terrorism. At the same time it is important to make considerable efforts to protect principal witnesses from acts of revenge, an issue which, however, is not to be deepened here.

2. *Temptations and Danger of Misuse*

A provision entailing substantial advantages for a perpetrator is at risk of being misused for his own advantages from the outset[8]. There is a danger that the offender could denounces other persons to benefit himself from a discharge or mitigation of sentence. It can be questioned whether the relevant provisions for the sanctioning of false testimony (sections 153 et. seqq.[9], 164, 145d, 185 et. seqq. of the German Criminal Code) have sufficient deterrent effect on a perpetrator who has to expect a high sentence[10]. This is why it was argued already during the legislative process that there is a risk of false accusations and misjudgement. In this respect, German Bundesrat even referred to a "constitutional denunciation" and requested the evidential value being critically scrutinized and in individual cases called into question as a whole[11]. Another concern raised is that ultimately the sentence can't be proportionate to fault anymore. Additionally, it was feared that law enforcement agencies would pressurize the accused person using the leniency program[12]. All of this, however, is not persuasive, as the conditions for the application of this provision counteract: the testimony has to be made voluntarily and needs to be connected to the perpetrator's

7 German Bundestag document 16/6268, p. 1.
8 On this aspect Maier, in: MK, 3rd ed. 2016, section 46b recital 5.
9 Et seqq = and the following.
10 König, NJW 2009, 2481 (2483); Maier, in: MK, 3rd ed. 2016, section 46b recital 5.
11 German Bundestag document 16/6268, p. 18.
12 In detail on this Maier, in: MK, 3rd ed. 2016, section 46b recitals 7 et seqq.; Streng, in: NK, 5th ed. 2017, section 46b recital 1.

own offence. Furthermore, the court owns discretionary power regarding the mitigation of sentence. I will get back to this later[13].

Legislature was well aware of the danger of misuse and tried to thwart efforts by implementing time limits[14]. Thus, mitigation of sentence or discharge are excluded if the offender discloses his knowledge only after the indictment against him has been admitted by the trial court (section 207 of the German Code of Criminal Procedure). The idea is that the voluntary nature of the testimony can be doubted if there already is probable cause against the offender and thus pressure has grown on him. However, this time boundary is not conclusive considering the key issue of the provision, which is to solve crimes. It's then the sole task of the judge to examine whether all of the legal prerequisites of the leniency program are fulfilled, despite the late point of disclosure[15]. It also needs to be taken into account that in cases of state crime the principal witness's individual offence is of diminished importance compared to the public interest in resolving the complex injustice committed by the main organizers. On the whole, it remains the prosecution' and especially the court's duty to survey the principal witness's testimony as to its truthfulness[16].

At least, leniency programs' advantages are that they comply with the principle of legality and that the crimes are investigated by the law enforcement agencies as opposed to being discontinued pursuant to elusive criteria, as it were the case with amnesty programs. Furthermore, the offender will be punished, which gratifies society's need for justice. Mitigation of sentence doesn't necessarily conflict with the principle of guilt, because the contribution to the discovery of the offences of other criminals alleviates the degree of guilt of the cooperating perpetrator, which has to be considered when determining the sentence; even undercutting the individual's guilt can be justified by taking into account that severe crimes are detected and a higher number of perpetrators are convicted[17].

---

13 See III. below.

14 German Bundestag document 16/6268, p. 14.

15 Critically also Eschelbach, in: SSW, 4th ed. 2019, section 46b recital 38.

16 For the closer examination Eschelbach, in: SSW, 4th ed. 2019, section 46b recital 28; Maier, in: MK, 3rd ed. 2016, section 46b recital 77 ff.

17 Applicable Maier, in: MK, 3rd ed. 2016, section 46b recital 8.

III. Prerequisites for Mitigation of Sentence

1. Voluntary Disclosure

It is crucial for the offender to voluntarily disclose his knowledge to the authorities. At the same time it is obvious that his testimony can't be free of any form of external influence, for the perpetrator is pressured by criminal proceedings or even the chance of being taken into pre-trial custody[18]. Besides, law enforcement agencies might reproach or push him to reveal information[19]. As long as prosecuting authorities don't use prohibited methods of examination (section 136a of the German Code of Criminal Procedure) and adhere to the principles of lawfulness, however, such conduct doesn't compromise voluntariness. The same applies to the offender worrying that accomplices disclose knowledge as well to benefit from a mitigation of sentence[20]. Otherwise, if an accomplice's testimony has led to detection of the offence first, mitigation would be ruled out. Yet such a "race" for cooperation with the law enforcement agencies complies with the provision's intention to discover offences effectively.

The motives underlying the perpetrator's disclosure are entirely irrelevant[21]. He doesn't need to act for the purpose of clearing up, he may even pursue opposite goals instead. It doesn't matter whether or not he regrets his own crimes or his participation in a complex organization[22]. The question of voluntariness must neither be answered with regard to a confession of his own offence[23]. It rather depends on voluntarily disclosing knowledge that leads to the discovery of accomplices' offences. Thus a perpetrator's own crime may have already been detected, but he may also benefit from a reduced mitigation of sentence if he gives information going beyond his own deed, and it's this aspect that's very important when dealing with state crime.

---

18 German Federal Court of Justice, StV 1990, p. 456 (457).

19 German Federal Court of Justice, NStZ 1983, p. 323.

20 German Federal Court of Justice, StV 1990, p. 456 (457); Maier, in: MK, 3rd ed. 2016, section 46b recital 26.

21 German Federal Court of Justice, StV 1991, p. 67; German Federal Court of Justice, NStZ 2011, p. 100; Maier, in: MK, 3rd ed. 2016, section 46b recital 28.

22 German Federal Court of Justice, NStZ 1986, p. 326; German Federal Court of Justice, StV 2011, p. 534.

23 German Federal Court of Justice, StV 1990, 456 (457); Maier, in: MK, 3rd ed. 2016, section 46b recital 27.

2. *Relationship between the offence committed and the offence to be discovered*

The next important aspect is the relationship between the offence committed by the principal witness and the crime that is to be detected. Until 2013 in Germany, no connection between crimes was necessary at all[24]. Therefore, a contribution to the discovery of any offence could lead to a mitigation of sentence and the perpetrator could collect or hold back information on other crimes as a precaution[25]. The legislature considered it necessary to obtain any testimony with high probative value from the perpetrator in order to discover or avert completion of offences[26].

So the provision now requires connection to an offence under section 100a (2) of the German Code of Criminal Procedure, i.e. an offence allowing the interception of telecommunications. In the opinion of legislature this relation is necessary for the offender's guilt to be diminished. Thus there must be a relationship between the perpetrator's offence and the offence committed by a third person that is to be discovered. There has to be a link to the testifying offender's guilt[27]. In view of the laws intent this connection is construed widely and extensively[28]. It does neither require a deed in a procedural meaning nor a concurrence of offences[29]. The principal witness's offence and the offence that is to be discovered don't need to be alike or similar. According to the legislature, it is sufficient if the deeds of the perpetrators share are common criminal nature. In this respect the grounds of the Law state[30]: "If the committed offence and the disclosed offence are committed out of a gang, group or any other organized plurality of perpetrators, which the principal witness belongs to, the mere affiliation with this plurality of persons, for example, will not suffice to constitute such connection. Rather, it will be necessary and sufficient that both the committed and the disclosed offence fit into the overall events which have been agreed upon." Therefore, involvement in the same group of perpetrators suffices. Connection is generally accepted in cases of a charged gang

24 On the old legal situation see only Kinzig, in: Schönke/Schröder, 28th ed. 2010, section 46b recital 4.

25 According to German Bundestag document 16/13094, p. 5, this should only be taken into account within the scope of discretion.

26 German Bundestag document 16/13094, p. 1, 10.

27 German Bundestag document 17/9695, p. 6; German Federal Court of Justice, StV 2014, p. 619.

28 Critical Eschelbach, in: SSW, 4th ed. 2019, section 46b recital 2.

29 Maier, in: MK, 3rd ed. 2016, section 46b recital 45.

30 Regarding section 31 of the German Narcotics Law: German Bundestag document 17/9695, p 8.

member revealing the identity or the offences of another member of the same gang[31]. Thus for the issue of authoritarian state crime, discovery of offences of the same organization or offences committed under the leadership of the same state functionary must be sufficient.

3. *Successful Discovery and Substantial Contribution*

a) *Successful Discovery*

Section 46b of the German Criminal Code does have a restricted scope of application though, because it requires an offence to be actually discovered. Merely, possible serious endeavours of the perpetrator aren't enough to mitigate sentencing of perpetrators[32]. This does seem problematic here, for if the discovery fails, the perpetrator bears the risk of his testimony, not being sufficient for having his sentence reduced. Thus, a design such as the one chosen for section 129 (7) No. 1 of the German Criminal Code, which is a special provision regarding Organized Crime, is to be preferred[33]. This provision only requires the perpetrator's voluntary and earnest efforts to prevent the completion of an offence. Although this section doesn't include the detection of an offence but merely its averting, genuine efforts of the offender, which don't depend on the prosecuting authorities' success, suffice. The leniency program concerning the offence of money laundering has been created similarly. It allows a discharge of sentence even in cases of the offence having already been discovered if the offender didn't know this and couldn't reasonably have known[34]. Irrespective of whether one requires a successful discovery or serious efforts only, plain informa-

31 German Federal Court of Justice, wistra 2015, p. 351; Maier, in: MK, 3rd ed. 2016, section 46b recital 47.

32 Kinzig, in: Schönke/Schröder, 28th ed. 2010, section 46b recitals 12 et seqq.; Streng, in: NK, 5th ed. 2017, section 46b recital 1.

33 Section 129 (7) No. 1 of the German Criminal Code: The court may in its discretion mitigate the sentence (section 49 (2)) or order a discharge under these provisions if the offender
1. voluntarily and earnestly makes efforts to prevent the continued existence of the organization or the commission of an offence consistent with its aims; (…).

34 Section 261 (9) of the German Criminal Code: Whosoever
1. voluntarily reports the offence to the competent public authority or voluntarily causes such a report to be made, unless the act had already been discovered in whole or in part at the time and the offender knew this or could reasonably have known (…).

tion such as a vague description of offence or perpetrator, which is inadequate to detect the crime *per se*, doesn't suffice[35]. It's necessary that the knowledge disclosed contains added value compared to the already existing evidence. If the information given is of adequate detail and the offence is discovered, it doesn't matter whether the offender will be arrested or even sentenced[36]. This seems to be especially important in cases of state crime, as the discovery of the crime and its backgrounds contains a substantial intrinsic value in truth and justice.

b) *Substantial Contribution*

Another prerequisite is that the knowledge disclosed has substantially contributed to the discovery of an offence. It is assumed that the perpetrator's testimony constitutes such a substantial contribution if otherwise the offence wouldn't have been discovered at all or at least not to the extent given. However, the knowledge presented only needs to be partially causal, it doesn't have to be the central reason for the discovery[37]. Provided that the perpetrator was involved in the offence to be disclosed, his contribution to discovery has to go beyond the scope of his own participation, i.e. it must regard the accomplices' actions. The court trying the principal witness's offence has to thoroughly examine the fulfilment of these requirements: Firstly, it needs to be convinced of the truthfulness of the principal witness's testimony regarding the offence to be discovered. Thereafter it has to establish that this testimony substantially contributes to the discovery of this offence[38].

3. *Discretion*

Under section 46b of the German Criminal Code the mitigation of sentencing isn't mandatory. Instead, the court has discretionary power. The decision whether or not to mitigate a sentence has to be based on an overall assessment[39]. The court of appeal may review this judgement on the

35 Closer Maier, in: MK, 3rd ed. 2016, section 46b recitals 52 et seqq.
36 Maier, in: MK, 3rd ed. 2016, section 46b recitals 53, 62 et seqq.
37 Maier, in: MK, 3rd ed. 2016, section 46b recital 66.
38 Maier, in: MK, 3rd ed. 2016, section 46b recital 77.
39 German Bundestag document 16/6268, p. 13.

grounds whether or not the discretionary power is being abused[40]. In accordance with section 46b (2) the court shall have particular regard to "the nature and scope of the disclosed facts and their relevance to the discovery or prevention of the offence, the time of disclosure, the degree of support given to the prosecuting authorities by the offender and the gravity of the offence to which his disclosure relates" as well as the relationship of these circumstances "to the gravity of the offence committed by and the degree of guilt of the offender"[41]. The latter point shows that it's not only the aspect of discovery which is decisive. Furthermore, the gravity of the offence has to be taken into account as well, considering the constitutional principle of fault[42]. The relationship between the principal witness's offence and the offence which is disclosed is of additional importance.

For dealing with serious crimes, however, an obligatory mitigation of sentence is to be preferred, as this guarantees uniform practice, preventing the risk of obscure and politically motivated decisions. In this respect, section 46b of the German Criminal Code is rightly criticized as reducing the incentive for disclosure and not providing sufficient assurance for the principal witness[43], who has to act upfront[44].

IV. Conclusion

Although section 46b of the German Criminal Code is rarely being applied due to its restrictions on certain offences and the other shortcomings I've pointed out, in my view there is nonetheless some truth in it, which can be used for the prosecution of severe crimes against humanity. Of

---

40 Eschelbach, in: SSW, 4th ed. 2019, section 46b recital 41.

41 In arriving at its decision under subsection (1) above the court shall have particular regard to:
1. the nature and scope of the disclosed facts and their relevance to the discovery or prevention of the offence, the time of disclosure, the degree of support given to the prosecuting authorities by the offender and the gravity of the offence to which his disclosure relates, as well as
2. the relationship of the circumstances mentioned in No. 1 above to the gravity of the offence committed by and the degree of guilt of the offender.

42 Maier, in: MK, 3rd ed. 2016, section 46b recital 118.

43 Closer Christoph, *Der Kronzeuge im Strafgesetzbuch*, 2019, p. 369 et seqq.; Eschelbach, in: SSW, 4th ed. 2019, section 46b recitals 32, 34 and 37.

44 On this aspect Hassemer, StV 1986, p. 550 (551); Kaspar, FS Kreutzer, 2018, p. 297 (304 et seq.).

course such a leniency program can't play the key role in dealing with the past, yet it can constitute an important complementary element.

While persons belonging to the senior management or higher levels of criminal organizations rather rarely make themselves available as principal witnesses[45], the opposite is true for relationships of equality or subordination[46]. Although one cannot expect that all state crimes committed will ever be discovered or resolved, yet individual pieces of information gathered from various criminal proceedings can form an accurate picture of the past and illuminate the context of injustice. Furthermore, empirical studies have found that in many cases principal witnesses' testimonies led to the perpetrator of the disclosed offence being sentenced[47]. If such a provision is to be created, the principle of guilt has to be observed, that means that the offence has to be punished appropriately in relation to the seriousness of the crime. In particular the reduction of the sentence mustn't result in the State being considered unwilling or unable genuinely to carry out the investigation or prosecution under Article 17 of the Rome Statute of the International Criminal Court.

45 Compare Stock/Kreuzer, *Drogen und Polizei*, 1996, p. 356 et seq., according to which the willingness to testify decreases the higher the position within the hierarchy of the organization.

46 Christoph, *Der Kronzeuge im Strafgesetzbuch*, 2019, p. 417 et seqq.; Kaspar, FS Kreutzer, 2018, p. 297 (310).

47 Christoph, *Der Kronzeuge im Strafgesetzbuch*, 2019, p. 337; Kaspar/Christoph, StV 2016, p. 318 (320).

Transitional justice, international duty to punish and leniency programs. The experience of Argentina

Prof. Dr. Natalia Barbero[*]

I. Transitional justice and the rights of victims

In cases of systematic and massive human rights violations to which transitional justice comes to give an answer, a sensitive confrontation arises between the rights of the victims and the persecution of peace by the State. A tool-box of legal and historically accepted mechanisms has been traditionally used to try to reach a peaceful end of human rights violations. We try to respond with justice to the claims of the victims but we also accept some legal mechanisms not so perpetrators may benefit from impunity but in order to negotiate peace. However, some of these accepted legal tools do not comply with current International Law standards which aim to completely satisfy the rights of victims.

Leniency programs and alternative dispute resolution measures are questionable in the eyes of the victims, because they do not get the full satisfaction that is assumed (pretended) in the event the State "negotiates" with the perpetrators of crimes. Why would those responsible for human rights violations benefit from amnesties, sentence reductions, leniency programs, criminal law defences, if the State has the international mandate to remove every legal obstacle that may lead to impunity? Is there an unavoidable duty of the State to "punish"?

How can truth, justice and reparation[1] be fulfilled if the State can "negotiate" with criminals? On the other hand, how can peace be achieved if the State does not have any tools to use at the negotiation table?

The majority of the victims demand criminal justice -in a traditional way- in order to fulfil their rights. However, transitional justice -not fol-

---

* Professor for Criminal Law, International Criminal Law and International Human Rights Law, University of Buenos Aires; Research Project Director; Member of the Admission Board of the LLM in Criminal Law Program, University of Buenos Aires; international counsellor and criminal law attorney.

1 As rights of the victims, Ambos, El Marco Jurídico de la Justicia de Transición, [2008], p. 39.

lowing the traditional way- still allows for some alternatives, such as leniency programs or other measures in order to make peace possible. These alternatives are not (always) fully accepted by the victims and now are also banned by international standards. So, we are beginning to doubt whether transitional justice will survive and whether leniency programs are acceptable in these cases at all.

1. *The right to truth*

Transitional justice tries to reach the truth as a primary purpose of the criminal procedure. We try to look for the determination of facts, of what has happened during the period of conflict and establish criminal liability, who were the perpetrators and to what extent[2].

In case law, the right to truth, that is to obtain verification of the facts and full and public disclosure of the truth, was established by the Inter American Court of Human Rights (ICHR) repeatedly, for instance, in the cases "Bámaca-Velásquez vs. Guatemala", 25/11/2000, Serie C Nº 70 par. 201; "Barrios Altos vs. Perú", 14/3/2001, Serie C Nº 75 par. 48; and, "Carpio Nicolle y otros vs. Guatemala", 22/11/2004, Serie C Nº 117 par. 128, among others[3].

According to the Report, "The Right to Truth in the Americas"[4], by the Inter American Commission on Human Rights, the right to truth implies: (1) the right to a fair trial and judicial protection, which includes the incompatibility of amnesty laws in cases of serious human rights violations, and the illegitimacy of the military criminal justice system in cases of human rights violations; (2) the right of access to information and the obligation to declassify documents; and, (3) the right to the truth as a measure of reparation.

Can we imply from these guidelines that traditional criminal justice is the only alternative to satisfy the right to truth? Is full punishment the only answer?

The Inter American human rights system has established that the guarantee of the right to truth as a corollary of the right to a fair trial, and judicial protection requires the judiciary to investigate and shed light on hu-

2 Naqvi, Review of the Red Cross, [2006], p. 2–5.

3 Ambos, (fn. 1), p. 41; Quinche Ramírez [2009], p. 51–53; p. 56–57; p. 70–72; p. 92–95; p. 97.

4 Inter American Commission on Human Rights, The Right to Truth in the Americas, OEA/Ser.L/V/II.152, Doc. 2, 13 August 2014.

man rights violations and overcome legal or de facto obstacles standing in the way of prosecuting those responsible. In that context, Argentina has taken significant steps in prosecuting cases of serious human rights violations.

According to the Report, "The Administration of Justice and the Human Rights of Detainees"[5], by the Inter American Commission on Human Rights, the right to truth is not simply the right of any individual victim or closely related persons to know what happened. The right to know is also a collective right, drawing upon history to prevent violations from recurring in the future[6].

So, the first question is if the right to truth is only satisfied by criminal justice or if it is enough to know the truth through extrajudicial commissions of enquiry, accepting leniency programs and other alternatives.

2. *The right to justice*

According to Joinet's Report, the right to justice includes the right to a fair and effective remedy, which implies that all victims shall have the opportunity to assert their rights and receive a fair and effective remedy, ensuring that their oppressors stand trial and that they obtain reparation. Because there can be no just and lasting reconciliation without an effective response to the need for justice.

The Report states that the right to justice entails obligations for the State: to investigate violations, to prosecute the perpetrators and, if their guilt is established, to punish them. What is more, though the decision to prosecute is initially a State responsibility, supplementary procedural rules should allow victims to be admitted as civil plaintiffs in criminal proceedings or, if the public authorities fail to do so, to institute proceedings themselves.

Besides, some traditional legal tools and defences are not accepted in these cases, because perpetrators may benefit from impunity, which is banned in this type of offences since the State has international obligations to fulfil. Thus, the statute of limitations is without effect in the case of certain serious crimes under international law, such as crimes against human-

---

5 Inter American Commission on Human Rights, "The Administration of Justice and the Human Rights of Detainees", Sub-Commission on Prevention of Discrimination and Protection of Minorities, E/CN.4/Sub.2/1997/20/Rev.1, 2 October 1997.

6 Fn. 5, par. 17.

ity; amnesty cannot be accorded to perpetrators of violations before the victims have obtained justice by means of an effective remedy; neither political refugee status nor territorial asylum, nor diplomatic asylum may be granted; due obedience cannot exonerate a perpetrator from criminal responsibility; and, human rights violations shall be investigated by ordinary courts, because military courts do not have sufficient statutory independence and their jurisdiction must be limited to specifically military infractions committed by members of the military[7].

Thus, the right to justice[8] implies a clear obligation for the State: no impunity. The question is, again, if the only answer to this duty of providing a judicial remedy means the obligation of engaging in a criminal procedure. The State has the duty to investigate, prosecute and punish the perpetrators of human rights violations that constitute crimes against humanity, so is this only at the criminal level? Would a truth commission or another kind of judicial procedure satisfy the right to justice?

3. *The right to reparation*

The right to reparation[9] has traditionally involved measures such as restitution[10]; compensation[11]; and, rehabilitation[12].

We may infer that leniency programs or benefits for the perpetrators of human right violations may not be related to this right of the victims, which can be fully guaranteed through measures determined by law, for instance. Thus, a criminal procedure and a sentence imposing punishment would not be needed. However, a judicial sentence has been considered a

7 Fn. 5, par. 26–39.

8 Ambos, fn. 1, p. 44–46; Quinche Ramírez, fn. 3, p. 57–58; p. 96; p. 98–99.

9 Ambos, fn. 1, p. 46–51; Quinche Ramírez, fn. 3, p. 101–113.

10 Restitutio in integrum, according to Palamara-Iribarne vs. Chile, 22/11/2005, Serie C, № 135, par. 234; *García-Asto y Ramírez-Rojas vs. Perú,* 25/11/2005, Serie C. № 137, par. 148; *Baldeón-García vs. Perú*, 6/4/2006, Serie C, № º47, par. 176. See Quinche Ramírez, fn. 3, p. 108.

11 Compensation for physical or mental injury, including lost opportunities, physical damage, defamation and legal aid costs. CIDH, *García-Asto y Ramírez-Rojas vs. Perú*, Fn. 10, par. 276; *Baldeón-García vs. Perú*, Fn. 10, par. 183.

12 Rehabilitation includes medical care, psychological and psychiatric treatment. CIDH, *García-Asto y Ramírez-Rojas vs. Perú,* fn. 10, par. 280; *Baldeón-García vs. Perú*, fn. 10, par. 206.

form of reparation in itself by the ICHR[13]. Following this idea, obtaining a sentence is still needed as form of reparation. No benefit for the perpetrator could, in this way, prevent him from being sentenced.

According to the international standards, reparation implies restitution, rehabilitation and satisfying measures, such as public apologies, public memorials, guarantees for no repetition[14] and changes in the law and legal practice, as well as "prosecuting the perpetrators of human rights violations to justice"[15].

In brief, the rights of the victim of human rights violations demand that the perpetrator of such violations be held to justice. So, to what extent is a leniency program still possible?

II. Alternative or complementary measures to criminal justice

Criminal justice is not the only way to overcome a widespread or systematic context of human rights violations and achieve a new peaceful scenario. It is clear that through criminal justice the three rights of the victims may be fulfilled. However, alternative measures may help to walk through a respectful transitional process and achieve stable peace. We know about commissions of enquiry, obtaining the truth about what happened, recommendations for the State and victims' reparation measures, even reconciliation[16]. There were successful truth commissions in Argentina, Colombia, Chile, Perú, Bolivia, Uruguay, El Salvador, Guatemala, Haiti, Ecuador, Panamá, Surinam, South Africa, and other countries[17].

Other alternatives to criminal justice are cleaning measures, UN programs and missions[18], domestic legislation and others.

---

13 For instance, Vélez Restreppo y familiares vs. Colombia, 3/9/2012; Masacre de Santo Domingo vs. Colombia, 30/11/2012; *Caso de las Comunidades Afrodescendientes desplazadas de la Cuenca del Río Cacarica (Operación Génesis) vs. Colombia*, 20/11/2013, *Rodríguez Vera y otros (Desaparecidos del Palacio de Justicia) vs. Colombia*, 14/11/2014.

14 ICHR, *Masacre de la Rochela vs. Colombia*, 11/5/2007, Serie C, № 163, par. 295.

15 HRC, General Comment 31, par. 16.

16 Seils, in: Almquist/Esposíto, Justicia transicional en Iberoamérica, [2009], p. 23.

17 Ceballos Medina, Comisiones de la Verdad, *La Carreta Política*, [2009]; Ross, Cuadernos de Antropología Social, [2006], p. 51–68; Bronkhorst, Comisiones de la Verdad y la Justicia de Transición, 2003; Rettberg (Comp.), Entre el perdón y el paredón: Preguntas y dilemas de la justicia transicional, [2005].

18 Such as UN missions in Kosovo, East Timor, El Salvador, Guatemala, Ivory Coast, Liberia and Haiti.

Is it necessary to go through criminal justice to satisfy the rights of the victims and fulfil the duties of the State at the international level? If the answer is "yes", we must analyse whether leniency programs and other tools are acceptable in order to make this criminal justice possible.

Are leniency programs tools for impunity or for a limited recognition of the rights of victims?

III. The experience in Argentina

1. Background

On March 24th 1976, a military coup took power[19] and began a systematic plan to finish with different groups and political organizations that had emerged and were acting in the country, such as "Uturuncos" (Tucumán), Ejército Guerrillero del Pueblo (Salta), Fuerzas Armadas Peronistas (FAP), Fuerzas Armadas Revolucionarias (FAR), Fuerzas Armadas de Liberación (FAL), Montoneros and Ejército Revolucionario del Pueblo (ERP).

The military coup planned a "fight against subversion" through a system of massive violations of human rights during which kidnapping, illegal detention, inhuman treatment, torture, killing and forced disappearance took place, from 1976 to 1983. After these years of terror, the military government started to decline and finally on September 27th 1983, as they were ready to leave power, they passed Act Nº 22.924, known as "Ley de Pacificación Nacional", which was an amnesty law for all crimes committed during the civic-military dictatorship[20].

---

19 The President María Estela Martínez de Perón was imprisoned. Commanders in Chief Jorge Rafael Videla, Emilio E. Massera and Orlando R. Agosti, conformed a Military Union and took over the government. The new "Reglamento del Proceso de Reorganización Nacional" was to lead the country and the Constitution of 1853/60 was diminished to a supplementary instrument.

20 According to the law: "Los beneficios otorgados por esta ley se extienden, asimismo, a todos los hechos de naturaleza penal, realizados en ocasión o con motivo del desarrollo de acciones dirigidas a prevenir, conjurar o poner fin a las referidas actividades terroristas o subversivas, cualquiera que hubiera sido su naturaleza o el bien jurídico lesionado. Los efectos de esta ley alcanzan a los autores, partícipes, instigadores, cómplices o encubridores y comprende a los delitos comunes conexos y a los delitos militares conexos". See Sancinetti/Ferrante, El Derecho Penal en la Protección de los derechos humanos, [1999], p. 256–258.

2. *Criminal Trial in Argentina in 1984*[21]

When democracy came to power on December 13th 1983, Decree 158/83 was passed and stated that the military chiefs were to be judged by a Supreme Council ("Consejo Supremo de las Fuerzas Armadas")[22].

On December 19th 1983, Decree 187/83 formed the truth commission known as CONADEP ("Comisión Nacional sobre la Desaparición de Personas")[23] which would later in 1984 publish the world-known Report called "Nunca Más"[24].

Finally, on December 29th 1983, by Act Nº 23.040 the amnesty law that had been passed by the military government was abrogated and declared null[25].

In this new scenario, a criminal trial against the military commanders was held by a newly formed tribunal[26]. The tribunal found the accused guilty[27], except for four of them who were acquitted[28].

---

21 Sancinetti, Derechos Humanos en la Argentina Post Dictatorial [1988]; Raffin, La Experiencia del Horror, Subjetividad y Derechos Humanos en las Dictaduras y Posdictaduras del Cono Sur [2006], p.146, p. 209; Ollé Sesé, Justicia Universal para Crímenes Internacionales [2008], p. 295.

22 The trial of Videla, Agosti, Massera, Viola, Graffigna, Lambruschini, Galtieri, Lami Dozo and Anaya for the crimes of murder, illegal detention and torture was decided.

23 Raffin, fn. 21, p. 244–248.

24 Parenti/Pellegrini, in: Ambos/Malarino/Elsner, Justicia de Transición [2009], p. 133–152.

25 Sancinetti, fn. 20, p. 260–294.

26 The tribunal was integrated by León Arslanián, Ricardo Gil Saavedra, Andrés D'Alessio, Jorge Torlasco, Jorge Valerga Aráoz and Guillermo Ledesma. Julio César Strassera and Luis Moreno Ocampo were the prosecutors. There were 23 defense attorneys.

27 Sentence published at El Diario del Juicio, National Congress Press, January 7 to 28th 1986. Videla: life imprisonment for 66 charges of murder, 306 charges of aggravated ilegal detention, 97 charges of torture (4 of them followed by death) and 26 charges of theft; Massera: life imprisonment for 3 charges of murder, 69 charges of illegal detention, 12 charges of torture and 7 charges of theft; Agosti: imprisonment for 4 years and 6 months for 8 charges of torture and 3 charges of theft; Viola: imprisonment for 17 years for 86 charges of illegal detention, 11 charges of torture and 3 charges of theft; Lambruschini: imprisonment for 8 years for 35 aggravated illegal detention and 10 charges of torture.

28 Graffigna, Galtieri, Anaya and Lami Dozo.

Those crimes were considered crimes against Argentinian Law and against Ius Cogens[29], and neither necessity nor due obedience were accepted as defences[30].

On December 30th 1986, the Supreme Court of Justice confirmed the sentence, although it changed the grade of participation in the events considering the ex-commanders as “accessory to the crime”, changing some of the charges and the punishment imposed to some of the accused.

So selected perpetrators were judged, sentenced and punished at a criminal trial. The rights of the victims and the duties of the State were fulfilled, mainly, through criminal justice. There was no leniency at all.

3. *Peace at jeopardy: Termination of criminal action, due obedience and pardon as a response*

Only two years after the famous trial, peace was at risk again. The country was being threatened by a possible military rebellion demanding to stop new trials that were in progress. This local claim from the military was too active and significant, so it conducted the Congress to pass two laws in order to recover peace: Act Nº 23.492 that stated the termination of criminal actions against crimes committed during the dictatorship[31] and Act Nº 23.521 of due obedience[32].

---

29 Par. 6.5), 4.16: “Los hechos que se han juzgado son antijurídicos para el Derecho interno argentino. Son contrarios al Derecho de Gentes. No encuentran justificación en las normas de cultura. No son un medio justo para un fin justo”.

30 Par. 6: “Examen de las Causas de Justificación Alegadas”, see ap. 2) a.1), a.2) and a.3), at 4.9.

31 Act Nº 23.492, 29/12/1986, article 1: "Se extinguirá la acción penal respecto de toda persona, por su presunta participación en cualquier grado, en los delitos del art. 10 de la ley 23.049 ("...de reprimir al terrorismo..."), que no estuviere prófugo, o declarado en rebeldía, o que no haya sido ordenada su citación a prestar declaración indagatoria, por tribunal competente, antes de los sesenta días corridos a partir de la fecha de promulgación de la presente ley". See Sancinetti, fn. 20, p. 330–334; Sancinetti, in: Beloff, Cuadernos de la Cárcel, 1st ed., [1991], p. 72–75; Ollé Sesé, fn. 21, p. 298–300.

32 Act Nº 23.521, 9/6/1987, article 1: "Se presume sin admitir prueba en contrario que quienes a la fecha de comisión del hecho revistaban como oficiales jefes, oficiales subalternos, suboficiales y personal de tropa de las Fuerzas Armadas, de seguridad, policiales y penitenciarias, no son punibles por los delitos a que se refiere el art. 10, punto 1 de la ley Nro. 23.049, por haber obrado en virtud de obediencia debida. La misma presunción será aplicada a los oficiales superiores que no hubieran revistado como comandante en jefe, jefe de zona, jefe de subzona o jefe de

Besides, the President decided to pardon perpetrators that were under process of law, convicted or detained, among other particular cases[33]. Thus, the military and high members of the forces of subversion were exonerated[34].

These laws and decrees were not well accepted. They were called "laws of impunity" or "laws of pardon", which confronted the most basic constitutional and international standards[35]. On the other hand, politicians presented them as legal tools needed for peace.

In this way, Argentina resorted to three legal tools: termination of criminal action, due obedience and pardon, which came to "interrupt" the process of justice. Can these tools be catalogued as "leniency" tools? They were not a reduction of punishment accorded at trial, at a process of law by a legally designed tribunal or commission in exchange of information or cooperation in the search of truth and justice. On the contrary, they were "exit doors" demanded by the perpetrators and applied after the main trial of the military was finished and even revised by the Supreme Court. They were political measures that implied no punishment at all, a full benefit for the perpetrators, total impunity.

More than ten years later, a new Law was passed. Act Nº 24.952[36] abrogated those "laws of impunity". However, this abrogation did not have a practical effect because it did not produce the reopening of judicial pro-

---

fuerza de seguridad, policial o penitenciaria si no se resuelve judicialmente dentro de los 30 días de la promulgación de esta ley que tuvieron capacidad decisoria o participación en la elaboración de las órdenes. En tales casos se considerará de pleno derecho que las personas mencionadas obraron en estado de coerción bajo subordinación a la autoridad superior y en cumplimiento de órdenes, sin facultad o posibilidad de inspección, oposición o resistencia a ellas en cuanto a su oportunidad y legitimidad". The Supreme Court at first approved Act Nº 23.521, Case "*Camps*", Fallos: 310:1162; and others: Fallos: 311:80, 715, 728, 734, 739, 742, 743, 816, 840, 890, 896, 899, 1042, 1085, 1095, y 1114; y 312:111. See Sancinetti, fn. 20, p. 334–340; Sancinetti, fn. 29, p. 75–77; Ollé Sesé, fn. 21, p. 300–302; Raffin, fn. 21, p. 164.

33 Decree Nº 1002/89 (pardon to more than 50 militaries under process of law), Decreee Nº 2741/90 (pardon to ex Commanders and Generals Camps and Riccheri), Decree Nº 2745/90 (pardon to ex Ministry of Economy Martínez de Hoz), and Decree Nº 2746/90 (pardon to Suárez Mason). See, Sancinetti, fn. 20, p. 342–360; Ollé Sesé, fn. 21, p. 302–305.

34 Ageitos, Historia de la Impunidad, De las Actas de Videla a los Indultos de Menem, [2002], p. 221–227.

35 López Garrido, in: García Arán/López Garrido (Coord.), Crimen Internacional y Jurisdicción Universal, [2000], p. 59.

36 25/3/1998, BO 17/4/98.

cesses against perpetrators of human rights violations[37]. The abrogation had effects for the future, not for the past. So, on August 21st 2003, under a new government, Act № 25.779 was passed and those laws of impunity were declared null and void. Now this new law allowed prosecutors to re-open legal proceedings that had been closed and perpetrators had to stand trial and be criminally judged[38].

The Supreme Court of Justice decided in the case SIMÓN[39] that the laws of impunity were not compatible with the American Convention on Human Rights (arts. 1, 2, 8 and 25), the American Declaration of the Rights and Duties of Man (art. XVIII), the International Covenant on Civil and Political Rights (arts. 2 y 9) and the Convention against Torture and Other Cruel, Inhuman or Degrading Treatment or Punishment.

Later, in the case MAZZEO[40], the decrees of pardon were declared to be contrary to the National Constitution.

In this way, Argentina removed the legal obstacles that had allowed perpetrators to avoid justice and prepared the legal scenario to judge and punish them.

Thus, no amnesty, no statute of limitations and no defences or exceptions were to be admitted in the case of serious human rights violations, as had previously been decided by the ICHR (case Velázquez-Rodríguez vs. Honduras[41] and case Barrios Altos vs. Perú[42]) and the Interamerican Commission (Report on Argentina, 2/10/1992). International standards were applied locally according to the basic principles of Ius Cogens (art. 118 of the National Constitution).

These decisions allowed criminal processes against the military to be re-opened. So new criminal trials began[43]. Criminal justice was the answer for criminal perpetrators and no leniency program applied. Full punishment stated by Criminal Law (of the time of the events) was to be applied.

---

37 Ollé Sesé, fn. 21, p. 306.

38 Ollé Sesé, fn. 21, p. 307.

39 Case № 17.768, "Simón, Julio Héctor y otros s/ privación ilegítima de la libertad, etc.", CSJN, 14/6/2005. The Supreme Court considered Act № 25.779 "valid" and laws 23.492 and 23.521 "of no effect". Cf. Sabelli/Santiago, Tiempo, Constitución y Ley Penal, [2008[, p. 105–154.

40 Case M. 2333. XLII, "Mazzeo, Julio Lilo y otros s/ rec. de casación e inconstitucionalidad", CSJN, 13/07/2007.

41 Sentence 29/7/1988, Serie C N º 4.

42 Sentence 14/3/2001, Serie C N º 75.

43 Since 2006, 915 have been found guilty in cases of crimes against humanity. Source: https://www.mpf.gob.ar/lesa/ (20/9/2019).

IV. Is leniency accepted in the case of widespread and systematic human rights violations?

When human rights violations constitute crimes against humanity, they must be judged and no amnesty, pardon or exoneration is possible. That is the international standard to be followed, that is the doctrine of the ICHR and Ius Cogens. What is more, since the creation of the International Criminal Court ("ICC"), no international crime can go unpunished. As long as the ICC can act in case the State does not judge or judges wrongly[44], this implies that criminal justice is the rule and a criminal punishment is expected.

However, leniency does not mean impunity. Leniency may imply lesser punishment, an alternative measure of penalty[45]. It can still be admitted as a tool for the State to try to fulfil with its international duty and, at the same time, try to reach peace. We cannot allow the avoidance of punishment, but we can allow lesser punishment.

Thus, leniency programs are to be allowed in cases of human rights violations only if they still permit punishment, may be a lesser punishment, but punishment at last. So criminal justice happens to be the only answer for these types of crime, according to international standards, because that is the only scenario where we can achieve punishment, though a lesser punishment may be allowed when needed for negotiating peace.

The rights of the victims and the rights of society as a collective victim are at stake. There is no possibility to admit no justice or no punishment. But there still is the possibility to resort to leniency programs aiming at peace.

---

44 Article 17, Rome Statute of the International Criminal Court.

45 See Duus-Otterström, Law & Philosophy Journal, URL: http://dx.doi.org/10.1007/s10982-012-9147-0 (20/9/2019).

Historical development of leniency programs in Germany

Prof. Dr. Bernd Heinrich[*]

I. Historical precursors

Contrary to English and American law, leniency programs have no legal tradition in Germany.[1] This is immediately apparent when looking at the German term for a leniency applicant ("Kronzeuge" is a direct translation of the English legal term "crown witness").[2] Conceptually, a leniency applicant is a criminal offender, who offers his knowledge about unknown or unconvicted third parties in return for leniency or remission regarding his own sentence.[3] A leniency applicant is usually a witness (with corresponding rights and duties), with the distinction to regular witnesses that the leniency applicant is a participant to a crime against whom separate criminal proceedings are possibly already pending.[4]

The only example of a legal instrument similar to a leniency program in German legal history before 1945 is § 398 of the Prussian Criminal Code of 1805. § 398 covered the evidential value of statements of a participant to the crime. Under Prussian law these statements carried no independent evidential value and could only be used as supplemental clues in support of

---

* Chair of Criminal Law, Law of Criminal Procedure and Copyright Law, University of Tübingen.

1 Frahm, *Die allgemeine Kronzeugenregelung* [2014], p. 20; Jaeger, *Der Kronzeuge unter besonderer Berücksichtigung von § 31 BtMG* [1986], p. 1; Jung, *Straffreiheit für den Kronzeugen?* [1974], p. 1 et seq.; concerning English and US law Jeßberger, *Kooperation und Strafzumessung, Der Kronzeuge im deutschen und amerikanischen Strafrecht* [1999]; Middendorff, ZStW 85 (1973), 1102 (1110); concerning North-Irish law Denny, ZStW 103 (1991), 269; however, Baumann, JuS 1975, 342, disagrees and refers to a German medieval legal tradition, according to which a criminal who delivers another perpetrator could be awarded freedom from punishment; see also Häusler, in: *30 Jahre ... kein Grund zu feiern, 30 Jahre Strafverteidigertag* [2007], p. 259 (260 et seqq.), who describes leniency programs before 1989.

2 The term is derived from the British term King's or Queen's Evidence, cf. Bernsmann, JZ 1988, 539 Mehrens, *Die Kronzeugenregelung als Instrument zur Bekämpfung der organisierten Kriminalität* [2001], p. 19 with further sources.

3 Denny, ZStW 103 (1991), 269 (270); Jaeger (fn. 1), p. 1; Mehrens (fn. 2), p. 19.

4 Frahm (fn. 1), p. 20; Jeßberger (fn. 1), p. 26; Mehrens (fn. 2), p. 20.

separate evidence. This provision is therefore not dissimilar to the rules of corroborated evidence found in US law.[5]

Additionally, there are isolated cases in German legal history before 1945 in which penal discount was granted using the rules of individualized sentencing in return for a confession to a crime or other forms of assistance towards an investigation. Thus the underlying thoughts and motivations of leniency programs themselves were not completely alien to German law, however, the need for a fully formulated concept and explicit regulation in the law did not really exist in Germany's legal tradition.[6]

II. Historic developments in the seventies – "small" leniency program in the German narcotics law

The first discussions in German law about leniency programs took place in 1970 with regard to the American criminal proceedings against Charles Manson, Susan Atkins, Leslie van Houten and Patricia Krenwinkel for six counts of murder. However, at first the discussion was focused only on the American court proceedings, which were closely followed in Germany as well.[7]

Shortly after, the focus of the discussion started to shift to German legal practices. With the advent and rising threat of the Red Army Fraction ("Rote Armee Fraktion", RAF) more people started to advocate for the adoption of a legally regulated leniency program in Germany. Even before any regulation came into being, the tendency of promising leniency to arrested members of the RAF in return for their cooperation with investigative authorities could be observed in the early seventies. This was used frequently and excessively by the authorities in the following years.[8]

To aid the fight against terrorism, the draft of a law to explicitly regulate leniency programs in German law was suggested at the Permanent Conference of Ministers of the Interior in 1972. The Ministers of the Interior of the Federal States were in favour of such a law, however, the exact wording was left to the Federal State Ministers of Justice. After the Ministers of Justice took a dismissive stance toward the proposed legislation, the idea was

5 Mehrens (fn. 2), p. 25 et seq.

6 Cf. the sample enumeration by Mehrens (fn. 2), p. 22 et seqq.; in addition Häusler (fn. 1), p. 259 (260 et seqq.).

7 Mehrens (fn. 2), p. 26; Middendorff, ZStW 85 (1973), 1102 (1110).

8 Stern, Strafo 2002, 185 (186).

abandoned at the end of 1972, because of the restriction of the principle of legality.[9]

In 1975, due to the abduction of Peter Lorenz, a politician of the Christian Democratic Union (CDU) and the subsequent attack on the German embassy in Stockholm, the Federal Council of Germany ("Bundesrat"), at the request of the state of North Rhine-Westphalia, presented a draft law introducing a leniency program aimed at combating criminal organizations.[10] As part of the fight against terrorism, the pros and cons of regulating the leniency witness were fought over for a long time. In 1977 the CDU/CSU parliamentary group introduced a draft law to combat terrorism, which also contained a leniency program.[11] The majority held by the Social Democratic Party (SPD) and the Free Democratic Party (FDP) in the Legal Committee of the German Federal Parliament ("Bundestag") at the time, however, prevented this draft law.[12]

In a completely different context, however, in the midst of the discussion on the fight against terrorism, the "small" leniency program[13] contained in § 31 of the German Narcotics Act came into force on 1 January 1982.[14] The introduction of this leniency program occurred "in relative silence" and was also far from controversial, which is probably due to the

---

9 Breucker/Engberding, *Die Kronzeugenregelung – Erfahrung, Anwendungsfälle, Entwicklungen*, [1999], p. 11.

10 Printed matter of the Bundesrat (BR-Drs.) 176/75 with the comments of the Federal Government at the time in: Printed matter of the Bundestag (BT-Drs.) 3734, p. 6; cf. hereto Breucker/Engberding (fn. 9); p. 11 et seq.; Meyer, ZRP 1976, 25; Stern, StraFo 2002, 186 (185).

11 Printed matter of the Bundestag (BT-Drs.) 8/996.

12 Protocol of the Legal Committee of the Bundestag 8/41; cf. also Breucker/Engberding (fn. 9), p. 12; König, NJW 2009, 2481 (2482); Stern, StraFo 2002, 185 (186).

13 The provision is called a "small" leniency program because the potential penalty discount only applies to narrowly defined offenses – in this case drug offenses. The terminology is derived from the contrast to the "large" leniency program contained in the later Article Law. According to the Article Law, the offender could obtain immunity or reduction of punishment not only for certain offenses, but for (almost) all offenses committed by him in connection with § 129a of the German Criminal Code.

14 BGBl. (Federal Law Gazette) 1981 I, p. 681 (690 et seq.); the provision of § 31 of the narcotics act stated then: „Das Gericht kann die Strafe nach seinem mildern (§ 49 Abs. 2 des Strafgesetzbuches) oder von einer Bestrafung nach § 29 Abs. 1, 2, 4 oder 6 absehen, wenn der Täter 1. durch freiwillige Offenbarung seines Wissens wesentlich dazu beigetragen hat, daß die Tat über seinen eigenen Tatbeitrag hinaus aufgedeckt werden konnte, oder 2. freiwillig sein Wissen so rechtzeitig einer Dienststelle offenbart, daß Straftaten nach § 29 Abs. 3, § 30 Abs. 1, von deren Pla-

fact that general attention was focused on other provisions of the narcotic criminal law at the time.[15] Nevertheless, the leniency program should achieve the same goals in drug-related crime as it should in the fight against terrorism.[16] It must therefore come as a surprise that for decades legislators were unable to reach a consensus on the regulation in the fight against terrorism, although a similar consensus was very quickly achieved in the area of narcotics crime.[17]

III. Historical Developments in the eighties – the „large“ leniency program in the Article Law

In the 1980s, the discussion about a leniency program in the field of counter-terrorism once again came into focus. Contrary to the field of narcotics crime, however, the leniency program here was still highly controversial until its adoption at the end of the decade. The ongoing debate prompted several attempts by lawmakers the legislature to tighten security laws,[18] against which there was often fierce opposition, especially from academics.[19] At the height of this dispute, more than 90 professors of criminal law issued a statement to the Federal Parliament (“Bundestag”) in which

---

nung er weiß, noch verhindert werden können“ (“The court may mitigate the sentence as it sees fit (§ 49 para. 2 of the Criminal Code) or may order a discharge if the offender 1. made a substantial contribution, by voluntarily revealing his knowledge, to the uncovering of the offense beyond his own contribution to the offense, or 2. voluntarily discloses his knowledge to a public authority in such a timely manner that an offense under section 29 para. 3 or section 30 para. 1 the planning of which he is aware of can still be prevented”).

15 Mehrens (fn. 2), p. 26 et seq.; in addition also Slotty, NStZ 1981, 321; Stern, StraFo 2002, 185 (186); Wieder, NStZ 1984, 392.

16 Printing matter of the Bundestag (BT-Drs.) 11/2834, p. 13 cites the goal of breaking out perpetrators from relevant groups who are not yet ideologically consolidated and the prevention of future criminal offenses in particular with regard to § 129a of the German Criminal Code. § 31 of the narcotics act also aimed to offer the perpetrator an opportunity to leave the scene, especially with regards to organized crime.

17 Similarly Jeßberger (fn. 1), p. 294 et seq.

18 Whereby – as far as can be seen – only in 1986 a draft contained a leniency program for the first time, cf. Art. 3 ETerrG, Printing matter of the Bundestag (BT-Drs.) 10/6286.

19 Summarizing Denny, ZStW 103 (1991), 269 (271 et seqq.); Kunert/Bernsmann, NStZ 1989, 449 (456).

they strongly warned against the introduction of a leniency program.[20] This statement brought down the current draft at the time in 1986.

However, the Federal Parliament ("Bundestag") eventually decided in 1989 to introduce a leniency program in a so-called "Article Law"[21] ("Artikelgesetz").[22] Article 4 of this Article Law contained the regulation of the leniency program in just five paragraphs. Article 4 was deliberately kept separate from any pre-existing codified law, in order to keep the leniency program detached from the existing doctrines of German criminal law, in particular the principle of legality. The essence of the leniency program was regulated in § 1 of Article 4[23], which permitted a facultative exemption

20 Statement of the Legal Committee of the Bundestag, reprinted in Breucker/Engberding (fn. 9), p. 158; additionally Mehrens (fn. 2), p. 27; Stern, StraFo 2002, 185 (186); cf. in addition the protocol of the Legal Committee of the Bundestag 10/101.

21 This term seems to be somewhat unique to German legislature. Conceptually it seems similar to the English term of the omnibus act, to the extent that the "Article Law" in question brought changes to multiple existing laws like the German Criminal Code and the German Criminal Procedural Code. However, the "Article Law" not only directed these laws to be changed but also carried the provisions to the leniency program separately from any other existing codification. It should be noted that this legislative procedure is irregular of normal legislative action. Herinafter this law will be referred to as "Article Law" and its provision specific to the leniency program will be referred to as "Article 4" (of the Article Law).

22 Gesetz zur Änderung des Strafgesetzbuches, der Strafprozessordnung und des Versammlungsgesetzes und zur Einführung einer Kronzeugenregelung bei terroristischen Straftaten („Act amending the Criminal Code, the Criminal Procedural Code and the Assembly Act and introducing a leniency program for terrorist forces"), BGBl. (Federal Law Gazette) 1989 I, p. 1059 (herinafter referred to as Article Law); on this law Kunert/Bernsmann, NStZ 1989, 449.

23 § 1 of Article 4 stated: „Offenbart der Täter oder Teilnehmer einer Straftat nach § 129a des Strafgesetzbuches oder einer mit dieser Tat zusammenhängenden Straftat selbst oder durch Vermittlung eines Dritten gegenüber einer Strafverfolgungsbehörde sein Wissen über Tatsachen, deren Kenntnis geeignet ist, 1. die Begehung einer solchen Straftat zu verhindern, 2. die Aufklärung einer solchen Straftat, falls er daran beteiligt war, über seinen eigenen Tatbeitrag hinaus zu fördern oder 3. zur Ergreifung eines Täters oder Teilnehmers einer solchen Straftat zu führen, so kann der Generalbundesanwalt mit Zustimmung eines Strafsenats des Bundesgerichtshofes von der Verfolgung absehen, wenn die Bedeutung dessen, was der Täter oder Teilnehmer offenbart hat, insbesondere im Hinblick auf die Verhinderung künftiger Straftaten, dies im Verhältnis zu der eigenen Tat rechtfertigt" (If the perpetrator or a participant of a criminal offense pursuant to § 129a of the Criminal Code or a criminal offence connected with this offence reveals to a prosecuting authority, either himself or through the inter-

from prosecution under certain circumstances[24] if the perpetrator or participant of a criminal offence under § 129a of the German Criminal Code (or a criminal offence in connection with this offence) discloses to the prosecution authorities his knowledge of facts which enable the authorities to prevent the commission of such a crime. The scope of application was thus limited to offences under § 129a of the German Criminal Code. However, offences that were merely "in connection" with the commission of a crime pursuant to § 129a of the German Criminal Code were also included in the leniency program, which greatly extended the scope of the leniency program compared with the regulation in the narcotics law.[25]

This provision was restricted by § 3 of Article 4, according to which the privileges of § 1 and 2 of Article 4 were limited in the cases of genocide (pursuant to § 220a of the old German Criminal Code) and murder and

mediary of a third party, his knowledge of facts the disclosure of which is conducive 1. to preventing the commission of such a criminal offence, 2. to facilitate the uncovering of such a criminal offence beyond his own contribution to the offence if he was involved in it, or 3. to lead to the apprehension of an offender or participant in such an offence, the Attorney General may, with the consent of a Senate of the Federal High Court of Justice, refrain from prosecution if the significance of what the perpetrator or participant has disclosed, in particular with regard to the prevention of future offenses, justifies this in relation to his own offense".

24 § 1 of Article 4 referred to refraining from prosecution by the Attorney General with the consent of a Senate oft he Federal High Court in the preliminary proceedings. § 2 of Article 4 expanded this regulation to criminal proceedings which are already underway. § 2 of Article 4 stated: „In den Fällen des § 1 kann das Gericht im Urteil von Strafe absehen oder die Strafe nach seinem Ermessen mildern; dabei kann es bis zum gesetzlichen Mindestmaß der angedrohten Strafe herabgehen oder statt auf Freiheitsstrafe auf Geldstrafe erkennen. Beabsichtigt das Gericht, das Verfahren nach § 153b Abs. 2 der Strafprozeßordnung einzustellen, so ist die nach dieser Vorschrift erforderliche Zustimmung der Staatsanwaltschaft vom Generalbundesanwalt zu erteilen" (In the cases of § 1, the court may order a discharge or, at its discretion, reduce the sentence to the statutory minimum or impose a fine instead of a prison sentence. If the court intends to terminate the proceedings pursuant to § 153b para. 2 of the Criminal Procedural Code, the consent of the Public Prosecutor's Office required under this provision shall be given by the Attorney General").

25 Due to its broad scope, the provision is also referred to as large leniency program.

manslaughter (§ 211 and 212 of the German Criminal Code[26]).[27] The Article Law came into force on 16 June 1989.[28]

The Article Law's leniency program was initially intended to be limited in duration, originally until 31 December 1992.[29] However, the leniency program was extended several times. First by the Leniency Program Extension Act until 31 December 1995,[30] then by the Act of 19 January 1996 until 31 December 1999.[31] A proposed further extension at the beginning of the year 2000 failed to reach the required majority in the Federal Parliament ("Bundestag"), with the result that the leniency program expired with effect from 31 December 1999.

In the same time frame, however, three further leniency programs came into force in other areas of German law in the 1990s: in 1992, the Act to Combat Organized Crime ("Gesetz zur Bekämpfung der organisierten Kriminalität")[32] created the provision of § 261 para. 10 of the German Criminal Code relating to leniency in money laundering; shortly afterwards, in 1994, the scope of application of the Article Law was extended to

---

26 However, the restriction to the offences in §§ 211 and 212 of the Criminal Code did not go far enough for many, who rightly argued that further offences should have been included in the catalogue which, according to the assessment of the legislator, are of equal gravity and are typical with regard to the terrorism background cf. Amelung/Hassemer/Rudolphi/Scheerer, StV 1989, 72 (79).

27 § 3 of Article 4 stated: „Die §§ 1 und 2 sind auf Straftaten nach § 220a des Strafgesetzbuches nicht anzuwenden. Bei Straftaten nach den §§ 211, 212 des Strafgesetzbuches ist ein Absehen von Verfolgung und Strafe nicht und eine Strafmilderung nach § 2 Satz 1 nur bis zu einer Mindeststrafe von drei Jahren zulässig; die Möglichkeit, von Verfolgung und Strafe wegen anderer, mit einer solchen Tat zusammenhängender Straftaten nach den §§ 1 und 2 abzusehen oder die Strafe nach § 2 zu mildern, bleibt unberührt. Satz 2 findet in den Fällen des Versuchs, der Anstiftung oder der Beihilfe keine Anwendung" (§§ 1 and 2 shall not apply to offenses under § 220a of the Criminal Code. In case of offenses according to §§ 211 and 212 of the Criminal Code, refraining from prosecution and punishment shall not be permitted and mitigation of punishment under § 2 sentence 1 shall only be permissible up to a minimum sentence of imprisonment of three years; the possibility of refraining from prosecution and punishment for other offenses under § 1 and 2 connected with such an offense or of mitigating the penalty under § 2 shall remain unaffected. Sentence 2 shall not apply in case of attempt or aiding and abetting").

28 According to Art. 6 of the Article Law, BGBl. (Federal Law Gazette) 1989 I, p. 1059 (1061).

29 Cf. § 5 of Article 4.

30 BGBl. (Federal Law Gazette) 1993 I, p. 238.

31 BGBl. (Federal Law Gazette) 1999 I, p. 58.

32 Art. 1 Nr. 19 OrgKG, BGBl. (Federal Law Gazette) 1992 I, p. 1302.

include offences under § 129 of the German Criminal Code (pertaining to the membership in criminal organizations)[33]; and in 1997, § 11a of the Federal Disciplinary Code ("Bundesdisziplinarordnung")[34] was created, which also provided for a corresponding leniency program. In the following period, scholars discussed in particular the practical experiences of the leniency program of the Article Law and also raised the question of whether a general leniency program should be introduced for all types of offences (such as the one that was created 2009 in § 46b of the German Criminal Code).[35]

IV. State of discussion at the time of enactment of the Article law in 1989

As was already mentioned, the leniency program in the area of terrorism was highly controversial from a legal policy point of view.[36] The concept of a leniency program was often rejected by academic literature.[37]

1. Justification for the Article Law

According to the legislature, the leniency program should serve several purposes. For example, it "aimed to 'break out' members of terrorist

---

33 BGBl. (Federal Law Gazette) 1994 I, p. 3186 (3193); this Law introduced a new Article 5 in the Article Law which stated: „Artikel 4 §§ 1 bis 5 [d.h.: das KronzG; Anm. d. Verf.] gilt sinngemäß für die Offenbarung durch einen Täter oder Teilnehmer einer Straftat nach § 129 des Strafgesetzbuches oder einer mit dieser Tat zusammenhängenden, mit zeitiger Freiheitsstrafe von mindestens einem Jahr bedrohten Tat, wenn die Zwecke oder die Tätigkeit der Vereinigung auf die Begehung von Taten im Sinne des § 100a Absatz 2 der Strafprozessordnung gerichtet sind". ("Article 4 §§ 1 to 5 shall apply accordingly to the disclosure by a perpetrator or participant of an offense pursuant to § 129 of the Criminal Code or an offense related to this offense and punishable by a fixed term of imprisonment of at least one year, if the purpose or activity of the organization is to commit offenses within the scope of § 100a para. 2 of the Criminal Procedural Code").

34 BGBl. (Federal Law Gazette) 1997 I p. 2038.

35 Cf. hereunto Jeßberger, Beulke-FS [2015], p. 1153; Kaspar, Kreuzer-FS 2018, p. 297.

36 Cf. Kunert/Bernsmann, NStZ 1989, 449, with many additional sources of information in fn. 7.

37 Baumann, JuS 1975, 342 (343); Hassemer, StV 1986, 550 (551); Kunert/Bernsmann, NStZ 1989, 449 (458); Lammer, ZRP 1989, 248 (251); viewed critically by Amelung/Hassemer/Rudolphi/Scheerer, StV 1989, 72 (80).

groups who have not yet been consolidated in the terrorist ideology, or who are no longer irrevocably committed to it, from the group by granting them an extensive reduction from their sentence in return for information suitable to assist in the investigation of crimes, and at the same time to facilitate their reintegration into society".[38] Furthermore, the regulation was regarded as suitable "to unsettle the members of a terrorist group by reducing the mutual trust of its individual members, which is created by the unconditionality of the threat of prosecution for every member and the shared fear of arrest and punishment, and thus weakening the organizational cohesion".[39] However, this could only succeed if the leniency program was adopted by practitioners and the existing terrorist organizations were thereby substantially disrupted. Therefore, the legislature had not so much the investigation of past offences in mind but rather the prevention of future offences:[40] "The main aim of the leniency program is to prevent future terrorist offences and thus avert serious threats to the highest legal interests. To the extent that is possible, taking into account its objective, it is modelled after the 'leniency programs' already in force in the applicable law (in particular § 129a para. 5 of the German Criminal Code in conjunction with § 129 para. 6 of the German Criminal Code, § 153e of the German Criminal Procedural Code and § 31 of the German narcotics law).[41] The leniency applicant should therefore first and foremost reveal his knowledge of specific offences, that have been planned and not yet committed, so that these could still be prevented. Only in a secondary capacity should the leniency program also lead to the solution of crimes already committed and to a general state of uncertainty and weakening of the terrorist scene.[42] It was also argued that the leniency program could avert a

38 Printed matter of the Bundestag (BT-Drs.) 11/2834, p. 13.
39 Printed matter of the Bundestag (BT-Drs.) 11/2834, p. 13.
40 Viewed critically by Amelung/Hassemer/Rudolphi/Scheerer, StV 1989, 72 (80).
41 Printed matter of the Bundestag (BT-Drs.) 11/2834, p. 13.
42 As claimed by Breucker/Engberding (fn. 9), p. 16.

"state of investigation emergency"[43] regarding the prosecution of RAF supporters.[44]

2. *Objections against the leniency program of the Article Law*

a) *Violation of the principle of legality*

As an integral objection to the leniency program, a violation of the principle of legality was raised by academics.[45] Scholars pointed out, that it follows from the principle of legality that the State not only has a right but also a duty to prosecute criminal actions, which it does not comply with if it grants persons who have committed a serious offence the "benefit" of criminal immunity from prosecution.[46] This not only leads to unequal treatment of offenders, it also impairs the enforceability and inviolability of the law when criminal prosecution may be waived in the case of serious violations.[47]

By contrast, the legislature did not regard the leniency program of the Article Law as an infringement of the principle of legality: "The fact that the fundamental significance of the principle of legality for the administration of criminal justice should not be affected is made clear by several specific aspects of the regulation: the regulation excludes the possibility of refraining the prosecution and punishment for criminal offences under

---

43 The original German term "Ermittlungsnotstand" is a reference to the corresponding term "Notstand" in the right to self-defense. It can be translated as state of emergency or more specifically as necessity as justification in regard to § 34 of the German Criminal Code and describes a situation in which a punishable action is justified if the action is necessary to effect self-defense. By referencing this state of emergency the German authors wanted to highlight that without a leniency program they lacked the necessary tools for an effective prosecution and that the leniency program was therefore necessary as a last measure of defense against this limitation.

44 Critics of the Article Law, however, always denied the existence of such a state of investigation emergency; cf. Kunert/Bernsmann, NStZ 1989, 449 (457 with additional sources.).

45 Cf. the statement of the minority of the Legal Committee of the Bundestag in printed matter (BT-Drs.) 11/4359, p. 16; furthermore Amelung/Hassemer/Rudolphi/Scheerer, StV 1989, 72 (80); Hassemer, StV 1986, 550 (551 f.); Kunert/Bernsmann, NStZ 1989, 449 (458); see also Baumann, JuS 1975, 342 (343); Lammer, ZRP 1989, 248 (251).

46 Hassemer, StV 1986, 550 (552).

47 Hassemer, StV 1986, 550 (552).

§ 211 and 212 of the [German] Criminal Code and in this respect only permits limited mitigation of punishment. Additionally, it is neither included in the Criminal Code not in the Criminal Procedural Code and does not amend any provisions of these laws, but is an independent 'offer' to the relevant offender groups. [...] Finally, the leniency program is limited in time, which emphasizes its exceptional character"[48].

b) *Lack of effectiveness*

The general effectiveness of a leniency program was also questioned by scholars in academic literature: Due to the nature of basic principles of German procedural law, the leniency applicant ultimately could not be provided with legally binding assurances in the preliminary proceedings.[49] If the leniency applicant admitted a confession in the preliminary proceedings or, by disclosing information, facilitated investigations and possibly convictions of others, the Prosecutor's Office could not give him an effective promise that he would actually benefit from such conduct (in particular, that the prosecuting authorities would refrain from prosecuting his case or that a judge would grant a reduction of his sentence). Under German criminal procedural law, the Prosecutor's Office is legally bound, by the principle of legality, to prosecute all cases in which there is sufficient grounds for suspicion.[50] Furthermore, the waiver of prosecution on the basis of the leniency program was phrased as a discretionary provision under § 1 of Article 4 of the Article Law.[51] Thus, there was always a risk for the future leniency applicant not to be rewarded for his assistance in prosecuting criminal offences of others. Even if the Attorney General ("Generalbundesanwalt"), as the "contact person" of the leniency applicant, were to advocate a waiver of prosecution, he would still be dependent on the consent of a senate of the Federal High Court of Justice ("Bundesgerichtshof –

48 Printed matter of the Bundestag (BT-Drs.) 11/2834, p. 13.

49 Amelung/Hassemer/Rudolphi/Scheerer, StV 1989, 72 (80); Kunert/Bernsmann, NStZ 1989, 449 (457 et seq.).

50 BGHSt 15, 155 (note: BGHSt is an official collection of decisions by the Federal High Court of Justice concerning criminal proceedings of particular importance); Münchener Kommentar zur Strafprozessordnung (MüKoStPO)-Peters, 2014 et seqq., § 152 recital. 20.

51 § 1 of Article 4: „[...] so kann der Generalbundesanwalt mit Zustimmung eines Strafsenats des Bundesgerichtshofes von der Verfolgung absehen [...]" („[...] the Attorney General may, with the consent of a senate of the Federal High Court of Justice, refrain from prosecution [...]").

BGH"), which was hardly predictable.[52] Finally, it was necessary to consider: Even if, with the consent of the Federal High Court of Justice ("BGH"), the case against the leniency applicant was dropped on the basis of § 1 of Article 4 of the Article Law, this decision would not have become legally binding, meaning that the case could have been reopened at any time.[53]

c) Lack of necessity

The supporters of the leniency program at that time always referred to a "state of investigation emergency", in particular in connection with the prosecution of supporters of the RAF. This view was often contested by scholars.[54] Many of them held the view that such a "state of investigation emergency" was just as poorly established as the question whether the (then) existing possibilities to grant a leniency applicant a reduction in penalty or to close his proceedings in accordance with other provisions of the Criminal Procedural Code would not be sufficient to adequately reward his willingness to cooperate.

d) Possible abuse without consequences for the leniency applicant

From the scholarly point of view, however, the leniency program also suffered from further weaknesses. For instance, information provided by the leniency applicant would often pose a risk to the prosecuting authorities and courts, which ultimately would promise the leniency applicant a "reward" for his information. The benefits for the leniency applicant were not dependent on a successful conviction at the trial resulting out of the leniency applicant's information (subsequent trial). Thus, if the leniency applicant provided information that would enable the conviction of many or serious criminal offences beyond his own contribution, and this information turned out to be worthless in the subsequent trial – for example, because the leniency applicant suddenly experienced gaps in his memory or even revoked his testimony – then this usually did not entail any risk for the leniency applicant himself or his sentence. If the trial of the leniency applicant was concluded with a sentence, the penalty reduction had al-

52 Hassemer, StV 1986, 550 (551); Kunert/Bernsmann, NStZ 1989, 449 (457 et seq.).
53 Kunert/Bernsmann, NStZ 1989, 449 (457 et seq., 460 et seq.).
54 Cf. Kunert/Bernsmann, NStZ 1989, 449 (457) with additional sources.

ready materialized for him. It was not possible to adapt the sentence or limit the reduction of penalty retroactively based on the usefulness of the leniency applicant's information. A reopening of the investigation into the leniency applicant was only possible in the case of closure of the proceedings in the course of the preliminary proceedings pursuant to § 1 of Article 4 of the Article Law, but not, however, if the case against him was decided by a legally binding (reduced) sentence.

A further problem one may see is that the leniency applicant, in order not to make his own contribution to the crime appear too serious, would often be enticed to make false statements and false accusations, which, especially if the leniency applicant could no longer be heard in the main trial for reasons of his own protection, would lead to misjudgements.[55] This, however, would detract from the discovery of the truth in criminal proceedings and not improve it.[56]

e) Counterproductive effects

In some cases, the regulation of the leniency program was even said to have counterproductive effects, especially if the regulation should prove to be ineffective. On the one hand, members of terrorist organizations could regard such a leniency program as a typical enemy attack on their "moral code",[57] which could have the (undesirable) consequence of bringing the group even closer together to oppose the provocation of "betrayal". If, moreover, it should turn out that the leniency program was not accepted, it was obvious that the groups would then in turn regard this as a "moral" victory, which would consequently have a solidarizing effect.[58]

f) Further difficulties in practice

But even from a practical point of view, the concept of a leniency program proved difficult. It remained unclear how exactly to handle the leniency

---

55 Hassemer, StV 1986, 550 (552).

56 Turner/Gallandi, ZRP 1988, 118, think that leniency programs are ineffective in the establishment of the truth; less strict on the other hand Mehrens (fn. 2), p. 113.

57 Kunert/Bernsmann, NStZ 1989, 449 (457).

58 Amelung/Hassemer/Rudolphi/Scheerer, StV 1989, 72 (80); Hassemer, StV 1986, 550 (551); Kunert/Bernsmann, NStZ 1989, 449 (457).

applicant in the subsequent trial: if the leniency applicant identified himself as a traitor in the subsequent trial, he exposed himself to the revenge of his former accomplices. If, for this reason, the witness remained anonymous in the main trial, it became difficult for the defence counsel of the later defendant to defend his client effectively against the then rather nebulous testimony of the leniency applicant.[59] Last but not least, it was also unclear how, for example, the family of the leniency applicant living abroad was to be protected from acts of revenge.[60]

V. *Practical experience with the leniency program of the Article Law*

At the beginning of the year 2000, a further extension of the period of application of the Article Law failed due to the necessary majority in the Federal Parliament ("Bundestag"). The leniency program of the Article Law was therefore in force for just over ten years. Although there have been isolated criminological studies of practical experience, the impact of the Article Law's leniency program has not been sufficiently documented statistically.[61] Precise statements on key questions, such as the frequency of use of the leniency program's provisions, the number of subsequent trials, as well as on the results of the leniency applicant's trial and the subsequent trials, and in the general effects of the leniency program in these trials, are difficult to establish due to the lack of precise statistics on these figures.[62] The only remaining possibility of investigating the effects of the leniency pro-

59 Amelung/Hassemer/Rudolphi/Scheerer, StV 1989, 72 (80); Kunert/Bernsmann, NStZ 1989, 449 (458).

60 This issue remained problematic; cf. practical experiences pertaining to this in Mühlhoff/Pfeiffer, ZRP 2000, 121 (124).

61 Jeßberger (fn. 1), p. 78; Mühlhoff/Pfeiffer, ZRP 2000, 121 (123); an additional hint can be found in printed matter of the Bundestag (BT-Drs.) 13/11320, p. 5, concerning convictions in the area of left-wing terrorism. This does not specifically refer to the leniency program, the total number of convictions however is very low with only 24 convictions in the year 1997; cf. also Breucker/Engberding (fn. 9), p. 154, who claim to have observed a weakening of the terrorist scene caused by the uncertainty introduced by the leniency program, even though they admit that this effect is not measurable.

62 Mühlhoff/Pfeiffer, ZRP 2000, 121 (123) point in their examination to an estimated number of application of the leniency program of the Article Law in approximately 20 – 25 cases in the field of counter-terrorism, as well as a similar number of cases in the field of organized crime; individual cases are referred to in Breucker/Engberding (fn. 9), p. 17 et seqq.

gram is to interview the professionals involved in practice and to examine their personal assessments.

These interviews show a characteristic split in opinions on the leniency program: While police officers, prosecutors, judges and other persons involved in practical prosecution are generally in favour of a leniency program in the field of organized crime and counter terrorism, scholars are almost unanimous in their disapproval of the leniency program.[63]

In practice, some problems have been identified in the application of the leniency program of the Article Law. The most problematic aspect was probably the high potential for abuse of the leniency program in several respects. On the one hand, this could be exploited by the prosecution authorities, since the leniency applicant had to provide his knowledge in advance. Due to the Prosecutor's Offices own obligations, in particular the obligation to prosecute in case of sufficient grounds for suspicion, which stems from the principle of legality, no assurances could be given to the leniency applicant with regard to a penalty discount,[64] for the approval of a penalty discount was entirely at the discretion of the competent court. If the leniency applicant was not granted this penalty discount for his confession and further information, he was disadvantaged by the disclosure of his knowledge compared to if he had remained silent or defended himself by conventional means. The closure of the proceedings pursuant to § 1 of Article 4 of the Article Law was also dependent on the consent of the Attorney General ("Generalbundesanwalt") and a Senate of the Federal High Court of Justice ("BGH"). In addition, the mere closing of the proceedings could be reversed at any time by a new indictment; as a result the threat of a trial continued to hover over the leniency applicant's head.[65]

On the other hand, the leniency program also allowed the leniency applicant himself to exploit considerable potential for abuse. the testimony of the leniency applicant was generally followed by extensive investigations and, if these investigations were successful, by a subsequent trial. It was likely that a considerable period of time would have passed since the leniency applicant's first testimony before this subsequent trial reached the stage of the main hearing. In fact, it was possible that the trial against the leniency applicant had already resulted in a sentence before the main hearing of the subsequent trial. Therefore, the leniency applicant could devel-

63 Mülhoff/Pfeiffer, ZRP 2000, 121 (122).

64 Cf. hereunto Breucker/Engberding (fn. 9), p. 148 et seq.

65 The situation was different, however, if the criminal proceedings were concluded with a sentence, see above IV 2d.

op sudden gaps in memory or withdraw his testimony entirely without any risk to his own sentence.[66] In addition, in view of the immense effort involved in investigating important subsequent trials, it would have been theoretically possible for shrewd leniency applicants to overtax individual Prosecutor's Offices by deliberately making false statements or at least to steer the investigations temporarily in the wrong direction and, in the most favourable case, even to obtain a penalty discount for it.[67]

Another practical problem of the Article Law's leniency program that emerged was the legal connection of the Article Law's provisions to § 129 and 129a of the German Criminal Code.[68] In view of the definition of the criminal organization in § 129 of the Criminal Code, but also in view of the definition of the terrorist organization according to § 129a of the Criminal Code, certain problems of differentiation arose in practice.[69] These made it difficult for the investigating authorities and the courts to prove membership in the respective organizations. Where the evidence was tried or even succeeded, mostly protracted investigations were necessary.[70] In comparison to the relatively low level of penalties in § 129 and 129a of the Criminal Code, it was therefore usually easier and more practical to focus on the typical, more serious accompanying offences in connection with the presumed membership. For the application of the leniency program,

---

66 This happened for example in the case against the airplane hijacker Souhaila Andrawes, cf. OLG Hamburg NStZ 1997, 443.

67 In view of the concrete wording of the Article Law, such a case would at least be conceivable if the Prosecutor's Office in question did not recognize the true circumstances for long enough. However, no evidence could be found that such a case had actually occurred in practice.

68 Section 129 [Forming criminal organizations]: (1) Whosoever forms an organization the aims or activities of which are directed at the commission of offenses or whosoever participates in such an organization as a member, recruits members or supporters for it or supports it, shall be liable to imprisonment not exceeding five years or a fine. [...]; Section 129a [Forming of terrorist organizations]: (1) Whosoever forms an organization whose aims or activities are directed at the commission of 1. murder under specific aggravating circumstances (section 211), murder (section 212) or genocide (section 6 of the Code of International criminal law) or a crime against humanity (section 7 of the Code of international Criminal law) or a war crime (section 8, section 9, section 10, section 11 or section 12 of the Code of International Criminal law); or 2. crimes against personal liberty under section 239a or section 239b, 3. [...] or whosoever participates in such a group as a member shall be liable to imprisonment from one tot en years. [...].

69 According to pertinent case law, among other things, the submission of the individual to a group will was necessary, cf. BGHSt 10, 16; BGHSt 28, 147; BGHSt 31, 202, 204 f.; BGHSt 31, 239 (240).

70 Mülheim/Pfeiffer, ZRP 2000, 121 (123).

however, it was crucial to establish a connection with the otherwise meaningless membership in a criminal or terrorist organization during the trial, which made the practice of applying the leniency program cumbersome for the courts.[71]

The treatment of the leniency applicant as a witness for the prosecution in the subsequent trial was initially unclear (at the time of the enactment of the Article Law). On the one hand, he was to be regarded as a regular witness who could now hardly invoke his right to refuse testimony on the grounds of self-incrimination, since he had already informed the authorities of everything within the scope of his testimony as a leniency applicant. On the other hand, he was exposed to considerable danger, since it must have been the concern of the defendants of the subsequent trial to "eliminate" the leniency applicant as the main witness for the prosecution. With the introduction of § 68 para. 3 of the Criminal Procedural Code in 1992, however, the legislature created the possibility of hearing witnesses in the trial hearing while keeping their identity confidential.[72] This provision was not exclusively aimed at the treatment of leniency witnesses, but is nonetheless applicable to them.[73] Since then, the differentiated case-law of the European Court of Human Rights has been concerned with the criticism by the academic literature presented above that such a procedure impairs the procedural rights of the defendant pursuant to Art. 6 para. 3 of the European Convention on Human Rights.[74] Over the years, the Criminal Procedural Code was amended with further methods of dealing with leniency witnesses. However, these were largely introduced only at the end of the 1990s or thereafter.[75] This issue was therefore subject to major changes during the period of application of the Article Law and thereafter.[76]

Despite the difficult research situation on the effects of the "large" leniency program of the Article Law, the sentiment seems to have changed towards the expiry of the Law. While the majority of voices in the litera-

---

71 Breucker/Engberding (fn. 9), p. 153 et seq.

72 BGBl. (Federal Law Gazette) 1992 I, p. 1302.

73 Cf. *Münchener Kommentar zum Strafgesetzbuch* (MüKoStGB)-Maier, 3rd ed. 2016 et seqq., § 31 BtMG recital 25 et seq.

74 MüKoStGB-Maier (fn. 70), § 31 BtMG, recital 29 et seqq.

75 Cf. §§ 168e and 247a StPO, BGBl. (Federal Law Gazette) 1998 I, p. 820 and § 223 et seq. StPO, BGBl. (Federal Law Gazette) 2004 I, p. 2198.

76 In 1983, according to the Federal High Court of Justice, the identity of the witness in criminal proceedings still had to be completely revealed, BGHSt 32, 115 (124 et seq.); Mülhoff/Pfeiffer, ZRP 2000, 121 (124) refer to the instruments of witness protection as insufficient in the year 2000.

ture were still critical of the various shortcomings of the Article Law, the majority seemed to have accepted that the introduction of a (new and general) leniency program was in principle necessary.[77]

This can be observed in particular in the regulation of the leniency program in narcotics law: the frequency of application of § 31 of the Federal Law on Narcotics was considerably higher than that of the leniency program in the Article Law, and due to the longer period of application it was possible to draw on a longer period of experience in this legal area.[78] While the Federal Government in a statement in 2007 made the blanket assumption of generally positive experiences by practitioners,[79] individual voices in academic literature viewed the success of the leniency program in narcotics law more cautiously[80]. Nevertheless, critical voices in the literature also acknowledge that there have been at least isolated cases of successful investigations which would not have happened without a leniency program.[81] The leniency program in narcotics law thus had a widely acknowledged positive effect, although this effect may have been less pronounced than had been hoped for at the time of introduction of the leniency program. Nevertheless, it should be critically noted that there are many doubts that a leniency program is an effective means of combating terrorists, as they are "politically motivated perpetrators".[82]

Consequently, on the basis of this experience, voices were raised shortly after the expiry of the Article Law calling for the introduction of a general leniency program for all types of offences while avoiding the shortcomings of the Article Law.[83] However, it took until 2009 before such a general le-

---

77 Breucker/Engberding (fn. 9), p. 156; Mülhoff/Mehrens, NK 2000, 12, 13 et seq.; Hamacher, *Kriminalistik* [1999], 795; Mülhoff/Pfeiffer, ZRP 2000, 121 (125 et seq.); different opinion held by Schaefer, NJW 2000, 2325.

78 Cf. the summary by Jeßberger (fn. 1), p. 78: according to him, in 1995, the leniency program in narcotics law is said to have been applied in every second case.

79 BT-Drs. 16/6268, p. 16.

80 MüKoStGB-Maier (fn. 70), § 31 BtMG recital 5.

81 Körner/Patzak/Volkmer-Patzak, Betäubungsmittelgesetz, 9th ed. 2019, § 31 recital 10.

82 The limited application practice of Article 4 of the Article Law could support this hypothesis, but in view of the numerous other problems of this provision, other factors could also be causal.

83 Breucker/Engberding (fn. 9), p. 156; Hamacher, Kriminalistik [1999], 795; Mülhoff/Mehrens, NK [2000], 12 (13 et seq.); Mülhoff/Pfeiffer, ZRP 2000, 121 (125 et seq.); different view held by Schaefer, NJW 2000, 2325.

niency program was created in the form of § 46b of the German Criminal Code.[84]

84 BGBl. (Federal Law Gazette) 2009 I, p. 2288. Section 46b [Contributing to the discovery or prevention of serious offenses]: (1) If the perpetrator of an offense punishable by an increased minimum sentence of imprisonment or a sentence of life imprisonment, 1. has substantially contributed to the discovery of an offense under section 100a (2) of the Code of Criminal Procedure which is relating to his own offense by voluntarily disclosing his knowledge, or 2. voluntarily discloses his knowledge to an official authority in time for the completion of an offense under section 100a (2) of the Code of Criminal Procedure related to his own offense, the planning of which he is aware of, to be averted, the court may mitigate the sentence under section 49 (1); a sentence of life imprisonment shall be replaced with a term of imprisonment of no less than ten years. In order to determine whether an offence is punishable by an increased minimum sentence of imprisonment, only aggravations for especially serious cases but no mitigation shall be taken into account. If the offender participated in the offense, his contribution to its discovery under the first sentence No. 1 above must exceed his own contribution. Instead of a reduction in sentence the court may order a discharge if the offense is punishable by a fixed-term sentence of imprisonment only and the offender would not be sentenced to a term exceeding three years. (2) In arriving at its decision under subsection (1) above the court shall have particular regard to: 1. the nature and scope of the disclosed facts and their relevance to the discovery or prevention of the offense, the time of disclosure, the degree of support given to the prosecuting authorities by the offender and the gravity of the offense to which his disclosure relates, as well as 2. the relationship of the circumstances mentioned in No. 1 above to the gravity of the offense committed by and the degree of guilt of the offender. (3) A mitigation of sentence or a discharge under subsection (1) above shall be excluded if the offender discloses his knowledge only after the indictment against him has been admitted by the trial court (section 207 of the Code of Criminal Procedure).

Leniency Instruments in the Colombian Criminal Procedure

Fabián Martínez, LL.M.[*]

I. Introduction

The frame and title of this symposium invite us to discuss about past conflicts, past autocracies and traditional criminal prosecution. In the case of Colombia, this topic is very much present both in political discourse and in legal practice. With this in mind, my presentation will aim to give an idea of two out of three of those elements in the Colombian legal system.

But before going into the specifics, I would like to make a disclaimer: I cannot say in the Colombian case that we are referring to a past conflict -since we are still suffering through one- and I do not think we are living in an autocracy -ask me again in a couple of years; instead I will concentrate on the last element: namely, the traditional criminal prosecution of the crimes related with the conflict in Colombia.

Up until today, Colombian criminal procedural law combines different normative systems with different orientations and logics. The State has tried over and over to find legal (procedural) ways to handle both organized crime and politically motivated violence. In a broad scope, the models of criminal procedural law in Colombia have oscillated between inquisitive and accusatorial systems[1].

Both systems have resorted to leniency programs and, at least to some extent, both still coexist today (the inquisitorial system is still applicable when investigating crimes that occurred before 2006). Thus, to have a full perspective of the criminal policy orientations that have influenced the shape given to the criminal procedure and the leniency programs, it is necessary to examine each of its components.

In this presentation I will offer an overview of the different approaches towards leniency, which were predominant in the 1980s and 1990s, in what tends to be perceived as an inquisitorial-leaning criminal procedure.

---

* Senior Legal Officer at the Jurisdicción Especial para la Paz, lecturer in criminal law at the Universidad Santo Tomás in Bogotá.

1 R. Posada Maya, *Una aproximación histórica a la evolución del proceso penal colombiano* [2008], p. 9 with further sources.

Then, I will focus on the leniency instruments within the framework of the current accusatorial-leaning criminal procedure. Finally, I will draw a few conclusions on the traditional approach to leniency in the Colombian criminal legal system.

II. Inquisitorial system and its instruments

1. Main characteristics and context

A procedural system can be called inquisitorial when the judge proceeds *ex officio* to the search, collection and evaluation of the evidence, arriving at the trial after a written and secret instruction from which the accused and his defence are excluded or, in any case, have limited rights of contradiction[2].

Prior to the 1991 constitution, the Colombian criminal system was characterized by an inquisitive tendency[3]. In the investigative phase of the proceedings, there was no separation between the prosecutorial and judging roles. In fact, the role of the prosecution, as an independent branch of the judiciary, was not permanently enshrined in the legal system until 1991[4].

Traditionally, the structure of Colombian criminal procedure was fairly rigid. It did not contain early termination mechanisms and gave almost no discretion to the judges. Between 1938[5] and 1987[6] criminal procedural law underwent numerous modifications but, in essence, the approach to criminal prosecution aimed at individual criminalization.

The 1980s were a decade of turmoil for Colombia and the State reacted in various ways to adapt its criminal law to deal with the new challenges of illegal armed groups of various political orientations and drug cartels[7]. The manifestations of both politically motivated violence and organized crime

---

2 L. Ferrajoli, *Derecho y Razón* [1995], pp. 562–563; J.F. Mestre Ordóñez, *La discrecionalidad para acusar* [2007], pp. 30–31.

3 R. Posada Maya (fn. 1) p.20.

4 Political Constitution for the Republic of Colombia, Articles 250 and 251.

5 First Criminal Procedural Act, Ley 94 de 1938.

6 Criminal Procedural Decree, Decreto 0050 de 1987.

7 One of the most significant ones was extradition. In 1980, the Colombian Government signed an extradition treaty with the United States. The treaty included drug trafficking as an offence for which a Colombian national could be extradited to the United States. See Ley 27 de 1980.

became more evident for Columbian society in the 80s[8]. Thus, the ability of the State to cope with these behaviours became increasingly insufficient[9].

Several criminal procedural bills were enacted, each being more restrictive of the rights of the accused[10]. The objective was to expand the attributions of the law enforcement agencies and give investigative judges more room to counterbalance the activities of organized crime, which was perceived as a threat to the States' existence[11]. These were the years of the drug cartels, the bombings in public buildings and shopping centres. In the countryside, away from the headlines, guerrilla groups tried to exercise control over large swaths of territory[12]. Similarly, paramilitary groups took arms under the excuse of being guerrilla-antagonists but serving more as private armies for the drug cartels in allegiance with the old political class[13].

2. *Leniency instruments*

Before the overflow of terrorist activities driven by criminal organizations, leniency was not an important factor in criminal procedure[14]. The only mechanism was the acceptance of guilty pleas, which were allowed as an accelerating mechanism of the process to decongest the justice apparatus and lighten the administrative burden that any criminal process would entail[15]. The wave of violence during the eighties and the indisputable evi-

8 M.T. Ronderos, *Guerras Recicladas* [2014] pp. 177–180.

9 1989 was a particularly violent year in Colombia. In that year alone a the long series of attacks that targeted Colombian politicians, officials, and journalists, which started with the January 18 killing of 12 judicial officials in Simacota, Santander and ended with the DAS building bombing in December 6. See: Grupo de Memoria Histórica, *¡basta ya! Colombia: Memorias de guerra y dignidad* [2013] pp.136 – 142.

10 Decreto 0050 de 1987, Ley 23 de 1991, Decreto 2699 de 1991, Decreto 2694 de 1992, Ley 81 de 1993, Ley 82 de 1993; Ley 104 de 1993, Ley 190 de 1995, Ley 201 de 1995, Decreto 1371 de 1995, y Decreto 1440 de 1995, Ley 228 de 1995, among others.

11 Cfr. Posada Maya (fn. 1) p. 24.

12 Grupo de Memoria Histórica (fn. 9) pp.138 – 140.

13 Ibid., p. 140.

14 J.C. Forero Ramírez, *Aproximación al estudio del principio de oportunidad,* 2ª ed. [2013] pp. 107–109.

15 R.G Gómez Velázquez/F.A. Castro Caballero, *Preacuerdos y negociaciones en el proceso penal acusatorio colombiano* [2009] pp. 39–40.

dence of organized crime paved the way for a broader approach to leniency as an instrument to strengthen the state in its efforts against it.

a) Narcotics control Act of 1986

In 1986 a comprehensive bill concerning narcotics control was passed through Congress. It created new drug-related offences and adjusted the criminal procedure for those offences[16]. It also contained a provision allowing a reduction of the sentence for a person who, being a subject of criminal prosecution for crimes related to drug trafficking, was able to provide substantial evidence against perpetrators and accomplices different to those investigated in the same case or unknown at the time of his arrest[17]. This became the first leniency mechanism used to stimulate cooperation with the judicial authorities against organised crime.

b) Guilty pleas

In the criminal procedure of the eighties and early nineties, in order to enter a guilty plea, the prosecutor would present the charges that had in accordance with the investigation arisen against the accused, having the possibility of accepting them at last, in whole or in part, receiving a penalty reduction[18]. The defendant could request to be granted the conditional execution sentence[19]. The judge had to validate the conformity of the facts presented to him with the legal description of the crime and the penalty imposed by law. Moreover, the judge had to confirm the existence of enough evidence for a guilty verdict, after which a sentence could be imposed.[20]

Although it was not formally regulated, in practice guilty pleas were the product of negotiations between the accused and the prosecution, which laid the groundwork the way for a regulatory approach to plea-bargaining in the future[21].

---

16 Ley 30 de 1986.
17 Ley 30 de 1986, art. 45.
18 Decreto 2700 de 1991, art. 37ª; Cfr. J.C. Forero Ramírez (fn. 14), p. 108.
19 Decreto 180 de 1988, art. 37.
20 Decreto 2700 de 1991, art. 37.
21 D. Niño Avendaño, *Reconstrucción histórico-práctica de la justicia negociada en* Colombia [2015] p. 28.

c) Benefits for effective collaboration

Following the path set forth by the Narcotics Control Act of 1986, the new criminal procedural statute in 1987 expanded the scope of the lenient treatment for those who provided information that facilitated the activities of the law enforcement agencies and the prosecution of kidnappings, extortion, terrorism and homicide[22]. This approach was carried over and expanded through several legal reforms[23] to the criminal procedure and proved to be an instrument of frequent use in the prosecutorial efforts against the gravest forms of criminality.

For instance, article 413 of the Criminal Procedural Act of 2000 established lenient treatment for a person who, being subject of investigation, standing at trial or even after being convicted, contributed effectively to the objectives of law enforcement[24].

The contribution of the beneficiary of this leniency program had to be useful for the administration of justice in terms of allowing the law enforcement agencies to gather evidence about ringleaders' activities and responsibilities, intelligence about their assets or information about the whereabouts of victims of kidnapping or enforced disappearance. The standard to measure the effectivity of the contribution was that the statement made by the collaborator had to be at least mentioned in indictments or used for the location of persons -victims or perpetrators- or assets related to the criminal activities[25].

The benefits for effective collaboration were considered to be a wide leniency mechanism[26]. It was no longer limited to certain types of criminal offences committed by the collaborator nor by the ringleaders. In this approach the goal was to debilitate criminal organizations, hence the emphasis on gathering information about their leaders or their assets, also for this reason the person who orders, instigates, nor the ringleader, financier or

22 Decreto 050 de 1987, art. 474; Decreto 1199 de 1987, art. 8.

23 Decreto 2700 de 1991, Ley 23 de 1991, Decreto 2699 de 1991, Decreto 2694 de 1992, Ley 81 de 1993, Ley 82 de 1993; Ley 104 de 1993, Ley 190 de 1995, Ley 201 de 1995, Decreto 1371 de 1995, y Decreto 1440 de 1995, Ley 228 de 1995, among others.

24 Ley 600 de 2000, art. 413.

25 Ley 600 de 2000, art. 413 para. 2, 3. See also R.G Gómez Velázquez/F.A. Castro Caballero (fn. 15), p. 23.

26 J.O Sotomayor Acosta, *Los estragos de la lucha contra la "Criminalidad Organizada" en el sistema penal: el caso colombiano*, Revista de estudios criminais 34, 2009, p. 122.

promoter was excluded of the benefits; the provision on the whereabouts of victims was not central to the program[27].

Proportionality was a condition for the program. This meant that the benefits to be granted had to gauged against the value of the evidence provided by the collaborator. Although the benefits contemplated could be accumulated in cases of multiple collaborations, it was not possible to completely exclude the penalty[28].

To some extent, the program aimed to be centralized, given that only the Attorney General or a direct delegate could officially validate the agreement prior to the control by the judiciary. Finally, the leniency program did not proceed ex officio, it could only be initiated upon request from the defendant or counsel, but the prosecutor was allowed to make the defendant aware of this mechanism[29].

III. Accusatory system and its instruments

1. Main characteristics and context

The 1990s began with peace negotiations that to some extent successfully achieved the demobilisation of an armed group in exchange for allowing its members to participate in the political debate and some commitments on reforms to the State.[30] In turn, the enthusiasm of civil society for this agreement prompted a process of institutional reform that concluded in the drafting of a new constitution.[31]

The 1991 constitution introduced considerable changes to the structure of the Colombian State and recognised fundamental rights as the most prominent role in the normative hierarchy of the Republic[32]. Accordingly, the criminal justice system should have also been adjusted shortly afterwards. This was not the case, at least not immediately. Although in 1993

---

27 Artículo 413 Ley 600 de 2000. With several critics to this provision see J.O Sotomayor Acosta (fn. 26) p. 124.

28 Ley 600 de 2000, art. 413 para. 6.

29 Ley 600 de 2000, art. 414.

30 Cfr. Grupo de Memoria Histórica (fn.9) pp. 146.

31 See Grupo de Memoria Histórica (fn. 9) pp. 148–149.

32 See A. Botero-Bernal, *Balance de los 25 años de la constitución colombiana de 1991*, Vniversitas 134 (2017), pp. 59–92, with further sources.

the code of criminal procedure was reformed again, the modifications carried on with the criminal policy orientations of the eighties[33].

A comprehensive reform of the criminal procedure was only first adopted in the year 2000. A mixed system was introduced, trying to build a bridge between an investigation phase of inquisitive tendency and a phase of a contradictory public trial with accusatory tendency. This legislative effort was short-lived: just three years later a thorough review of the criminal procedure system brought about the implementation of an accusatory system[34]. This new model was introduced with a constitutional amendment, which was later completed with the adoption of the Criminal Procedural Act of 2004 (CPA of 2004)[35]. These legislative efforts were strongly supported by the United States Department of Justice[36].

A procedural system is accusatory when the judge has a passive role in the proceedings, is rigidly separated from the parties, and the trial takes the form of a debate initiated by the accusation, to which the burden of proof lies. There, both parties are confronted in a contradictory, oral and public trial, which is resolved by a judge according to a free weighting of the evidence and submissions of the parties[37].

In Colombia, it had been understood that regardless of how the prosecution of a crime is carried out, it must always comply with the principle of legality to defend the rights of the defendants and of the citizens in general[38]. However, the implementation of a more accusatory system with the CPA of 2004, made it necessary to incorporate mechanisms of prosecutorial discretion and early termination of the criminal process[39]. The accusatory model tries to decongest the judicial system, since the requirements for an accusatory trial make it unlikely for most matters to reach that stage[40]. Those mechanisms were written following the example of the legislation

---

33 Cfr. Posada Maya (fn. 1), pp. 24–27.

34 On the characteristics of the new criminal procedure reform of 2004 see Corte Constitucional, Sentencia C-591 de 2005.

35 D. Niño Avendaño (fn.21), pp. 50–53.

36 A.J. Cancino Moreno, *Reforma al Código de Procedimiento Penal y a la Fiscalía General de la Nación* [2004] p. 13.

37 L. Ferrajoli (fn. 2) p. 564.

38 J.C. Forero Ramírez (fn. 14), p. 39. See also Corte Constitucional, Sentencia C-891 de 2012.

39 Corte Constitucional, Sentencia C-095 de 2007. Artículo Preacuerdos y negociaciones de culpabilidad; C. Gómez Pavajeau, *Preacuerdos y negociaciones de culpabilidad* [2010] pp. 137–142.

40 A.C. Navarro Navajas, *La inmunidad y el principio de oportunidad en el proceso penal* [2015] p. 63. J.C. Forero Ramírez (fn. 14), pp. 49–50.

of the United States and Puerto Rico but were quickly assimilated to the traditional leniency programs or at least ended up fulfilling a similar role[41].

2. Leniency Instruments

One way to prevent most criminal investigations from reaching the trial stage is to establish a system of incentives that will allow the reduction of penalties to be imposed, in exchange for waiving the debate at trial or in exchange for the acceptance of criminal responsibility[42].

Although –as it was shown before– some leniency instruments were used in the Colombian criminal procedure, the reconfiguration of the criminal system towards a model of accusatory characteristics made it necessary to redesign the leniency instruments as well.

With the CPA of 2004, some leniency instruments such as the benefits for effective collaboration and the exemption of punishment were eliminated while the possibility of obtaining benefits for the guilty pleas was maintained. Interestingly, some provisions for regulating the plea bargaining were included and the scope of the principle of legality was restricted[43], allowing a regulated discretion in the prosecutor's proceedings, that is, admitting the principle of opportunity in the criminal procedural system[44].

The change of mentality that such an ambitious reform required, weakening the supremacy of the principle of legality and explicitly allowing negotiations and the discretionary exercise of criminal prosecution, produced effects that have not yet been fully consolidated in the Colombian legal system.

a) Plea-bargaining

Plea-bargaining and the negotiation on the charges to be imposed were not alien to the Colombian legal practice[45]. The fact that the CPA of 2004

41 R.G Gómez Velázquez/F.A. Castro Caballero (fn. 15), pp. 26–27, 42–43.

42 A.C. Navarro Navajas (fn. 39), p. 64. J.C. Forero Ramírez (fn. 14), p. 151.

43 D. Niño Avendaño (fn. 21) pp. 70–75. J.F. Mestre Ordóñez (fn. 2) p 91–96.

44 J.C. Forero Ramírez (fn. 14), p. 62.

45 J.C. Forero Ramírez (fn. 14), p. 108; D. Niño Avendaño (fn. 21) pp. 23–25; R.G Gómez Velázquez, F.A. Castro Caballero (fn. 15), pp. 23–26.

recognised, regulated and considered them inherent to the system was the real novelty. This brought more transparency and better control of these endeavours, both from the judiciary but also from public opinion[46].

Article 348 of the CPA of 2004 sets ambitious objectives for the plea-bargaining mechanism: "to humanise the process and the penalty", "to obtain prompt and effective administration of justice", "to activate the resolution of social conflicts", and "to promote the reparation of the damages caused by the crime"[47]. There are no provisions or further explanations on how the "humanisation" is supposed to occur. Also, there is no empirical evidence on whether the resolution of social conflicts is activated by it. Regarding the reparation of damages, Article 349 mandates that when the charges involve an increase in the assets of the accused, the agreement cannot be concluded until at least half of the patrimonial benefit obtained is reimbursed and the collection of the other half is secured[48].

According to Article 350 of the same statute, the prosecution and the defendant agree to a guilty plea on specific, previously discussed, charges[49]. On the side of the prosecution, the goal of the provision is to avoid reaching the trial stage, achieving thus the closure of the proceedings in less time and with fewer resources. For the defendant, the plea bargaining offers the possibility of lenient charges and eliminates the uncertainty of more severe punishment[50].

The scope of the agreement is set forth in Article 350 as follows: a) the elimination of aggravating circumstances (generic or specific) attached to the charges; b) the discard of a specific charge; or c) the characterisation of the offence in a concrete way, in order to achieve the subsequent reduction of the penalty. The agreement reached between prosecution and defence is binding for the judge, who can only quash it if the deal ignores the fundamental rights of the accused or the victims. It is worth mentioning that the victims do not take in the negotiation process and they usually oppose the agreement when it is presented to the judge.

46 A.C. Navarro Navajas (fn. 39), p. 67–69.
47 Ley 906 de 2004, Artículo 348.
48 Ley 906 de 2004, Artículo 349.
49 Ley 906 de 2004, Artículo 350.
50 C. Gómez Pavajeau (fn. 39) pp. 121–123.

b) *Opportunity-principle*

Pursuant to Article 323 of the CPA of 2004, the opportunity-principle has been defined as the constitutional power that allows the Attorney General's Office (AGO) to suspend, interrupt or renounce it, although there is a basis to advance criminal prosecution, for reasons of criminal policy, according to the grounds defined in the law and in the regulations issued by the AGO itself. The use of the opportunity-principle must be submitted to a legality control before a judge[51].

In the Colombian legal tradition, the principle of legality had been an undisputed pillar, designed to guarantee the primacy of the law in criminal procedure so that neither state prosecution nor defendants are exposed to subjective bias. It assures that no defendant may be punished arbitrarily or retroactively by the state and that the AGO has an obligation to press charges when there is enough evidence available on the commission of a crime. There is no margin of discretion[52].

In contrast, the opportunity-principle allows for the AGO to decide whether to charge a suspect of a crime if this is considered appropriate or convenient considering its criminal policy guidelines[53]. In Colombian criminal procedural law, it is a regulated as a discretionary faculty. In other words, the legislature has established a legal framework for the exercise of discretion that confers the principle of opportunity[54].

In the framework of the CPA, the accused has no right to demand the resignation, suspension or interruption of the prosecutorial efforts[55]. Conversely, the power of the prosecution is subject to mandatory control by a judge[56]. The judge's examination is not only formal but also material for the rights of both the accused and the victims[57]. Moreover, the application of the opportunity-principle will only proceed if there is evidence about the existence of a crime and of the accused's involvement in it[58].

---

51 Ley 906 de 2004, Artículo 323.

52 J.C. Forero Ramírez (fn. 14), pp. 39–44.

53 L.F. Bedoya Sierra et al., *Principio de Oprtunidad. Bases conceptuales para su aplicación* [2010] p.33; J.C. Forero Ramírez (fn. 14) pp. 125–128.

54 J.C. Forero Ramírez (fn. 14) p. 268; J.F. Mestre Ordóñez. (fn. 2) pp. 97–99.

55 Corte Constitucional, Sentencia C-738 de 2008.

56 Corte Constitucional, Sentencia C 979 de 2005.

57 Corte Constitucional, ibid.; L.F. Bedoya Sierra et al. (fn. 53) p. 50.

58 Corte Constitucional, Sentencia C-095 de 2007; L.F. Bedoya Sierra et al. (fn. 53) p. 101.

Article 324 establishes eighteen grounds on which it is possible to consider not to prosecute, namely, to apply the opportunity principle. However, for the purposes of this text they can be synthesized in six categories: a) Cases in which the statutory penalty is reduced or the enforcement of it seems disproportionate; b) Cases of so-called petty criminality, in which the damage caused by the crime is not of sufficient entity to merit State intervention; c) Cases in which the criminal prosecution could create social problems of greater importance; d) Cases in which the accused has suffered moral or physical damage; e) Cases in which the criminal prosecution puts the external security of the State at risk; f) Cases of effective collaboration with the authorities to prevent the commission on new crimes, or to prevent others from continuing in criminal activities, or when it helps to dismantle criminal organizations[59].

To include the opportunity-principle in the catalogue of leniency programs may seem misleading. However, in Colombian judicial practice, the possibility of conditioning (or deferring in time) the exercise of criminal action to collaboration with the investigative bodies, has been used more frequently and it constitutes a mechanism of certain utility and preference for prosecutors to approach complex criminal phenomena[60].

c) Agreements upon guilty-pleas and deferral of prosecution

A third approach to leniency, not expressly allowed in the CPA or other provisions originates from a mixture of the plea bargaining and the opportunity-principle. In legal practice it is often the case that negotiations for pre-agreements also include the possibility of using the principle of opportunity with respect to at least one charge resulting of the prosecution's case[61]. Considering that the agreement on a guilty plea is binding and final once it is approved by the judge, and that the limitations of the principle of opportunity can make effective collaboration more difficult, prosecutors often do not agree on all possible charges with the defence and leave some of them subject to the principle of opportunity on condition that the defendant testifies in court against the persons he has previously accused[62].

---

59 Cfr. J.C. Forero Ramírez (fn. 14) p. 145–208; J.F. Mestre Ordóñez. (fn. 2) pp. 241–299.

60 J.O Sotomayor Acosta (fn. 26) pp. 254–255.

61 A.C. Navarro Navajas (fn. 39), pp. 67–68.

62 Ibid.

IV. Conclusions

Leniency programs have been a part of Columbia's criminal procedural system for the better part of the last 40 years. During the early years of this period, the State practically did not need the collaboration of the citizens investigated, so the leniency mechanisms were reduced to reward those who did not wear out the judicial apparatus[63]. In the face of more complex criminal phenomena, such as organised crime or crimes committed in the context of the armed conflict, leniency mechanisms were used to obtain information that would not otherwise reach the authorities' knowledge, either for the dismantling of those organizations or for the effective criminal prosecution of its members[64].

In the procedural system of accusatory tendency introduced by the CPA, the structure of the criminal process by phases granted the defence a better standing in the procedure[65]. This, in addition to the higher evidentiary standards, made it necessary for the AGO of the State to have to resort more frequently to leniency, to avoid the congestion of the system[66]. However, the lack of a coherent approach in criminal policy led to the closure of certain legal avenues for the use of leniency instruments. For example, the general hardening of penalties and the exclusion of leniency through legislative reforms to the CPA in which such possibilities were originally contemplated, resulted in a greater number of defendants willing to go to trial, to the point of heavily congesting all judicial instances[67].

The ever-evolving and more complex activities of organized crime, a surge in politically motivated violence in the first decade of the 2000s and the growing pains of the accusatory system rendered the State barely capable of offering an effective operation of the criminal system. This is even more noticeable in the action against criminal organisations. Investigations against the members of these organisations are often difficult, long, resource-intensive, and therefore wear down the judicial apparatus. The State's answer has been to extend the terms for the investigation or trial phase, or even for the prescription of criminal action.

This response has also been insufficient and has not produced satisfactory effects. However, outside transitional justice mechanisms created in the

---

63 R.G Gómez Velázquez, F.A. Castro Caballero (fn. 15), pp. 22.

64 L.F. Bedoya Sierra et al. (fn. 53) p. 89; J.C. Forero Ramírez (fn. 14) p. 68.

65 Cfr. Posada Maya (fn. 1), pp. 31–32.

66 J.C. Forero Ramírez (fn. 14), pp. 67–69.

67 Corporación Excelencia en la Justicia (CEJ), *Balance diez años del funcionamiento del Sistema Penal Acusatorio en Colombia* [2014] pp. 118–119, 127, 184.

legal framework of the peace agreements of 2016, the Colombian State is reluctant to consider structural alternatives to deepen the mechanisms of leniency that either in general terms or aimed exclusively at combating organized crime could increase the efficiency of prosecution, reduce judicial congestion and significantly fight impunity.

Conditioned Leniency Instruments in the Special Jurisdiction for Peace*

*PhD Alejandro Ramelli Arteaga*** *& Laura Acosta Zárate*

I. Introduction

After almost four years of negotiations carried out between the Colombian Government and the Colombian Revolutionary Armed Forces – Popular Army (the FARC, hereafter,) the Final Peace Agreement to End the Armed Conflict and Build a Stable and Lasting Peace (the Peace Agreement, hereafter,) was signed on 24th November 2016. The initial Agreement was submitted to the plebiscite on the 2nd October 2016 for the endorsement of the Colombian people. Due to the disapproval of the population, the Parties were forced to modify some parts of the Agreement, which was finally submitted for approval by Congress. The Peace Agreement encompasses six points: (i) rural reform, (ii) political participation, (iii) ceasefire and disarmament, (iv) illicit drugs, (v) victims' rights and (vi) post-agreement monitoring and verification mechanisms[1].

Addressing point (v), the Peace Agreement included the consolidation of an Integrated System of Truth, Justice, Reparation and Non-Repetition (the ISTJRNR or the System, hereafter,). The main purpose of the System is to contribute to the realization of the victim's rights to the truth, justice, reparation and non-recurrence and the establishment of responsibility of those who took part in the conflict[2].

It was established as a mixed transitional justice system, since it combines administrative institutions and judicial and extrajudicial measures.

---

* Many thanks to Paola Acosta and Fabián Martínez for their insightful discussions, contributions and their extraordinary support in the elaboration of this paper.

** Judge at the Jurisdicción Especial para la Paz Alberto Yepes Palacio Coordinator at Observatorio de Derechos Humanos y Derecho.

1 Colombia. Final agreement to end the armed conflict and build a stable and lasting peace. (2016). Available in: http://especiales.presidencia.gov.co/Documents/20170620-dejacion-armas/acuerdos/acuerdo-final-ingles.pdf. [Accessed on June 4th, 2019].

2 See Olasolo/Ramirez Mendoza, *Journal of International Criminal Justice*, Volume 15, Issue 5, December 2017, Pages 1011–1047.

The System is integrated by the Truth, Coexistence and Non-Recurrence Commission (The Commission of the Truth, hereafter,), a Special Unit for the Search for Persons deemed as missing in the context of and due to the conflict, the Special Jurisdiction for Peace as well as comprehensive reparation measures for peacebuilding and guarantees of non- recurrence[3].

Perhaps one of the most innovative contributions that the Peace Agreement has brought, is the implementation of the Special Jurisdiction for Peace as the judicial component of the System. This transitory mechanism differs from the ordinary justice system since it will only address serious human rights violations related to the armed conflict. Its objectives aim to guarantee the victims' rights by providing justice, offer truth to the Colombian society and decide the legal outcome for those who were involved in the conflict. With these purposes in mind, the Jurisdiction is based on a transitional justice model designed to investigate, clarify, prosecute and punish serious human rights and international humanitarian law violations committed before 1st December 2016.

Along with the Peace Agreement implementation, Congress issued Law No. 1820, also known as the amnesty law. This Act regulates the widest lenient system granted by the Colombian Government to former FARC combatants and special and distinctive treatment has been conceded to members of the Security Forces of the State. The regulation encompasses theoretical and procedural aspects of amnesties, pardons and waiving of prosecution. Finally, it includes the rules that should be used to impose sanctions in cases in which none of the lenient measures could be applied.

Overall, this lenient system can be seen from two different perspectives: First, as a mechanism that enclose the imposition of sanctions for those crimes which are not eligible for amnesty. And second, as a system that regulates different lenient treatments that could be granted for political crimes and related offences[4].

The main objective of this article is to evaluate the implementation of lenient systems as a mechanism for the restoration of human rights violations, peacebuilding and reconciliation in the current Colombian context. To do so, the judicial component of the Integrated System of Truth, Justice, Reparation and Non-Repetition and the leniency instruments established for former FARC members and to members of the Security Forces

---

3 Bustamante-Reyes, New Zealand International Revie,. Jan/Feb2017, Vol. 42 Issue 1, p14–17.

4 Ambos/Cote, *Ley de Amnistía. Comentario completo y sistemático (Ley 1820 de 2016)* [2019].

will be examined. Then, the conditional regime will be assessed as an essential part of the leniency instruments adopted by the Special Jurisdiction for Peace. Therefore, it will be concluded that the leniency instruments embraced by the SJP do not infringe international human rights law or international criminal law or represent a risk for the rights of victims.

II. Integrated System of Truth, Justice, Reparation and Non-Repetition

The System´s objective is to contribute to the realization of the victim's rights to the truth, justice, reparation and non-recurrence and the establishment of responsibility of those who took part in the conflict. It was established as a mixed transitional justice system since it combines administrative institutions, judicial and extrajudicial measures. The System is integrated by a Truth Commission, a Special Unit for the Search for Persons deemed as missing in the context of and due to the conflict, the Special Jurisdiction for Peace as well as comprehensive reparation measures for peacebuilding and guarantees of non-recurrence[5]. However, to satisfy this article's purpose, we need to delve into the role of the Special Jurisdiction for Peace, as addressed below.

1. Special Jurisdiction for Peace

The Special Jurisdiction for Peace is the judicial component of the ISTJRNR. This transitory mechanism differs from the ordinary justice system since it will only investigate serious human rights violations related to the armed conflict[6] that occurred before December 1st, 2016. Its objectives are to address victims' rights through guaranteeing justice, offering truth to Colombian society and deciding the legal outcome for those who were involved in the conflict[7]. With this purpose in mind, the SJP is based on a transitional justice model which is designed to investigate, clarify, prose-

5 See Presidencia de la República, Final Agreement to End the Armed Conflict and Build a Stable and Lasting Peace. Point 5: Agreement regarding the Victims of the Conflict, title II, 32 [2016].

6 Bustamante-Reyes, New Zealand International Review,42(1) [2017], 14.

7 See transitional article No. 5 from the Legislative Act No. 01/2017.

cute and punish serious human rights and international humanitarian law violations[8].

As such, in contrast to the previous peace processes held in Colombia, the SJP is framed for placing victims at the centre of the agenda[9]. More specifically, it is designed to explicitly respond to their rights to truth, justice, reparation and guarantee of non-repetition[10]. Through the incorporation of restorative justice –as a guidance criteria–, the Jurisdiction objective is to repair the damage caused to the victims by the conflict.

Hence, a paradigm was developed of restorative measures instead of having applied a punishment model of retributive justice by the system[11]. This is understood as a holistic approach that combines the victim's rights restoration and a retributive ingredient in terms of alternative sanctions and sentences[12].

This special jurisdiction is designed to ensure the appearance in court of individuals who participated directly or indirectly in the conflict. Thereby, former FARC combatants, members of the public security forces and non-military state agents will be able to stand before the SPJ[13]. In exchange for their cooperation with the SJP and their commitment provide full truth and reparation to the victims, they will benefit from transitional sanctions[14].

---

8 Jurisdiccion Especial para la Paz. Count with us for peace never for war. [Available in https://www.jep.gov.co/Infografas/englishversion2.pdf].

9 Maldonado, *Early lessons from the Colombian peace process* [2016]; See article 13, Law 1957/2019.

10 Herbolzheimer, *Innovations in the Colombian peace process* [2016].

11 Rojas Andrade/Dietmair, *Transitional Justice in Colombia Under Attack: An Interview with GABRIEL ROJAS. VerfassungsBlog. [Available in:* https://verfassungsblog.de/transitional-justice-in-colombia-under-attack-an-interview-with-gabriel-rojas/] [2019].

12 Pabón, *Truth, justice and reconciliation in Colombia: Transitioning from violence* [2018].

13 Oficina del Alto Comisionado para la Paz. Preguntas y respuestas sobre el Sistema Integral de Verdad, Justicia, Reparación y no Repetición. [Available in: http://www.altocomisionadoparalapaz.gov.co/Documents/informes-especiales/abc-del-proceso-de-paz/preguntas-respuestas-victimas.html].

14 Harper/Sonneland, Explainer: Colombia's Special Jurisdiction for Peace (JEP). Americas Society Council of the Americas. [Available in: https://www.as-coa.org/articles/explainer-colombias-special-jurisdiction-peace-jep] [2018]; Tavares/Zuluaga/Cohelo, *El proceso de paz en Colombia y las nuevas alternativas penales. Revista da Faculdade de Direito UFPR,* [2017], v. 62, n.Jan jan./abr. 2017, p. 255 – 271. ISSN 2236–7284. [Availble in: file:///C:/Users/JEP/Downloads/50792–203781–1-PB.pdf]. (Accessed in: June 25th, 2019).

By participating in this process and complying with the requirements, perpetrators are granted with the following leniency instruments.

2. *Leniency instruments for former FARC members and for members of the public security forces*

The SJP encompasses three main leniency instruments: amnesty, the conditional withdrawing of the criminal prosecution and a system of restorative sanctions[15]. Although they constitute the elements of clemency of the system, they all differ among themselves in terms of who they are addressed to, which authority grants its application, as well as which are the requirements for obtaining each one of them.

As such, Law 1820/2016 encompasses the widest leniency treatment[16] adopted by the Colombian government within a peacebuilding process. These three instruments will be granted to those who have been sentenced for acts committed directly or indirectly, in relation to or during the internal armed conflict[17]. The application of these measures to the different actors of the armed conflict is described as follows:

a) Amnesties

According to Law 1820/2016, amnesty entails immunity from legal consequences of the individual's criminal deeds[18]. As such, this is a mechanism that extinguishes existing criminal investigations, administrative or disciplinary proceedings against the individual[19]. In the case of the SJP, amnesties are linked to the type of crime committed and the person to whom it is directed. Thus, the granting of these instruments is limited to the following standards:

---

15 Comisión Internacional de Juristas, *Colombia: Jurisdicción Especial para la Paz, análisis a un año y medio de su entrada en funcionamiento* [2019].

16 See article 8, Law 1820/2016 and article 40 Law 1957/2019.

17 See article 3, Law 1820/2016.

18 Ntoubandi, *Amnesty for crimes against humanity under international law* [2007].

19 See paragraph 2, article 7, Law 1820/2016.

b) *Types of amnesties*

aa) Amnesty de jure

This amnesty is granted in accordance with the law to former FARC combatants who participated in criminal acts before the Peace Agreement was signed[20]. To apply the benefit, former fighters must subscribe to a commitment document[21] in which they promise to leave their weapons and obey the constitution and the law[22].

This particular amnesty "de jure" is granted for political offences[23]. Law 1820/2016 establishes that the crimes of rebellion, sedition, rioting, illegal possession of weapons, murder in combat that is compatible with international humanitarian law, conspiracy to commit the crime of rebellion, and other related crimes, are eligible for amnesty[24].

bb) Amnesties granted by the Judicial Chamber for Amnesty or Pardon

The Special Jurisdiction for Peace is compounded by two main bodies: (i) the Peace Tribunal which encompasses four Sections and (ii) three judicial Chambers. Additionally, the Jurisdiction has an Investigation and Prosecution Unit, an Analysis of the Information Group, the Office of Executive Secretary, the Office of Judicial Secretary, the Presidency and a Governing Body. The Judicial Chamber for Amnesty or Pardon is part of the three judicial chambers together with the Chamber for Acknowledgement of

---

20 Article 17, Law 1820/2016.

21 Law Act 1820/2016, article No. 36.

22 Jurisdiccion Especial para la Paz. [2019]. JEP en cifras. [Available in https://www.jep.gov.co/Infografas/cifras-junio-12.pdf]: Until June 13th, 2019, 9,704 former FARC members, 2,059 members of the public security forces and 52 non-military state agents have subscribed a commitment act.

23 It is possible to refer those included in Tittle XVIII of the Colombian Penal Code. Thi is norms which aim to protect the constitutional and legal regime. Furthermore, decision C-557/2014 issued by the Constitutional Court Political crime is defined and linked to transitional justice processes. By establishing this relation, the government guarantees an easiest path to reintegration of former combatants; Taraupes Sandino, in: Ambos/Cote, *Ley de Amnistía. Comentario completo y sistemático* (Ley 1820 de 2016) [2019].

24 Articles 15 and 16, Law 1820/2016. Article 16 enounces a list of criminal conducts which may be understood as connected crimes.

Truth, Responsibility and Determination of Facts and Conducts and the Chamber for Determination of Legal Situations.

According to Law 1820/2016, the role of the Judicial Chamber for Amnesty or Pardon is subsidiary[25]. Therefore, the Chamber is in charge of deciding whether special treatments could be granted for those cases that do not comply with the requirements set for the application of amnesties *de jure*[26]. This assessment is carried out by the Chamber in accordance with article 6.5 of the Geneva Conventions and Additional Protocol II thereto on war crimes[27].

The Judicial Chamber has an essential role regarding the granting of amnesties in cases in which the relationship between the crime and its political motive is unclear[28]. Thereby, its task is to review case by case and exclude those in which the crime does not comply with the criteria stated by article 23 of the Law 1820/2016[29]. Thereafter, an investigation and prosecution will be necessary[30].

c) *Waiver of Prosecution*

The amendment to Constitution No. 01/2017 established that the SJP will also operate for public officials who have committed crimes related to the armed conflict.

However, its application will follow a different criterion, granting an equitable, balanced, simultaneous and symmetrical treatment[31]. Therefore, the leniency instrument intended for these cases is not amnesty but the waiver of prosecution[32]. This instrument which has been compared to other plea barraging instruments[33], –under determined conditions–, extinguishes the criminal prosecution and sanction.

---

25 Cote Barco G. E., in: Ambos/Cote, *Ley de Amnistía. Comentario completo y sistemático* (Ley 1820 de 2016) [2019].
Ibid.

26 Article 21 and 28, Law 1820/2016.

27 Ibidem.

28 Op. Cit., Cote Barco G. E., (2019).

29 Op. Cit., Cote Barco G. E., (2019).

30 Article 25, Law 1820/2018.

31 Article 17, Legislative Act 01/2017.

32 See article 46, Law 1820/2018.

33 Salazar Solarte, (2017, August). Naturaleza jurídica de la renuncia a la persecucion penal [Blog post]. Retrieved June 28, 2019, from http://jepjusticiatransicional.net/naturaleza-juridica-de-la-renuncia-a-la-persecucion-penal/.

As is the case with amnesties, waiver of prosecution is conditioned to the type of crime committed. Hence, it does not apply (i) in case of serious war crimes[34] enlisted in Law 1820/2016, article 46.1[35]; (ii) those which were not committed in relation to or during the internal armed conflict; and (iii) public force crimes.

For this instrument in particular, it is the responsibility of the Judicial Chamber for Determination of Legal Situations to decide whether the instrument can be applied or not[36]. The granting of this benefit does not exempt the perpetrator from his obligation to contribute fully to truth and to comply with the compensation to victims[37].

III. Conditionality regime for the leniency instruments in the SJP

The conditionality regime is established as a core element that limits the granting and the preservation of leniency instruments. The bases of this regime were settled by the Colombian Congress in 2012, with the issuance of a constitutional reform known as the "Integral Legal Framework for Peace" (Act 01/2012)[38]. The purpose was to determine the required instruments needed to obtain truth, justice and compensation. Therefore, the constitutional amendment established a balance between the special treatment given to perpetrators for their criminal acts and, the conditionalities[39] that must be fulfilled to benefit from this[40].

---

34 Jean-Baptiste, Marie-Claude [2017] Notre Dame Journal of International & Comparative Law: Vol. 7: Iss. 1, Article 4. Available at: http://scholarship.law.nd.edu/ndjicl/vol7/iss1/4.

35 This benefit will not be eligible in cases of crimes against humanity, genocide, war crimes, the taking of hostages, serious deprivations of liberty, torture, forced displacement, enforced disappearance, extrajudicial executions, sexual violence, child abduction, and the recruitment of child soldiers, in addition to the recruitment of minors in accordance with the provisions of the Statute from Rome.

36 Article 47, Law 1820/2016.

37 Article 50, Law 1820/2016.

38 Colombia, Congreso de Colombia, Acto Legislativo 01 de 31 de julio de 2012, "Por medio del cual se establecen instrumentos jurídicos de justicia transicional en el marco del artículo 22 de la Constitución Política y se dictan otras disposiciones"; Colombia, Corte Constitucional, sentencia C-579/2013.

39 Conditionalities included the lay down of weapons, the recognition of liability, contribution to clarify the truth, the release of prisoners and of recruited children.

40 Colombia, Corte Constitucional, sentencia C-674/2017.

Later, the ISTJRNR endorsed these principles by integrating them to the leniency instruments established for the SJP[41]. According to the Constitutional Court, these benevolent treatments are necessary within a transitional justice context, but they cannot have an unconditional nature[42]. Therefore, Law 1820/2016 limited the granting of amnesties and waiver of prosecution to the compliance of specific requirements established for each case. The purpose of this regime is to render a balance between the given flexible consequences for perpetrators and the rights of the victims[43]. The system entails two main conditioned benefits:

1. *Conditional release*

This benefit is understood as a non-retributive measure which aims to enable the combatant's demobilisation and reintegration process[44]. It is granted to those former members of the FARC who have been in prison for more than five years and fulfilled the requirements set in the commitment document[45].

In order to benefit from this measure, the former combatant has to comply with a temporary, personal and material criteria[46]. As such, the conditional release can only be granted for crimes committed before the Peace Agreement was signed[47]. Moreover, the ex-combatant has to be in prison due to any of the criminal conducts enlisted by the Law

---

41 Ibid.

42 Colombia, Corte constitucional, sentencia C-077 de 2018.

43 Zuluaga, J./Vargas, J., *Regimen de condicionalidad y acceso a la Jurisdiicción Especial para la Paz*, Instituto Colombo-Aleman para la Paz, [2019].

44 Jurisdiccion Especial para la Paz, Sala de Amnistia e Indulto. (2019) Resolución que resuleve solicitud de libertad condicionada. [Available in: https://www.jep.gov.co/Sala-de-Prensa/SiteAssets/Paginas/Sala-de-Amnist%C3%ADa-o-Indulto-otorga-libertad-condicionada--a-Omaira-Rojas-Cabrera/Resoluci%C3%B3n%20que%20Resuelve%20Solicitud%20de%20Libertad%20Condicionada%20Omaira%20Rojas%20Cabrera.pdf].

45 According to article 36, Law 1820/2016, beneficiaries of this conditional release have to inform any change of residence and they cannot leave the country without the SPJ's previous authorization.

46 Op. Cit., *Jurisdiccion Especial para la Paz*, Sala de Amnistia e Indulto, [2019].

47 Article 5 Legislative Act 01/2017 and article 3 Law 1820/2016.

1820/2016[48] and have signed the commitment pledge. Finally, the granting of this benefit is linked to the obligation of satisfying the victims' rights[49].

2. *Transitional, conditional and anticipated release*

Likewise, the regime entails a transitional, conditional and anticipated release for members of the State's security forces[50]. This leniency treatment is also conditioned on compliance with the requirements established in article 52 of Law 1820/2016[51]. Hence, the benefit is exclusive for State Agents who have been convicted for crimes related to the armed conflict. However, the individual cannot benefit from this instrument when the crime committed was qualified as a serious war crime[52]. Additionally, this implies the individual commitment to contribute with full truth, to repair the damages caused and the non-repetition[53].

Hence the full truth will be evaluated based on the exhaustiveness and level of detail of the information provided[54]. Finally, due to the importance of the conditionality regime for the transitional justice model, failure to comply with its terms can lead to the loss of the leniency treatments[55]. Consequently, the criminal procedure will be referred to the ordinary justice, so the prosecution and further trial will be carried out without any transitional instruments[56].

---

48 Articles 15,16,17,22 and 29.

49 Colombia, Corte Constitucional, sentencia C-007/2018.

50 Article 51, Law 1820/2016.

51 This leniency instrument is excluded for those members of the public security forces who have been sentenced for serious war crimes.

52 See article 52.2, Law 1820/2017.

53 Op. Cit. C-007/2018.

54 Article 5, Legislative Act 01/2017; Article 20 (i), Law 1957/2019.

55 Colombia, Corte Constitucional, sentecnia C-080 de 2018, párr.4.1.8.; article 67, Law 1922/2018.

56 Uprimny Yepes/Güiza Gómez, Reflexiones sobre la reforma constitucional que crea la jurisdicción especial para la paz y regula el tratamiento especial a fuerza pública [2017].

IV. Conclusions

1. Justice for victims is a central issue to the peace process

The objective of implementing a model of transitional justice within the ISTJRNR has been framed as a mechanism through which the victims and perpetrators of the Colombian armed conflict can engage in the pursuit of the provision of justice, reparation and truth. Therefore, contrary to the previous peace processes implemented in Colombia, the objective of this new model is not focused on the political participation of former rebels or the simply demobilisation of the armed group. Here, the main objective is to recognise the victims' role within the conflict and to satisfy their fundamental rights.

2. Colombia's Special Jurisdiction for Peace does not violate international standards.

With the implementation of the ISTJRNR, Colombia is found to be in compliance with the international obligations set by the American Convention on Human Rights[57]. This situation is evidenced in light of other transitional measures adopted in peacebuilding States[58]. As such, it is noted that the Colombian system has assumed its obligation to investigate, prosecute and punish serious human rights violations[59].

Therefore, by excluding the most serious crimes from the list of conducts that could be forgiven (application of leniency treatments), the Colombian transitional peace system guarantees compliance with international obligations. Additionally, the SJP adopts a selection and prioritisa-

57 Acosta-López, *The Inter-American Human Rights System and the Colombian Peace: Redefining the Fight Against Impunity. AJIL Unbound,* [2016], 110, 178–182.

58 This is the case of the amnesty model that is now discussed within the El Salvador congress, known as "Ley Especial de Justicia Transicional y Restaurativa para la Reconciliación Nacional". The diverse issues of this law Project and the risk it represents to the satisfaction of the victims' rights has leaded to the Inter-American Court of Human Rights to order the suspension of its approval. Specifically, the Court has stressed the inconveniences of articles 5, 12 and 13.

59 Gutiérrez Ramírez, La obligación internacional de investigar, juzgar y sancionar graves violaciones a los derechos humanos en contextos de justicia transicional [2014] 16(2), 23–60.

tion model[60] through which the admissibility of each case is linked to the assessment of the scale, nature and impact of the crimes[61]. This evaluation is carried out constantly in order to determine the admissibility of new cases, criminal behaviours and which of them should be selected for investigation[62]. This process guarantees that the operation of the system is not limited to a single set of crimes and secures for the victims the possibility of bringing the case upon the system.

Also, by integrating a conditionality model into the granting of leniency instruments, the States guarantees compliance with its international duties. As such, the system leaves aside those crimes which under any circumstance are suitable for the application of leniency instruments. This implies a necessary investigation, judgement and determination of sanctions. The process will also ensure the satisfaction of the victims' rights, since the benefit is conditioned to the contribution made by the perpetrators to the construction of the truth and their engagement with compensation mechanisms.

Finally, even if the Colombian transitional justice model is based on an indulgent model, sanctions are included as possible outcomes. Perpetrators who contribute to the truth will be sentenced with the restorative measures of the system, consisting of rights restrictions between 5 and 8 years, as well as carrying out work on behalf of the victims. Those who do not recognize their responsibility and are defeated in court will be subject to imprisonment of up to twenty years. In the same way, those who violate their commitments lose the benefits received, which can lead to the loss of freedom.

This is to say, that the amnesty and pardon instruments adopted by Colombia's peace model is not automatic or unrestricted. On the contrary,

---

60 Jurisdicción Especial para la Paz. "Criterios y metodología de priorización de casos y situaciones. En la Sala de Reconocimiento de Verdad, de Responsabilidad y de Determinación de los Hechos y Conductas", 28 de junio de 2018.

61 Situation on Registered Vessels of Comoros, Greece and Cambodia, Office of the Prosecutor, Article 53(1) Report, 138–141 (Nov. 6, 2014), https://www.icc-cpi.int/iccdocs/otp/otp-com-article_53(1)-report-06nov2014eng.pdf.

62 Up to the moments, the SJP has prioritised seven cases regarding: (i) Case 001: Illegal retentions; (ii) Case 002: Human Rights violations in Tumaco, Ricaurte y Barbacoas and Nariño municipalities; (iii) case 003: Illegal deaths presented in combat; (iv) case 004: Human Rights violations in Turbo, Apartadó, Carepa, Chigorodó, Mutatá, Dabeiba (Antioquia) y El Carmen del Darién, Riosucio, Unguía y Acandí, Chocó; (v) case 005: Santander de Quilichao, Suárez, Buenos Aires, Morales, Caloto, Corinto, Toribío y Caldono municipalities; (vi) case 006: victimization towards UP members; (vii) case 007: child recruitment.

the system entails the prosecution and sanction of those who bear the greatest responsibility[63]. According to the Constitutional Court decision C-579/2013, this condition is linked to the significance of the person's role in the execution of the crime. This is, leading, controlling or financing the illegal act[64]. Thus, those whose participation was decisive for the crime to be committed will not be granted automatically with leniency instruments, but their participation will be evaluated by the SJP. This final decision could lead to granting benefits or the application of sanctions[65]. In conclusion, the system guarantees that the most serious crimes and therewith, the greatest perpetrators do not remain in impunity.

Bearing the possible risks derived from the application of leniency instruments, the Inter-American Court of Human Rights (the Court hereafter) assessed similar measures created in other post-conflict countries. Specifically, the Court reviewed the case of the Massacres of El Mozote and nearby places against El Salvador[66]. After noting the possible violations to the victim's rights and the risk of impunity, the Court ordered to suspend the legislative action of the draft amnesty law.

Albeit, the leniency instruments included in Law 1820/2016 are quite similar to El Salvador amnesty system, Colombia's measures were built based on an equilibrium between the centrality of the victim's rights and the right to due process. Additionally, these transitional measures are established as a mechanism of restoration, yet it is limited so there is no impunity for the perpetrators involved in serious criminal acts.

In conclusion, the peace model that is currently being implemented in Colombia is substantially different from the previous ones since it implies a transitional justice component. This feature provides a balance between the victims' rights and the due process of justice for perpetrators. As discussed, the judicial component of the system offers a model of leniency instruments that are conditioned to the achievement of justice, truth and compensation for the damage caused. The positive results reflected in the granting of these measures are a clear example of the success of implement-

---

63 See Agreement between the United Nations and the Government of Sierra Leone and Statute of the Special Court for Sierra Leone, 16 January 2002.

64 Financing is understood by the Constitutional Court as providing the economic resources needed to commit the crime or to make the organisation function.

65 Articles 12 and 16, Legislative Act 01/2017; articles 28.8 and 30.1 Law No. 1820/2018.

66 Inter-American Court of Human Rights (IACrtHR),*The Massacres of El Mozote and nearby places v. El Salvador*, 25 October 2012, available at: https://www.refworld.org/cases,IACRTHR,564ecfee4.html [accessed 4 July 2019]

ing these sorts of transitional models in peacebuilding processes held in post-war countries.

III. Truth Commissions and Reconciliation

Experience with Truth Commissions in Africa

Prof. Dr. Hartmut Hamann

I. Introduction

What is a truth commission? Lawyers like definitions. In legal literature, a truth commission is defined as an institution established to collect information about the facts of a conflict to provide an accurate picture of what occurred.[1]

Being an attorney in private practice, I prefer a practical approach. I will share with you my experience with and my thoughts on Truth Commissions in Africa inviting you to look at three examples:

- South Africa
- Burundi
- The Gambia.

The Truth and Reconciliation Commission in South Africa is considered a success. Burundi´s Truth and Reconciliation Commission never really started its work. In The Gambia, the latest truth commission on the African continent took up its work last year. It is an ongoing example, which you can follow online.

II. South Africa

1. Legal Framework

The Truth and Reconciliation Commission of South Africa ("TRC") is governed by the "*Promotion of National Unity and Reconciliation Act 34*" of 1995. The Act makes reference to the Interim Constitution of the Republic of South Africa of 1993, which was later replaced by the Constitution of 1996. The Interim Constitution states "*that the pursuit of national unity, the*

---

1 O´Shea, Truth and Reconciliation Commissions, MPEPIL, para 1 (Dezember 2008), www.mpepil.com; in detail Werle/Vormbaum, Transitional Jusice-Vergangenheitsabwicklung durch Recht, [2018] 83 ff.

well-being of all South African citizens and peace require reconciliation between the people of South Africa and the reconstruction of society", Chapter 15, Section 251 of the Interim Constitution of 1993. An essential part of the legal framework is the establishment of a new Constitutional Court,[2]Chapter 7, Section 98 of the Interim Constitution of 1993.

2. *Competence*

TRC was established for the purposes of investigation and establishment of nature and causes of human rights violations committed during the time of apartheid since 1 March 1960 (Preamble of the Act 34 of 1995). The TRC of South Africa consisted of three main Committees:

- The Human Rights Violations Committee collected the relevant facts.
- The Reparations Committee recommended reparations.
- The Committee on Amnesty could grant amnesty to perpetrators who gave full disclosure.[3]

The competence to grant amnesty is a specific feature of the South African TRC.[4]

3. *Historical Background*

When establishing its truth and reconciliation commission after the end of apartheid South Africa could build on experiences made in Latin America, especially in Argentina.[5] South Africa could also build on the work of the domestic "*Goldstone Commission on Public Violence and Intimidation*" which had been established in 1991. Richard J. Goldstone, the chairman of that commission, describes the results as follows:

> "*The commission held over forty inquires. In my view it resulted in three major achievements. The first was that it produced sufficient evidence of serious human rights abuses during the last of the apartheid years to justify the establishment of a truth commission. The second was that its report on senior police involvement in violence as late as 1994 caused substantial disarray*

2 In detail Werle/Vormbaum, fn. 1, at 184 et seqq.
3 O´Shea, fn. 1, recital 16.
4 In detail Werle/Vormbaum, fn. 1, recital 186.
5 O´Shea, fn. 1, recital 6, Werle/Vormbaum, fn. 1, recital 84.

> *within right-wing circles and averted more serious violence in the weeks preceding the April 1994 election. The third, and most important, was that timely public inquiries into serious incidents of violence helped keep the South African nation calm and so avoid a bloody end to the negotiation process that led to the death of apartheid and the birth of a democratic system of government. … The Goldstone Commission assisted in creating the political climate in which the Truth and Reconciliation Commission could be established with the agreement of the major parties*."[6]

The TRC could also build on the work of other domestic commissions established to examine cruelty and human rights abuses against African National Congress (ANC) prisoners and detainees, the "*Skweyiya Commission*" established in 1991 and the "*Motsuenyane Commission*" established in 1993.[7]

4. *Results*

The Commission operated from December 1995 to June 2002. It allowed for a broad public participation. It had several regional offices and an annual budget of about 18 million US Dollars. It had the power to name the perpetrators in its final report.[8]

The Commission produced a report, five volumes of which were published in 1998, two more volumes in 2003.[9] Government regulations on reparations were promulgated in 2003.[10] The amount paid to victims was much lower than what the TRC had recommended.[11]

6 Richard J. Goldstone, For Humanity, Reflections of a War Crimes Investigator [2000] 57, 58.

7 See Charles Manga Fombad, Transitional Justice in Africa: The Experience with Truth Commissions, GlobaLex, [2008] 13), URL: https://www.nyulawglobal.org/globalex/Africa_Truth_Commissions.html.

8 Fombad, fn. 7, recital 13.

9 Accessible at http://www.justice.gov.za; Werle/Vormbaum, fn. 1 recital 186.

10 Gordon O´Shea, fn. 1, recital 17.

11 Fombad, fn. 8, recital 13; Werle/Vormbaum, fn. 1, recital 188; William Gumede, in: Swart/van Marle, The limits of Transition: The South African Truth and Reconciliation Commission 20 years on, [2017] 59 et seqq.

5. Evaluation of Results

The TRC of South Africa is widely considered to be a success.[12] Critical commentators note that more perpetrators should have been punished.[13] This is about the balance between reconciliation and punishment. From victims' perspective, it is understandable. In my view, it does not put into question the good results of the TRC but leads to the question, whether prosecutors have done enough. Amounts paid to victims felt short in comparison to what the TRC had recommended (see above). However, this is not a shortcoming of the TRC, either. Rather, this is a political issue.

Major elements of the success are as follows:

- Acceptance by all major groups of society, who actively asked for the TRC and participated in its establishment and followed its work.
- A credible, sound legal framework including a new constitution and a newly established constitutional court.
- A sound basis to start work, building on the results of the work of commissions which had been established earlier.
- The transparent publishing of the results, which helps to assure the visibility of the truth of what happened.

III. Burundi

1. Legal Framework

The Arusha Peace and Reconciliation Agreement for Burundi of 28 August 2000 ("Arusha Agreement") provides for the establishment of the International Judicial Commission of Inquiry on genocide, war crimes and other crimes against humanity, Art. 6 (10) Protocol I Arusha Agreement, and the National Truth and Reconciliation Commission ("TRC") to investigate acts of violence committed after gaining independence in 1962, Art. 8 Protocol I Arusha Agreement.[14]

---

12 Werle/Vormbaum, fn. 1, recital 94, 184 ff.; Fombad, fn. 1,recital 16.

13 Werle/Vormbaum, fn. 1, recital187; in detail Antije Krog, Rethinking Reconciliation and Forgiveness at the South African Truth and Reconciliation Commission, in Mia Swart, Karin van Marle, fn. 11, recital 11 et seq.

14 In detail Hamann/Berger, Burundi, MPEPIL, para 30 et seqq. (July 2017), www.mpepil.com.

Art. 7 (18) Protocol I Arusha Agreement provides for a number of measures which shall accompany the establishment of the TRC:

"*(a) Promotion of impartial and independent justice. In this respect, all petitions and appeals relating to assassinations and political trials shall be made through the National Truth and Reconciliation Commission established pursuant to the provisions of article 8 of the present Protocol;*
(b) Reform of the judicial machinery at all levels, inter alia with a view to correcting ethnic and gender imbalances where they exist;
(c) Amendment of laws where necessary (Criminal Code, Code of Criminal Procedure, Civil Code, Nationality Act, etc.);
(d) Reform of the Judicial Service Commission so as to ensure its independence and that of the judicial system;
(e) Organization of a judicial training programme, inter alia through the establishment of a National School for the Magistracy;
(f) Provision of adequate human and material resources for the courts;
(g) Establishment of the post of Ombudsperson."

After national consultations had been completed, the establishment of the TRC was scheduled for January 2012. On 15 May 2014, fourteen years after signing of the Arusha Agreement, a law for the creation, operation and mandate of the TRC was signed into force. In December of the same year the Burundian National Assembly elected the foreseen 11 TRC commissioners.[15] Finally, the TRC was officially launched in 2016[16], sixteen years after signing the Arusha Agreement. On 6 November 2018 a new law was enacted replacing the law of May 2014.[17]

2. *Competence*

The Arusha Agreement included the establishment of a National Truth and Reconciliation Commission with a strong position to examine crimes, embedded in an international framework and complemented by a strong national judiciary. However, the Burundian TRC has never gained such a strong position. Neither an international framework was made available, nor was the national judiciary strengthened. The nomination of the mem-

15 Report of the UN Secretary-General on the United Nations Office in Burundi of 19 January 2015, UNDOC S 2015/36, paras 24–25.

16 Hamann/Berger, fn. 14, recital 36.

17 In detail https://www.uantwerpen.be/en/projects/centre-des-grands-lacs-afrique/droit-pouvoir-paix-burundi/justice-transitionnelle/.

bers of the TRC was dominated by the ruling power, an efficient work of the TRC was not intended, even though the law provided for a competence to establish responsibility of individuals and public institutions.[18]

The law of May 2014 requested the TRC to examine Burundian history since its independence in 1962 until 2008. The law of November 2018 extended this period asking TRC to also cover the colonial period starting in 1885[19].[20]

3. *Historical Background*

Following its independence on 1 July 1962 from *United Nations (UN)* trusteeship under Belgian administration, Burundi suffered from a highly violent non-international armed conflict, culminating in the 1972, 1988, and 1993 massacres as well as the pre- and post-election violence of 2015–2016. All of these crimes have never been investigated, punished or reconciled. Some people who have spent much time in Burundi say "*There is no innocent in Burundi*".[21] Among the striking features of Burundi are the late response of the *international community* to the Burundian civil wars, regional peace initiatives which led to first *peacekeeping* activity of the *African Union (AU)* in 2003, subsequent UN peacekeeping from 2004 to 2006, and the fact that mechanisms of transitional justice are still not in place, perpetuating a culture of impunity. Furthermore, the case of present Burundi illustrates a reluctant approach of the AU and the East African Community (EAC) to take resolute measures against massive human rights abuses by the current Burundian authorities.[22]

18 Id.

19 End of the Congo-Conference in Berlin, which also defined Burundian borders.

20 For regular updates on the situation in Burundi see https://www.uantwerpen.be/en/projects/centre-des-grands-lacs-afrique/droit-pouvoir-paix-burundi/justice-transitionnelle.

21 In detail on the historical background: Jean-Pierre Chrétien, Great Lakes of Africa: Two Thousand Years of History [2003]; S. Vandeginste, Stones Left Unturned: Law and Transitional Justice in Burundi [2010].

22 Hamann/Berger, fn. 14, recital 2.

4. Results

In the end of 2018 the TRC presented a report. In summary the report states that no investigation had been realized, only some preparatory work. In other words: The TRC has not started its work. The new law on the TRC of November 2018 does not mention this report altogether. The TRC is now asked to examine not only the period from 1962 to 2008 – which is already a long period – but to examine the period of 123 years from 1885 to 2008. There are no time limits set for the work of the TRC.

The political situation in Burundi – governed by an autocratic regime – is not an advantageous one for conducting an independent examination of crimes committal in the past. Nineteen years after the signing of the Arusha Agreement, there is not much hope for a seriously working TRC. There are no tangible results to be expected.[23]

5. Evaluation of Results

There is one lesson to be learned: The implementation of the Arusha Agreement was systematically delayed and obstructed by the Burundian Government. The UN, the AU, the EAC and major donors such as the EU and its Member States tolerated this Burundian approach instead of insisting on a consequent and immediate implementation of the agreement. Doing so, the international community has not respected a core element of the rule of law: rules have to be implemented, breaking rules has to be sanctioned. Not insisting on this basic element is either negligent or cynical.[24] The case of Burundi shows how a national government determined to systematically hinder the establishment of truth can be successful.

IV. The Gambia

1. Legal Framework

The legal base in The Gambia is the "*Truth, Reconciliation and Reparations Commissions Bill*" of 2017[25]aiming "*to provide for establishment of a Truth,*

23 Political chronicles of the African Great Lakes Region (F. Reyntjens ed. 2018).
24 Quote from Hamann/Berger, fn. 14, recital 47.
25 Accessible at http://www.trrc.gm/.

Reconciliation and Reparations Commission; to investigate and establish an impartial historical record of the nature, causes and extent of violations and abuses of human rights committed during the period July 1994 to January 2017 and to consider the granting of reparations to victims and for connected matters."

2. Competence

Art. 15 of the Bill provides for the following competence of the TRRC:

- gather any information it considers appropriate;
- visit any place without giving prior notice;
- interview any individual;
- to compel the attendance of any person to appear;
- to issue summonses and subpoenas;
- to request and receive police assistance;
- identification and recommendation for prosecution of persons who bear the greatest responsibility for human rights violations and abuses;
- granting of reparations to victims;
- recommend the granting of amnesty in appropriate cases.

Pursuant to Art. 15 para 3 of the Bill, TRRC may undertake investigation and research into key events, causes, patterns of abuses or violations and hold public sessions on such themes and institutions as it considers appropriate. However, not explicitly within its competence is the preparation of possible prosecution of the former dictator Jammeh. His name is not mentioned in the bill.

3. Historical Background

From 1994 to 2016 The Gambia was under the autocratic rule of Yahya Jammeh. In December 2016 Adama Barrow surprisingly won presidential elections. With pressure from neighbouring Senegal, other West African countries and the ECOWAS (Economic Community of West African States) Jammeh left the country and Barrow took over.

He revised Jammeh's decision to leave the jurisdiction of the International Criminal Court. He agreed to abolish the death penalty, ordered to free political prisoners, re-established freedom of the press and launched a process to draft a new constitution.[26]

The establishment of the Truth and Reconciliation Commission is one important element of The Gambia's way to the rule of law and democracy.

The "*Guide on transitional Justice in Gambia*"[27] published by the Attorney General's Chambers and Ministry of Justice in July 2017 makes reference to experiences made in other African countries, especially in South Africa, as well as to international support. In addition, it points out that "*Nationals must own the full processes and mechanisms put in place*" (para 6.7).

4. Results

TRRC's official website[28] regularly informs on the work of the commission:

In April 2019 it ended its fourth three-week session of hearings. Up to that date all alleged perpetrators had appeared and given their statements voluntarily. The commission is also engaged in what it calls "robust outreach activities," such as encouraging students to attend hearings and conducting town hall meetings and village dialogues. The relatively small size of The Gambia (the smallest country on the African continent) and low number of inhabitants (ca. 2 million) may help to achieve an active engagement of a large number of citizens. A free access to video recordings of hearings over the official website and through YouTube, Facebook, television and radio allows for maximum of transparency.

5. Evaluation of Results

It is too early to evaluate results. As far as I can see, the commission had a promising

start. However, it remains unclear, whether there will be a negative impact due to lack of a well functioning judiciary trusted by people, or whether The Gambia will be able to rebuild an effective and trusted judiciary.

---

26 https://www.auswaertiges-amt.de/de/aussenpolitik/laender/gambia-node/bilaterales/213614.

27 Accessible at http://www.trrc.gm/.

28 www.trrc.gm.

V. Lessons to be Learned

1. Criteria for Success

a) Major parts of society and their leaders feel a need to establish a truth and reconciliation commission and put it into place. The driving force are internal players and their need to look for and make visible the truth.
b) Those internal players can make sure that a truth and reconciliation commission fits into the historical, cultural and political background.
c) Participation of the society and transparent proceedings are guaranteed.[29]
d) Only if the criteria above are met, is the support from foreign countries or international institutions helpful.
e) The truth and reconciliation commission has a clearly defined competence. Members of the commission are carefully chosen and accepted by all major parts of the society.
f) Support by traditional judicial institutions is assured. The work of the truth commission and the work of the judiciary complement each other. The legal framework should define the relationship between both: Do truth commissions assist prosecution by collecting facts? Or do they hinder prosecution by granting amnesty?[30] Prosecution is necessary to facilitate reconciliation. It may even be "*a prerequisite for true reconciliation*".[31]

   A strong, efficient and independent judiciary is therefore of enormous help. If it does not exist, measures to implement or strengthen such a judiciary should accompany the work of the truth commission.
g) The starting point makes a difference: Up to which extent facts have already been established when the truth commission starts its work? On what material can the commission base its work? The more facts are already well documented the better the truth commission can work, the more likely it is that perpetrators will decide to pronounce the truth instead of hiding it.

29 O´Shea, fn. 1, recital 43.
30 Id. recital 40.
31 Ambos, in: Building a Future on Peace and Justice: Studies on Transitional Justice, Peace and Development [2009].

These criteria have been met in South Africa. The results are widely accepted as good. The criteria a) to e) seem to be met in The Gambia. It is less evident for criteria f) and g) The outcome remains to be seen.

2. Criteria for Failure

a) External players pressure for truth without serious support from within society and its leaders. I don´t think that the Nuremberg trials could have been replaced by a truth and reconciliation commission. The widespread need for truth was expressed by German society only as late as in the 1960s.
b) A weak judiciary can motivate perpetrators to hide the truth. Only a strong judiciary with a credible threat of punishment motivates perpetrators to confess. Lack of traditional criminal prosecution weakens the work of truth commissions.
c) Unclear competence and relationship with the judiciary undermine the work of truth commissions. The risk to a truth commission's work is that it may be seen only as window-dressing.
d) A lack of transparency and participation of society takes away major possible effects: public recognition of wrong-doings as well as public reparation and recognitions toward the victims.

Unfortunately, these criteria are met in Burundi.

VI. Alternative or Additional Means to Legal Instruments of Traditional Criminal Prosecution

1. Prosecutors' Perspective

Facts and testimonies collected by a truth and reconciliation commission can help to establish prosecution. However, TRCs should be more than mere assistants of prosecutors. Also, from the perspective of prosecutors it should be clear from the outset, what role the findings of TRCs should play in later prosecution and what effects admitting the truth by perpetrators ("full disclosure") shall have.

2. Perpetrators' Perspective

Perpetrators get a chance to actively unveil criminal acts in order to contribute to healing of suffered damage.[32] It is not up to perpetrators or to truth commissions to decide on forgiveness, this is up to the victims. Perpetrators should not get a chance to play with the TRC, but they deserve a fair trial. That includes a clearly defined competence of the TRC and of possible prosecution.[33]

3. Victims' Perspective

Victims' honour might be reestablished by making the truth public. Also, in the interest of victims, an adequate balance of punishment and reconciliation is necessary. It might be very hard for victims of serious crimes to see perpetrators get away without consequences.

4. Effects on Society

Reconciliation can build bridges. But establishing the truth may not be enough to achieve reconciliation. Serious crimes may need visible punishment, which can contribute to reconciliation.[34]

VII. Conclusion

Truth and reconciliation commissions can help to deal with past conflicts. To achieve good results their work must be accompanied by efficient traditional criminal prosecution. TRCs are not an alternative to traditional criminal prosecution. Both means can complement each other.

---

32 Krog, fn. 13, describes in detail a case of one of the major perpetrators in South Africa.

33 This seems to be unclear in The Gambia, where perpetrators have been liberated after confessions before the TRRC without clear perspective of prosecution or amnesty, see e.g. http://www.rfi.fr/emission/20190806-liberation-junglers-est-impunite-regne-gambie.

34 Ambos, fn. 31, recital 25.

Memory, Truth and Justice: criminal trials or truth commissions?[1]

Prof. Dr. Gabriel Pérez Barberá[*]

I. Introduction

My gratitude goes to the Elisabeth Käsemann Foundation for giving me the opportunity to speak in this debate, which is intended to discuss not only the suitability, but also the moral and legal admissibility of criminal trials for crimes against humanity carried out in Argentina. I am referring, of course, both to the trial of the military juntas of the 1980s and to those that began with the annulment of the impunity laws in 2004 and the case "Simón" ordered by the Supreme Court in 2005.

At this point, my talk will not address the legal problems related to the trials. I did that on another occasion, in an article I published with Alejandro Agüero in 2012.[2] Here I would like to deal, from a perhaps more philosophical-legal point of view, only with a thesis supported by authors such as Claudia Hilb and Claudio Tamburrini, according to whom it would be possible and desirable to cede a little in justice to obtain more truth. And this without ignoring, later on, the important differences in emphasis and nuances that exist between the positions of these two authors.[3] My intention is to criticize that thesis.

II. Definition of Justice and Truth

There is some imprecision in the thesis that I intend to object to here. Because, as it has been formulated, it suggests a possibility of gradation of

1 A preliminary version of this text was published as a lecture in: Beade/Penna (eds.), *Memoria y castigo en los juicios de lesa humanidad* [2018], p. 145 et seqq.

* Professor of Criminal Law at the University of Córdoba and at the University Torcuato Di Tella, Buenos Aires, federal public prosecutor.

2 See Pérez/Barberá/Agüero, Revista de Derecho Penal y Criminología, 2012, p. 249 et seqq.

3 See Hilb, Discusiones, 2013, p. 31 et seqq; Tamburrini, Res Publica, 2010, p. 153 et seqq.

both justice and truth, and that would be at the very least inaccurate. What can be graduated, in any case, is the thoroughness of the epistemic processes that we set in motion in search of justice or truth. But not justice or truth. Something is just or unjust, true or false. And what is just now will always have been; what is true now will always have been true. As long as the term "truth" is understood in its most intuitive sense of truth as correspondence – as it is understood in criminal proceedings – if there is anything that characterizes it, it is precisely that bivalence and invariability.[4] Also, some constructivist versions in metaethics support the thesis of the "only correct answer" in moral matters.[5]

Even clearer is the question at the level of theoretical discourse: as far as I know, there is no theory of truth, at least among the most important, that is willing to say that truth is "adjustable". It would not be claimed by a naive realist; nor a realist, let's say "à la Tarski-style" or "à la Popper";[6] nor a deflationist "à la Horwich";[7] nor a minimalist "à la Crispin Wright";[8] nor even a pragmatist " à la Rorty";[9] nor "à la Rescher" coherentists;[10] nor even supporters of epistemological concepts of truth, such as Putnam[11] or the early Habermas.[12] It was precisely Habermas who, influenced by a very fine critique by Cristina Lafont, ended up abandoning his epistemological conception of truth (which, like Putnam, assimilated truth to justification under ideal conditions), by recognizing that this earlier point of view forced him to renounce the irreducible, invariable and non-perspectivist character of the concept of truth.[13] What is true, in short, will be completely independent of our attitudes towards truth.

---

4 Such us, among others, Carnap, Philosophy and Phenomenological Research, 1946, p. 590 et seqq.; Popper, *"Wahrheit und Annäherung an die Wahrheit"* [1960], Karl Popper. *Lesebuch.* [2000], p. 164 et seqq.; Davidson, The Journal of Philosophy, 1990, p. 305 et seqq.

5 As, explicitly, Lafont, in: Aboulafia/Bookman/Kemp (eds.), Habermas and Pragmatism, p. 185 et seqq.; implicitly Nino, Ética y derechos humanos, [1989], p. 117 et seqq.

6 See Tarski, Philosophy and Phenomenological Research, 1944, p. 341 et seqq. Popper, op. cit. (fn. 5).

7 See Horwich, in: Jackson/Smith/ (eds.), *The Oxford Handbook of Contemporary Philosophy* [2013], p. 454 et seqq.

8 See Wright, *Truth and Objectivity* [1994].

9 See Rorty, in: Rorty, *Objectivity, Relativism, and Truth* [1991].

10 See Rescher, Review of Metaphysics, 1985, p. 795 et seqq.

11 See Putnam, *Reason, Truth, and History* [1981], section 3.

12 See Habermas, in: Habermas, *Vorstudien und Ergänzungen zur Theorie des kommunikativen Handelns* [1984], p. 127 et seqq.

13 See Habermas, *Wahrheit und Rechtfertigung* [1999], p. 256.

As I said, it is possible, on the other hand, to graduate the epistemic strictness that we apply to justification, i.e., to the procedure we use to find out the truth or to determine whether something is just. At the level of a theoretical discourse (i.e., that relating to the factual world), since we can never be sure that a statement is true, we need a justifying process that guarantees us, at least, that we have done everything possible to reasonably (justifiably) believe in the truth of a statement.[14] Hence, in a judicial process, the justification consists of the evidentiary procedure, as I have substantiated in a previous work on the problem of truth.[15] So, we can put more or less effort into the justification procedures, depending on how much (and with how much precision) we want to find out something, i.e., depending on how much we want to "get closer to the truth". That's why it can be said that justification is adjustable. But you never get more truth, or less truth, or one truth, or a "clipped" truth.[16] You get the truth, or you don't get it.

Truth, then, is always independent of justification.[17] Therefore, while a rigorous justification may give us better reasons to believe in the truth of a statement, the fact is that its truth does not depend on that strictness, but only on the world. Now, as a rigorous justificatory procedure guarantees us those "best reasons to believe", in certain contexts particularly interested in truth and therefore depending on the way of its inquiry (such as that of the natural sciences or that of a criminal trial), it will be necessary to implement sophisticated justificatory procedures.

Having made all these clarifications, then, Hilb and Tamburrini's thesis could – and should – be formulated in a different way, perhaps like this:

In relation to the trials in Argentina for crimes against humanity, it is possible and desirable to give way a little in justice in order to undertake a justifying or evidentiary procedure that will give us more reasons to believe that it is true that the crimes occurred in such a way.

---

14 See about Röhl, *Allgemeine Rechtslehre*, 2nd ed. 2001, p. 117 et seqq.; Grundmann, *Analytische Einführung in die Erkenntnistheorie* [2008], p. 223 et seqq., 277 et seqq.

15 See Pérez Barberá, Isonomía, nº 52, in print.

16 Grossly incorrect in this respect is the dominant view among proceduralists in the continental European tradition, who distinguish between "material truth" (or objective truth) and "forensic truth" (or judicial truth). See for example v. Canstein, 1880, pp. 297 et seqq., 306 et seqq.; Walter, [1979], pp. 77 et seqq.; Hassemer, 1990, p. 153; Beulke, [2016], p. 5. In Argentina, on the other hand, fortunately even the classical proceduralists have always rejected the idea of different kinds of truths (see, by all, Maier, *Derecho procesal penal, t. I: Fundamentos*, 2ª edic., [1996], pp. 848 et seqq.).

17 As Wright, Truth and Objectivity, [1994], pp. 71 et seqq.

Before moving on to the core of my objection to this thesis, it is necessary to bear in mind that there is a conceptual connection between justice and truth, in the sense that truth is a necessary condition of justice; truth being understood as the correspondence between statement and world, on the one hand, and justice as retributive justice, on the other.[18] It is that kind of justice, archetypal in discursive processes in which a criminal or a moral sanction is applied (and not in others, such as processes that result in civil compensation, for example), that is inextricably linked to the concept of truth as correspondence. Because retribution is a "deserved reaction", and it can only be deserved by those who have done what justifies that reaction, that is: the one who has actually done it. Only if it is true that the accused of a crime committed it, the accused will deserve a criminal and a moral reproach (and a criminal punishment and a moral sanction).[19]

It is precisely in this, in reacting against someone because they deserve it and to the extent that they deserve it, that the normative core of retributive justice consists. As I argued in a previous article on justification of punishment, responding to one evil with another evil is only the descriptive core of that kind of justice. I reproduce that argument here:

> *"There is a certain consensus that punishment, conceptually, contains two elements that must be analytically differentiated: disapproval and the irrogation of an evil. Disapproval is always a reaction, a response. As such, it is directed towards the past. Only a fact that has already happened can be approved or disapproved. But this is also what caracterizes retribution. Does this mean that retribution already plays a role in the definition of punishment? It is necessary to differentiate. Conceptually, retribution is a deserved reaction. It therefore contains a descriptive element (reaction) and a normative element (deserving). Here I would like to support the thesis that the descriptive element of retribution, that which characterizes it as reaction or response, is part of the concept of punishment. The normative element of retribution – deserving – belongs instead to the justification of the punishment."*[20]

Hence those who focus on the question of the answer to one evil with another evil (such as Tamburrini and, to a lesser extent, Hilb) give only an

---

18 More detailed I explain it in Pérez Barberá, Isonomía, nº 52, cit. (note 16), in print.

19 Ibid.

20 Pérez Barberá, InDret Penal, núm. 4/2014, p. 1 et seqq.. URL: https://indret.com/wp-content/themes/indret/pdf/1081.pdf.

account of one aspect of retribution (the descriptive), and leave out its normative essence, which is the most interesting here. Because it is precisely this normative aspect, related to the idea of deserving, that makes the answering of one evil with another evil into an act of justice and not another crime.[21] That is why in this work I grant retribution an essential (albeit partial) role in the justification of punishment.

Now, even if a) it were descriptively clear that retributive justice plays an essential role in criminal proceedings; b) it were demonstrated that retribution (as a deserved response) plays in turn an essential normative role in the justification of punishment; and c) it were accepted that in order for being deserved it is necessary for it to be true that whoever is accused of committing a crime has committed it, it would still remain to be seen to what extent our criminal proceedings are designed in such a way that they are suitable to provide truth and, based on it, retributive justice.

It should be like this. If we claim that retribution must play a fundamental role in the justification of punishment (even if partial because preventive or consequentialist arguments are also given a place), then we are committed to designing criminal proceedings consistent with the idea of retribution, that are interested in the truth (not in the oxymoron of a truth) and that are therefore able to provide at least something that we can justifiably believe to be true.

III. Necessity of truth-finding

But can it really be said that, in our criminal proceedings, obtaining the truth is a necessary condition for imposing a penalty? If not, Hilb and Tamburrini would have an additional argument to support their position. Because in this case, they might claim that truth and reconciliation commissions can be a better means of obtaining truth than criminal proceedings, and they also might even add that the design of legitimate criminal proceedings does not consider truth to be indispensable. The contemporary epistemology interested in judicial processes, on top of that, offers a very solid argument in favor of that thesis, which basically reads as follows: for a judicial process of any type -civil, criminal, etc.- to end validly, it does not matter if "it is true that p", but only if "it is true that it is proven that

21 As for example Moore, Placing Blame. A Theory of the Criminal Law [1997], p. 157 et seqq., 719 et seqq.; Berman, *Ethics*, [2008], p. 258 et seqq.; Pawlik, Das Unrecht des Bürgers [2012], p. 82 et seqq.

p". The relation between proof and truth would not be, therefore, a conceptual relation, but merely empirical or contingent.[22]

Rebutting this argument requires a major effort of substantiation which, for reasons of time, I cannot comprehensively carry out here. I tried to do that in an article on the connection between proof and truth.[23] I still believe the argument that I referenced is correct, and that it therefore helps to consolidate the idea that, in criminal matters, there is a conceptual, and not merely contingent or empirical, connection between legitimate evidence and truth; at least, if we are talking about evidence to convict. So we can really say that we have processes genuinely interested in the truth; that they can also obtain truth (even if we do not know it for sure, which does not matter as long as we have no reason to believe that what we have found is false or probably false); and that, consequently, their design is suitable for applying retributive justice.

IV. Differences between criminal trials and truth commissions

Faced with this, one might ask what the situation is like in a truth commission such as the South African one or any other that follows the rule of "amnesty as a response to the voluntary and sincere confession of crimes". Or, more precisely, if the connection between the truth and the mechanism for finding it is different from that of a criminal trial. I think it shouldn't be very different if you want to find truth. A truth commission is supposed to look for the same thing as a criminal trial like the one we know here in Argentina, and even in a very similar way: the truth will be sought and sought through devices comparable to what in a criminal process is called "evidence".

Now, are there differences between the epistemic strictness of a criminal trial and that of a truth commission? I do not think it is possible to generalize, that is to say: we will have to see how each commission is designed and each process in particular. But beyond that, it cannot be disregarded the fact that, to be legitimate, a truth commission need not be particularly rigorous in its evidentiary procedure; basically because it will not result in the application of punishment.

---

22 Claimed for example in Ferrer Beltrán, Prueba y verdad en el derecho, 2nd ed. [2005].

23 See Pérez Barberá, Isonomía, nº 52, in print.

A criminal proceeding, on the other hand, does have to meet certain strict epistemic standards regarding evidence in order to be legitimate in constitutional terms (at least in a liberal rule of law). Because if it ends with a conviction, it will have as a consequence the imposition of punishment and, therefore, of an evil. This, of course, may be justified as being deserved, but for that, as was said, it is necessary that it be true that the accused committed a crime. And since the evil of punishment is serious, because it consists of pain or loss of rights (hard treatment), then the procedure from which we determine whether a criminal charge is true or false must be especially rigorous.

That is why the evidentiary procedure of the criminal process is highly sophisticated and demanding. Since it must be true that the accused is guilty in order to impose punishment, and that it implies real suffering, it is necessary to implement evidentiary procedures that give us as much assurance as possible of the truth of the factual statements in the trial. That is the reason why a criminal process is not content with voluntary confessions of the accused. Even if there are, in order to consider them credible it must confront them with the rest of the evidentiary material: other testimonies, expert opinions, reconstructions of the crime, recognition of persons, listening to telephone conversations, etc. And all of this, at least in the oral trial stage, within the framework of a procedure in which parties with opposing interests intervene under a strict "contradictory" regime, that is, one that allows everything said by each of those parties to be contradicted (both with evidence and with arguments related to that evidence) by the other. In the face of this, an impartial tribunal assesses which of the hypotheses put into play by the parties is the most credible, and considers it to be true, after giving reasons in this regard.

If all this also happens in a truth commission, and with the same thoroughness, then it may well be said that this particular committee (commission) has no greater epistemic deficits (or virtues) than those of criminal proceedings, and that it can therefore offer approximately the same quantity and quality of reasons for justified belief in the truth of what is said there as those provided by criminal proceedings. But if this is not the case, that is: if the procedure with which a truth commission is designed is not contradictory, if there is no confrontation between the confessions and testimonies of the victims and other objective data (in addition to contrasting the testimonies of victims and perpetrators), if there is no impartial tribunal that should base with arguments why it believes what it believes, then there will be no reason to suggest that a truth commission is in better conditions than a criminal process to find out the truth.

By this I do not intend to make an irresponsible plea for criminal proceedings, as if they were a panacea. That is not the case, almost nothing works there ideally and there is much to criticize. But the same goes for truth commissions. I would just like to emphasize that, to the extent that a position such as Hilb's has failed to take account of these nuances, I have the feeling that it is a little rushed, both when it underestimates criminal proceedings as real suppliers and when it overestimates truth commissions as such.[24]

It is true that, as Hilb points out, the threat of punishment can inhibit sincere confessions.[25] But just as the promise of forgiveness can stimulate false confessions. The only way to compensate for these epistemic deficits that originate in truth-finding processes based on the promise of benefits or punishments is, as I said, to shore them up with sophisticated epistemic strictness, so that it is feasible to confront such confessions with other highly credible evidence.

For the rest, we all know that the South African process of "truth and reconciliation" was extremely flawed in terms of epistemic strictness, or that it was very deficient in that sense in comparison with the thoroughness that characterized both the trial of the juntas and the current trials in Argentina. In South Africa, testimonies were only collected from victims and perpetrators and there was no serious and systematic confrontation of these statements with other evidence obtained from trustworthy investigations. This was for the simple reason that these data were not obtained, or at least not to any appreciable extent.[26] If one compares this with what was done in Argentina by forensic anthropology teams and by the National Genetic Data Bank (just to mention two very convincing examples, which are by no means the only ones), the balance in favor of our country's option seems evident.

It is true that what I have just pointed out is purely contingent, because, as I have already insinuated, nothing prevents the design and organization of an epistemically sophisticated truth commission. But it is no less true that, even if this were achieved, it would be difficult to surpass the probative rigor that is characteristic of criminal proceedings, at least of those that are constitutionally legitimate.

---

24 See Hilb, op. cit. (fn. 4).

25 Ibid.

26 See, for example, the findings of the International Center for Transitional Justice in this regard: https://www.ictj.org/es/news/ignorando-sus-demandas-de-justicia-sudafrica-fracasa-ante-las-victimas-del-apartheid.

V. Benefits of criminal proceedings

The immediate question that arises then is: if not only criminal proceedings have an epistemic deficit of origin (because of the threat of punishment), but that type of deficit is also found in truth commissions (because of the promise of forgiveness); and if the greatest imaginable epistemic thoroughness for a truth commission would not be different from that of a standard (legitimate) criminal proceeding, then why opt for a truth commission and not for a criminal proceeding to investigate the course of events in relation to these type of crimes?

The answer could be: because if everything I have just said about truth commissions is correct, then one should assume that even so they offer more opportunities for reflection on what has been done. And that it would be so because of the absence of the threat of punishment and the promise of forgiveness in their design. Hence, they would be taken by the accused of the crimes as a better basis for sincere repentance and reconciliation, which is a core reason of Hilb's proposal.[27] However, the question should be asked again: if only sincere repentance counts, to what extent is it stimulated by a procedure that offers a benefit in return? To what extent, in such a framework, will its sincerity be credible?

Proceedings such as criminal ones, or those of expiation of guilt in certain religions, which are characterized by the threat of punishment, also make it possible, by their design, for the perpetrator or sinner to confront what has been done, reflect on it and, on that basis, repent sincerely. Of course not everyone does, but the structural conditions in which they develop (to the extent that they confront the alleged perpetrator with his facts and his victims, whether through the oral presentations of accusations and the physical presence of the victims in their vicinity in criminal proceedings, or through examination of conscience in religious atonement) create an adequate framework for this, which, at least in principle, is no more defective than the one that can achieve the best design of a truth commission. And, contrary to what happens in these, the threat of punishment makes sincerity more credible if repentance occurs, because at least it cannot be said that it is motivated in an attempt to gain an advantage.

I would like to emphasize a point that I have tried to make clear so far, but which perhaps needs special clarification: I am not interested in the empirical contingencies of these truth inquiry processes. In any of them, criminal or non-criminal, due to very different historical, social and per-

---

27 See op. cit. (fn. 4).

sonal circumstances, it can happen that true or false confessions, sincere remorse or liars are produced, or that none of this happens. What matters to me is only the extent to which the institutional design of each of these procedures is structurally capable of producing certain effects of strong epistemological importance. And what I think that I have made clear so far is that it does not appear that truth commissions can be said to be better or more apt – at finding out the truth than criminal proceedings.

VI. Retrospective

Here I'd like to return to a couple of central notions and explain what I think is my main criticism of Hilb. A criminal proceeding, in order to provide justice, requires truth, because it is a matter of retributive justice, which requires desert, and there is no desert if it is not true that one acted wrong. Without truth, then, there is no justice. Enlarging the argument, with little truth, there will be little justice. By this I am not admitting that the truth can be graduated: I am only referring, with a metaphorical expression, to the possibility that, in a certain context, the truth of some factual statements has been ascertained, but not that of many others also relevant to that context.

Well, the most disturbing thing about Hilb's opinion seems to me is that she is suggesting precisely this: that in the trials in Argentina the truth would not have been ascertained of enough factual statements. And this is disturbing because, if so, she would be questioning not only a lack of truth in the trials, but also, as a consequence of this, a lack of justice. Having cleared the relationship in terms of the necessary condition that exists between truth and justice in that context, her argument inevitably leads to that conclusion. So, does Hilb really thinks that already obtained justice should be sacrificed, or does she suggest, strictly speaking, that there has not been sufficient justice? Since it is her reasoning that generates this doubt, I believe that it is she who should answer this question in her next inquiries on the subject.

Especially because, in this drama, nobody is waiting to exploit discursive advantages. Think for a moment about who might take advantage of Hilb's argument to directly question the justice obtained after the trials.[28]

28 One possible example is the following, published by the Argentine press in 2015: "The Catholic Church disavowed retired Bishop Alcides Jorge Pedro Casaretto, who a month ago said at the Pontifical Catholic University, PUCA, that truth

Are they concerned about the same as Hilb? Obviously not. But I think, anyway, that it is not unreasonable to guess that, if apologists or at least defenders of the dictatorship use these ideas of Hilb, it is because they have found in them a tool to subtly question also – and especially – what trials represent in justice, because that is, strictly speaking, what this sector is interested in.

Of course, Hilb can say that she does not have to correct what she thinks if she believes in it, even if it serves as an input for those who in no way she wants to benefit. But, as I said, what I wonder is whether Hilb has noticed that, with her argument, she is actually also questioning the justice of the outcome of our criminal proceedings against the dictators. It would be important to listen to her at this point.

VII. Conclusion

For my part, I believe that both the trial of the juntas and the subsequent trials restarted in 2004 have provided innumerable factual statements that can be considered true. Enough in fact to form a narrative of that past – as long as no new data becomes available – that does not generate relevant doubts. At least regarding certain core matters, in particular everything related to the guilt or innocence of those who have been condemned and acquitted up to now. And if this is so, then the result of the trials, in this very important aspect, has been just.

The self-critical reflection of notable intellectuals and contemporaries of those years, such as Hilb and Oscar Del Barco,[29] among others, has contributed in a very relevant way to peace pacification in Argentina, and to the abandonment (hopefully definitive) of violence as a tool of political struggle. But the trials have also made a decisive contribution to this. I know Hilb does not deny this. But in any case, I do not share her hypothesis that, once impunity has been eliminated as an option – as she has ex-

---

should be privileged over justice for the crimes of the last dictatorship... Casaretto had said that justice 'is not totally impartial' and that 'the more justice we apply, the less truth we recover, and the more truth we want to recover, the softer we have to be in the justice applied. We have to undo that equation of so much justice, which is in contrast to truth'". (URL: https://www.pagina12.com.ar/diario/elpais/1-281050-2015-09-06.html).

29 See his letter, known as "No matás", originally published in La intemperie, Córdoba, 2004. Available for example at https://lectoresdeheidegger.wordpress.com/2011/09/22/oscar-del-barco-no-mataras-carta-a-schmucler/.

pressly clarified -, everything could have been better without the trials. Here, I believe, I have demonstrated that there are no reasons of institutional design on the basis of which it can be said that a truth commission is in a better position to provide truth and sincere remorse than a criminal trial.

The rest – it should be repeated – is contingent: Whether or not sincere remorse occurs in one area or another depends on each social context and therefore on exogenous circumstances to that institutional design. And then it will be on the pulse of politics, attentive to the historical processes that are really taking place, to warn which path is the most conducive, in a given territory and at a given time, to generate memory, truth and justice in the face of situations of horror such as those we have experienced here. In these terms, I still think that Argentina's option in favor of criminal trials has been the right one.

On the other hand, this option does not prevent reductions of sentence in exchange for more information from the accused, as Tamburrini wishes.[30] In the monumental trial of the concentration camp "La Perla", carried out in Córdoba, on more than one occasion there was an outline of this in my opinion legitimate transaction, which later vanished because it was verified that what was initially presented as an opening to provide data was nothing more than a grotesque mockery by some of the accused.[31]

Notwithstanding the foregoing, I think it can be said that the factual contingencies are also against Hilb's ideas. As Diego Tatián has emphasized in his discussion with her,[32] the truth is that neither military nor insurgent leaders with direct participation in the violence showed any remorse when there was no threat of punishment, it is to say, while the impunity laws were in force and there was no indication of what would happen if they confessed (almost five years can be counted from Menem's pardon to Scilingo's confession,[33] during which there were in fact truth com-

30 See op. cit. (fn. 4).

31 On what the Argentine press has published about this episode, see, for example: https://www.clarin.com/politica/derechos_humanos-lesa_humanidad-la_perla-ernesto_barreriro_0_Sy_qedv9Pmg.html.

32 See Tatian, in: Discusiones, 2013, p. 59 et seqq.

33 Adolfo Scilingo is the only (former) Argentine military officer, a participant in the dictatorship, who confessed to the crimes (in particular the so-called "death flights") and showed repentance. He did so before the journalist Horacio Verbitsky (see Verbitsky, *El vuelo*, [1995]).

missions, even though they functioned in the courts under the label of "trials for historical truth").[34]

According to this experience, it would undoubtedly have been a mistake, in 2004, to repeal the impunity laws and then to propose not the carrying out of criminal trials, but a path of amnesty in exchange for information. And it is this same experience that allows us to infer as more plausible the counterfactual that nobody would have admitted anything if Alfonsín had chosen to complement the Conadep report with a process similar to that of South Africa, instead of propitiating to carry out the trial to the juntas.

However, we can only be grateful for texts such as Hilb's and others that are in her line, because they really help us to think better. And if I have quoted especially some of Hilb's contributions, it is because she has managed to make the depth of her suggestions, threaded together with the beauty of her prose, work in me like a song of sirens similar to and at the same time different from that of the Homeric tragedy, while it generated in me not only the need to move away, but also to get closer to her mistake in order to achieve more clarity in my ideas.

34 On this subject, see Andriotti Romanin, *Review of Latin American and Caribbean Studies*, [2013], p. 5 et seqq. Also available at https://www.jstor.org/stable/23408419?seq=1#metadata_info_tab_contents.

The Truth Comissions as a mechanism for repair societies traversed by mass violence

Alberto Yepes Palacio[1]

I. Introduction

In this paper I propose to analyse the social conditions in which the Truth Commission in Colombia arose out of and has evolved from. I examine the work of other Truth Commissions (henceforth TC) that have been established during the last four decades in some Latin American countries. I also consider the evaluation of these TCs by the Inter American Commission of Human Rights (IAHCR) in order to compare the efficiency of these Commissions with the mechanisms focused on criminal trials. Hence, I intend to show the conditions under which they can be successful to face past crimes in societies that have gone through situations of mass violence in the context of wars, armed conflicts or periods of dictatorship and face the challenge of building peace or restore democratic life.

These reflections are the product of my experience of almost 30 years working in the defence of human rights, supporting victims of war and from the struggle for building peace in Colombia.

II. Peace Processes and Clarification of the truth in Colombia

Colombia is a society that has been immersed in multiple and prolonged armed conflicts since its independence from Spain at the beginning of the 19th century. The current armed conflict between the State and the leftists Guerillas has been in process for the past 60 years. Nonetheless, there have also been multiple peace agreements to overcome these conflicts in the last 200 years. The historian Mario Aguilera details 63 pardons and 25

1 Coordinator of the Human Rights Observatory of the Colombia – Europe – United States Coordination, network that groups 275 organizations for the promotion and defense of human rights in Colombiain the face ofth and justice uld gr.

amnesties between 1820 and 1995[2]. These were agreed through political negotiation between the State and rebel groups. However, the processes of political negotiation with illegal armed groups in the last 15 years show that politics alone can no longer define the paths to overcoming armed conflicts and allow for a transition from war to peace[3]. The arrangements to end violence need to be made in the context of a solid and growing internal and external humanitarian consciousness, and restrictions marked by demanding international and national human rights standards, referring above all to the rights of victims of the truth, justice and reparation. The "judicialization of politics" today marks the field of the possible and the desirable in the formulas of justice for the transition from war to peace and from dictatorship to democracy.

In of the case of Colombia, where war and internal armed conflict continues after 6 decades, neither the State is in a position to defeat its rebel adversaries by arms nor are the rebels capable of defeating the State[4]. Therefore, criminal trials and proportional retributive penalties are not viable options for a political negotiation that would allow for a cessation of war and hence peace. The rebel groups will not be willing to demobilize their militant structures, lay down their arms and submit to state law when the prospect offered is to spend a good part of the rest of their days in jail. There is also the complexity of the armed conflict in which the State, its armed forces and judiciary are not neutral and impartial actors. They are even responsible for a greater percentage of human rights abuses and violations. For example, they have caused a situation in which more than 8.5

2 Aguilera, in: El Espectador. 2 Dec. 2015, URL: https://www.elespectador.com/noticias/judicial/colombia-una-tradicion-de-amnistias-e-indultos-i-articulo-603001.

3 The process of universalization of human rights treaties, the raising of humanitarian awareness in the world, the activism of non-governmental organizations and the creation of institutions such as the International Criminal Court as well as the expansion of universal jurisdiction for international crimes have drastically limited the options of states to negotiate or impose Transitional Justice arrangements that ignore the minimum standards required for truth, justice, reparation and guarantees of non-repetition.

4 Apart from the FARC-EP guerrillas that concluded a peace and demobilization process in 2016 with the government of President Juan Manuel Santos (2010–18), in Colombia there are other leftist guerrilla organizations with which the government of Iván Duque, which came after Santos (2018–2022) has refused any negotiation process and even recognition as actors of the internal armed conflict. These are the Ejercito de Liberación Nacional, the Ejercito Popular de Liberación and the recently formed FARC dissidents, known as Nueva Marquetalia that allege the breach of the Duque Government as a reason to resume the armed uprising.

million people are registered as victims of the internal armed conflict[5], which make it infeasible, factually, legally, ethically and politically to apply the criminal law to prosecute all those who perpetrated each and every one of these criminal acts. Faced with these factual, political and legal limitations, it is necessary to rethink the punitive claims of imposing trials and retributive punishments. The consideration of a combination of formulas that aim to overcome the armed conflict through negotiation is imposed and the recovery and/or construction of a process to move from an "unfair legal system" to a project of Social State under the rule of Law is necessary in order to represent and be recognized by all sectors of society. Under these circumstances and with these perspectives, a Peace Agreement was signed between the Colombian State and the FARC-EP[6], which represented the main and most powerful guerrilla organizations. In this context, the need for the creation of the Commission for the Clarification of Truth – CEV is also understood[7].

5 República de Colombia, Unidad para la Atención y Reparación Integral a las Víctimas Registro Nacional de Información in: https://cifras.unidadvictimas.gov.co. (last consultation on January 23 2020).

6 The peace negotiations between the Government of Colombia and the FARC-EP guerrillas carried out in Havana between 2012 and 2016 concluded with the signing of the Final Agreement for the End of the Conflict and the Construction of a Stable and Lasting Peace, through which ended 52 years of armed uprising of these guerrillas, including agreements on rural reform, extension of democracies and political participation, security guarantees for the legal exercise of politics, strategies for the substitution of illegal crops and an accountability system for all those who committed crimes within the framework of the armed conflict. This agreement allowed the demobilization of about 13,000 members of the FARC guerrillas (Vid. Oficina del Alto Comisionado para la Paz [2016]. El Acuerdo final de Paz, Oportunidad para constuir la Paz, http://www.altocomisionadoparalapaz.gov.co/herramientas/Documents/Nuevo_enterese_version_6_Sep_final_web.pdf).

7 For the entities of the transitional justice system created under the Peace Agreement between the Government of Colombia and the guerrillas of the Fuerzas Armadas Revolucionarias de Colombia -Ejército del Pueblo (Revolutionary Armed Forces of Colombia – Army of the People, FARC-EP), the current acronym in Spanish is used in this article: CEV, Comisión para el Esclarecimiento de la Verdad (Commission for the Clarification of Truth, Coexistence and Non-Repetition); UBPD for the Unidad de Busqueda de Personas Desaparecidas (the Unit for the Search of Missing Persons); JEP, Jurisdicción Especial para la Paz (Special Court for Peace) and SIVJRNR for the Sistema Integral de Verdad, Justicia, Reparación y Garnatias de No Repetición (Comprehensive System of Truth, Justice, Reparation and Guarantees of Non-Repetition), although for other Truth Commissions we use the acronym TC.

The Colombian case is also complex, because in addition to the direct responsibility and complicity of the State in political violence against the population, the State and the political and economic power groups have promoted and encouraged the formation and performance of paramilitary groups with whom they maintain close links with and tolerate. The State always hides their links and even denies the existence of these criminal structures, making the procedures for clarifying the truth about state responsibility more necessary, both for covert actions and for claims to divert responsibility with the use of war mechanisms by delegation or commission through proxies, which lead many sectors to mistakenly think that it is a war with multiple sides or "all against all"[8].

III. The Truth Commission in Colombia

In December 2015, in the framework of the peace negotiations in Havana between the Government and the Revolutionary Armed Forces of Colombia – FARC agreed to create a Commission for the Clarification of Truth, Convenience and Non-Repetition – CEV, an independent and impartial mechanism, of a non-judicial nature, that would enter into force once the peace agreement was signed, with the purpose of satisfying the right of victims to the truth and society to know the facts of the conflict, contribute to the construction and preservation of historical memory and achieve a broad understanding of the multiple dimensions of the truth of the conflict, including the historical dimension, in such a way that not only the right to the truth be satisfied, but also to help build the basis of convenience, reconciliation, and non-repetition. The goal is to contribute to the clarification of what happened within the framework of the armed conflict, to promote and contribute to the recognition of the victims and the promotion of coexistence in the territories.[9]

---

8 In recent years, and after a partial demobilization culminated in 2006, paramilitary groups have evolved into a series of criminal groups that are linked to drug trafficking and other illegal income, who exercise social and territorial control in large regions through terror and are primarily responsible for an atrocious campaign of extermination of social leaders and human rights defenders that worsened after the signing of the Peace Agreement with the FARC.

9 The Commission for the Clarification of Truth was established in Article 2 of Legislative Act 01 of 2017 that incorporates into the National Constitution the Comprehensive System of Truth, Justice and Non-Repetition included in the Peace Agreements, and was regulated by Presidential Decree 588 from April 5, 2017.

However, the CEV is not an isolated entity or one that can function in a disjointed way because, within the framework of the Agreement for the Termination of the Conflict and the Construction of a Stable and Lasting Peace, the parties agreed that the CEV would become part of an Integral System of Truth, Justice, Reparation and Non-Repetition, SIVJRNR, made up of 5 mechanisms, in which the CEV is only one of them. The other 4 mechanisms that constitute the system are made up of a) a court for peace (Special Jurisdiction for Peace, JEP) that will deal with the prosecution and punishment of the most serious and representative crimes committed by those who were most responsible in the context of the armed conflict; b) a Missing Persons Search Unit – UBPD that has the task of searching, identifying and returning to their families more than 120,000 people who were victims of enforced disappearance[10]; c) measures for material and symbolic reparation to the victims of the conflict, and lastly, d) a series of measures to avoid the non-repetition of atrocities such as administrative reforms and revision of legislation that may lead to human rights violations. The 5 mechanisms should work in a coordinated manner, bearing in mind that criminal trials will be carried out only through the Jurisdiction for Peace.

The integrality is established by means of a "conditionality regime" in which access to pardon and amnesty measures for less serious crimes and for attenuated penalties in the case of the most serious crimes can be granted by the JEP[11]. These measures are conditioned on the realization of concrete contributions towards peace, the delivery of the truth to the CEV and information about the missing persons in front of the UBPD. However, both the UBPD and the CEV had established that their activities could not be used for criminal charges in front of any jurisdictional authority, and that "the information received or produced by the CEV cannot be transferred to judicial authorities to be used in order to attribute responsibilities in judicial proceedings or to have probative value, nor may the judicial authorities require it". In this way, an important part of its effectiveness depends on the perpetrators of the most serious crimes having decided to

10 El tiempo (29-V-2019), *'Hay que encontrar a más de 120.000 desaparecidos por el conflicto'*. URL: https://www.eltiempo.com/justicia/jep-colombia/unidad-de-busqueda-de-personas-desaparecidas-ya-empezo-trabajo-territorial-368222.

11 On the "conditionality regime", the JEP Appeal Section has said that it consists of "concrete, programmed and clear commitments" through which whoever submits to the JEP reveals how they will make their contribution to the truth and the future reparation of the victims as a commitment to access provisional or definitive benefits (JEP, Sala de Reconocimiento de Verdad, Responsabilidad y de determinación de los hechos y conductas, Auto 0079 de 2018).

submit to the JEP and collaborate with the clarification of the crimes and the assumption of responsibility[12].

In the case of former demobilized FARC combatants, compliance with this conditionality regime is unavoidable in order to access the benefits of amnesties, pardons, or alternative or reduced penalties. In the case of State agents, very few of the officers involved in serious human rights violations have requested their submission to the JEP, because the investigations of their crimes never advanced and there is no will to prosecute in ordinary justice, and therefore they will not go through the transitional justice system. In the case of unarmed agents of the State and other individuals who have been linked to the formation and support of paramilitary groups, they managed to impose in the regulations of the agreements that their appearance in front of the instances of the Transitional Justice System would be voluntary, wherewith few have come to the JEP and less therefore in front of the CEV. In the case of the military agents who have appeared in front of the system, recently the military command issued a directive to build a unique narrative to coordinate their versions in front of the CEV[13], which greatly weakens the ability of the system and the CEV to clarify the truth about crimes committed by the State. The Agreement ensured that former presidents were not required to be accountable to the system, and also, after the defeat of the Agreements in the plebiscite, the military imposed the non-application of the rules on responsibility of command enshrined in the Rome Statute or in international criminal jurisprudence for the accountability of military superiors[14].

(The enormous power of extreme right-wing political groups, led by former President Álvaro Uribe, a fierce opponent of the peace accords and great promoter of the military submission and extermination of the guerrilla without any type of negotiation, and economic and military leaders who have been implicated in crimes in the context of the war for their involvement in violations of human rights or the conformation of paramilitary groups, has led them to carry out a strategy of population polarization

---

12 To access the benefits of the system those who submit to it are obliged to provide truth to both the Special Jurisdiction for Peace, as well as the Truth Commission and the Unit for the Search of Missing Persons.

13 Oquendo, (2019, August 21). *El Ejército de Colombia prepara una versión coordinada sobre el conflict*, URL: https://elpais.com/internacional/2019/08/19/colombia/1566244001_904750.html.

14 Olasolo/Canosa, *La Responsabilidad del Superior en el Acuerdo de Paz en Colombia a la luz del Derecho Internacional*, [2018] URL: http://dx.doi.org/10.4067/S0718-33992018000100444.

against the peace agreement, which allowed them to reach a majority against the agreements reached between the Government and the FARC in the referendum called by the Government to validate the agreements in October 2016.)

The victory in the elections by the NO to the peace agreements coalition, obliged a renegotiation of the agreed text that allowed the so called "third parties" (politicians and businessmen who financed paramilitary groups and benefited from their criminal actions and loot, but did not participate directly as armed actors in the war) were not obliged to go to the Truth Commission or be accountable to the peace tribunal, unless they did so voluntarily, and also managed to ensure that the command responsibility rules enshrined in the Rome Statute and in international criminal law did not apply to high-ranking military officers. Furthermore, these groups have regained political power, placing in the government a president who, together with his party and their allied Attorney General of the Nation have led an aggressive campaign against the JEP and the other institutions and mechanisms of the transitional justice systems, paralysing the implementation of agreements signed by the former administration and carrying out measures that have re-established war in the regions formerly occupied by the guerrillas. When those responsible for past crimes returned to power in the 2012 presidential and congressional elections, they resisted applying peace agreements, leaving intact the structures and military command involved in illegal actions in the context of the conflict, as well as the allied paramilitary structures that not only were not dismantled but expanded throughout the country, carrying out a ferocious campaign of extermination of the social leaders and the demobilized members of the guerrillas who signed the peace. Under these conditions, the work of entities such as the CEV and the JEP have become very difficult.

This weakens the possibilities for clarifying the truth, especially in relation to state crimes. However, victims' organizations, human rights organizations and an important sector of Colombian society and the international community are struggling so that the country does not return to war, for the already signed agreements to be implemented and for conversations with other guerrilla groups to be resumed. If peace as a whole does not advance, neither will the measures for the clarification of the truth nor the criminal sanction of the perpetrators of state crime be advanced.

IV. The Commissions of Truth and the right to the truth

There is not a single conception of what truth commissions should be. Their configuration, their assigned purposes and functions, as well as the degree of effectiveness in their fulfilment depend on the political, socio-economic and political culture contexts in which they must carry out their work. For the Inter-American Commission on Human Rights[15], "... The Commissions of Truth are "official, temporary and fact-finding bodies that are not judicial in nature and are responsible for investigating human rights or humanitarian law abuses that have been committed over several years". In this regard, both the Commission and the Court have highlighted the importance of the TC as an extrajudicial mechanism of transitional justice, aimed at clarifying situations of massive and systematic violations of human rights. (OEA, parr. 30)

The Inter-American Court of Human Rights has argued that "the establishment of a TC, depending on the object, procedure, structure and purpose of its mandate, may contribute to the construction and preservation of historical memory, clarification of facts and the determination of institutional, social and political responsibilities in certain historical periods of a society". (OEA, Parr. 321).

Apart from these functions, the experience of the TCs shows how they have assumed different functions according to the countries in which some of these have also worked to clarify the truth from restricted mandates to establish the fate of missing persons (Argentina, Chile and Bolivia), to establish formulas and programs for the reparation of the victims of such atrocities (Argentina and Chile), to recommend measures of institutional reforms and purification of judicial and security agencies (El Salvador), to prevent the return to atrocities, and in cases like South Africa even from the granting of amnesties[16]. In fact, the South African TC is the only one that has taken care of offering amnesties, so it would not seem very appropriate to assimilate the TCs to inefficient processes of granting

---

15 OEA, Comisión interamericana de Derechos Humanos, El Derecho a la Verdad en América Latina [2014]. Documento OEA/Ser.L/V/II.152. Doc. 2. 13 agosto 2014.

16 The sources for the study of this segment were mainly taken from a detailed study of the experience, conformation, mandates and results of the work of the Truth Commissions in various parts of the world that can be found in Hayner, *Unspeakable Truths, Transitional Justice and the challenge of the Truth Commissions.* [2010] 376 p. URL: https://www.mcgill.ca/isid/files/isid/priscilla_b._hayner_unspeakable_truths_transitibookzz.org_.pdf.

amnesties to produce truth and justice in the face of the greater a priori effectiveness that criminal trials would have. The TC have also contributed to discovering the names of perpetrators of the most decisive atrocities that have led to their separation from office and have contributed with their findings to the judicial system or these have been used to promote judicial prosecutions both in national and international courts. (El Salvador).

The experience of various Latin American TCs shows that the practice of the TC and criminal trials are not divergent and have mutually fed back on another. Criminal trial information has provided information to build a more comprehensive truth about the atrocities of the past and the TCs have served to feed, provide evidence, stimulate the judicial system to open trials in internal courts, and even when the publication of names has been restricted, they have sometimes opened the possibility of adjudicating responsibilities of the principal perpetrators (Guatemala). On other occasions even their information has been the support for decisions that have promoted the fight against impunity at an international level and the activation of international jurisdiction, as happened with the decision of the Spanish judge who requested the extradition of Pinochet, who based this determination largely on information from the Chilean TC.

In this regard, the IAHCR has also held that on many occasions both organs of the inter-American system have used the information provided by the final reports of the TC as a source of information and evidence in relation to cases processed in front of the system of cases and requests (v.gr. cases of the TC in Chile, El Salvador and Guatemala). (OEA, Parr, 30).

V. Criminal judgements and the right to investigate, judge and punish

Within the framework of political transitions from authoritarianism to democracy or from war to peace, which are often faced with a legacy of massive human rights violations, it may be essential to implement transition processes, agreed or negotiated, in which transitional justice formulas are imposed that make the universal application of criminal trials with retributive penalties impossible for all those involved. Nevertheless, the international obligation of the State to investigate, prosecute and punish serious human rights violations still persists. However, these obligations should not be understood as an absolute rule but as a principle that must be realized as much as possible so that victims' rights are maximized and convenience is ensured. Since judicial or procedural truth cannot be established in all cases, it is then necessary to establish mechanisms for clarification and construction of historical memory that account for all the complexities of periods of violence that want to be overcome. The TCs are well-suited entities in order to establish the institutional responsibilities, the causes, effects and affectations to the victims. The truth of criminal trials, which arises from the application of the state duty to investigate, prosecute and punish in transition contexts, generally focuses on the determination of unlawful conduct and responsibilities. Therefore, they run the risk of being insensitive to the expectations of victims. The truth that arises from the processes unleashed by the TC seeks to focus on social harm and the victim, that is framed in the social and economic context in which prolonged damage and systematic violations were perpetrated. Beyond the forensic, factual or procedural truth that determines that if A committed N, and therefore is worthy of X, there are other dimensions of the truth that the TCs help to build, such as narrative or interpersonal truth, which is built from the stories of victims and perpetrators, or social and dialogic truth, built from dialogue and debate between different actors in society, or the restorative or healing truth, that arises from the exercises of recognition of truth, assumption of responsibility and request of forgiveness in front of the victims. They are truths that build inputs for historical memory and that can generate the necessary consensus to delimit what happened historically and above all, what should not happen again[17].

VI. Conclusions

The success of both truth commissions and criminal trials in democratic transition processes depends largely on the valuation that a society makes of both the past that it wants to overcome or compensate as well as the context in which the measures to restore the rule of law will have to be applied. There is no single formula on how much proportion of restorative truth or retribution penalty should be agreed upon for each transition in each type of society, but the simultaneous achievement of peace and justice, of the search for cohesive societies that at the same time guarantee the

---

17 La reflexión sobre las diferentes dimensiones y usos de la "verdad" o "verdades" y las posibilidades de su recuperación en un proceso de transicion ha sido desarrollada generalmente a partir del informe de la Comisión de la Verdad y Reconciliación de Sudáfrica, que abordaba cuatro tipos diferentes de verdad: la verdad fáctica y forense, la verdad personal y narrativa, la verdad social y la verdad sanadora y restauradora (Vid. Uprimny, Sánchez, L.M/Sánchez, N.C, Justicia para la Paz. Crímenes atroces, derecho a la justicia y paz negociada [2014] pp. (91–153).

rights of victims to the greatest extent possible, requires a balanced combination between different mechanisms and purposes that in general terms, according to Duggan (2005), should include 4 mechanisms:

i) legal actions against the perpetrators, always necessary, ii) initiatives to search for truth and construction of historical memory, iii) both material and symbolic reparations to the victims and, iv) reform of key institutions to re-establish the democratic order and Rule of law[18].

The possible and acceptable arrangements in each society always imply taking into account the factual and political conditions as well as the establishment of minimum international human rights parameters related to the victims' rights to truth, justice and reparation that can guarantee coexistence, peaceful, non-repetition of violence and at the same time the guarantee that the parties involved negotiate in good faith while maintaining their commitment to implement and comply in good faith with the agreements reached.

Unlike the processes of transition to democracy after the end of a dictatorship, the processes of transition after civil wars or internal armed conflicts generally show greater difficulties for the exercise of state duty to investigate and punish transgressors of state law both for the reluctance of the combatants to leave their weapons in exchange for jail and for the inability of the judicial system to investigate and prosecute all those responsible within a reasonable time frame. The aspiration for total judicialization and proportional retributive punishment of all actors involved are unthinkable in the face of a peacemaking process or to give it sustainability because the possibilities of truth and justice that can be compatible with peace could only arise in conditions of mutual concessions and resignations between the parties.

The issue of merit as a basis for compensation has been deeply questioned when it comes to political crime, in which those who break the law do so by offering society a more just and legitimate model of organization than they affront. Therefore, even if they are defeated and submitted, most of the legal systems contemplate for them the granting of the widest possible amnesty, although humanitarian conscience demands effective accountability processes for those who could be responsible for war crimes or against humanity that satisfies the rights of the victims to truth, justice and reparation to the greatest extent that can be attainable.

18 Duggan, *Prologo.* Entre el perdón y el Paredón: preguntas y dilemas de la justicia transicional, [2005] (pp. vi-xii).

The TC are more likely to succeed when the relative power of the perpetrators has been previously defeated or weakened in the course of transitions (Argentina or Chile). The passage of time, when it weakens the relative power that the perpetrators had, can enable more space for criminal trials. In the initial phases it is the TC who can carry elements to legitimize future justice actions. As long as the perpetrators remain in power, or return to power (Guatemala and Colombia), the effectiveness of the TC is weakened and criminal trials become practically impossible.

Within the framework of transitions that have had to be agreed or negotiated, the total judgements and the universal economic sanctions show more difficult conditions to be applied (Guatemala, El Salvador or Colombia). Here the Truth Commissions seem to show better results comparatively, which appear to be more effective if their mandates are more precise or limited. General or unconditional amnesties or self-amnesties in the case of agents of the State (Argentina or Chile) do not generate appropriate conditions to stimulate those involved to provide truth to the TC. The effectiveness of criminal trials for those responsible, compatible with benefits proportional to the contribution of truth and reparation to victims, are essential for the progress of the mechanisms of clarification with which they must be articulated or tuned.

The commitment of international mechanisms for the protection of human rights (such as the inter-American system, the application of universal jurisdiction or the advancement in the mechanisms of complementarity of the International Criminal Court) are an important factor in contributing to the success of the mandates of the Truth commissions and transitional justice in general. In Colombia, human rights organizations insist on seeking progress in the processing of cases of serious human rights violations perpetrated by state agents in both the IAHCR and the CPI in the hope that they will stimulate the appearance and effective collaboration of the perpetrators before the entities of the system of truth and transitional justice.

There is not a single type of TC, neither do they all have the same functions or chances of success. It is not very feasible then to compare the accomplishments of the different truth commissions without taking into account the contexts in which they should act. Nor is it feasible, omitting references to the context, to establish that criminal trials or TC are the most effective or successful in terms of producing truth or justice.

Neither the TC nor the criminal trials act in a void of political, economic or cultural conditions, but both are more or less viable and may be more or less successful by virtue of the context, but above all if they can act in an articulated manner with each other, and with other mechanisms that facilitate the justice of the transition such as reparation programs for victims, institutional reform measures, the purification of security apparatus and the judicial system, criminal prosecution strategies based on the selection of the maximum responsible and attenuated forms of punishment and even amnesties for those less responsible in articulation with the fulfilment of conditions to contribute to the truth, justice and consolidation of peace and democracy. The success of the TC and the criminal trials reinforce each other when both articulate and condition the benefits of the perpetrators to undergo their procedures.

As a summary and final conclusion of this reflection, it is possible to affirm that in Colombia, the Peace Agreement between the Government and the FARC-EP guerrillas, in addition to social and economic reforms, agreed on a comprehensive system of truth, justice, reparation and guarantees of non-repetition, in which all those responsible for crimes against rights human and International Humanitarian Law should report to three institutions: the Commission for the Clarification of Truth (CEV), the Unit for the Search for Missing Persons (UBPD) and the Special Jurisdiction for Peace (JEP). However, the mobilization of very powerful political and economic sectors of the extreme right wing, linked to perpetration of serious crimes of the past, managed to get the population to vote against the peace agreements in a popular consultation to validate the agreements, and then later won the congressional and presidential elections thus controlling the power, preventing the implementation of the agreements and seeking to reinstate the war strategy. This implies that the perpetrators of the past are those who are in power today, so accountability to the Truth Commission and the JEP has ended up being limited to members of the guerrillas and a few middle-level commanders of the Armed Forces. Therefore, both the CEV and the JEP will have limited effectiveness and to overcome this situation criminal trials in the ordinary criminal justice system against those responsible for state and business crimes need to be carried out. However, in absence of such will, as it seems to be happening, it is required that the mechanisms of international justice to be put into operation (both in the inter-American system of Human Rights and in the International Criminal Court), as well as that other states carry out their collaboration in the fight against impunity by implementing the available mechanisms of universal jurisdiction to meet the demands of Colombian society to end impunity for those most responsible for these crimes.

IV. Final Speech

Past and Future. New Ways of Dealing with Past Conflicts and Past Autocracies Versus Traditional Criminal Prosecution

Memory, Truth and Justice

Prof. Dr. Mónica Pinto[1]

I. Introduction

Massive human rights violations produce painful wounds. In the move from dictatorial to more democratic systems of governance, Memory, Truth and Justice play a special role. They encapsulate what the great majority of the survivors is looking for in order to elaborate on the past and, more importantly, to face a present able of protecting us all from those risks.

Jacques Le Goff quoted by Tzvetan Todorov in *Les abus de la mémoire*[2] holds that "Memory, which both fuels and feeds on history, only strives to serve the past in order to serve the present and the future. Let us endeavour to ensure that collective memory serves human liberation rather than human enslavement."

The phenomenon of human rights, a creation or "invention" of the second half of the 20th century[3], helped in the establishment of criteria and tools to envisage this completely new chapter regarding democratic transitions.

A set of international legal standards has been adopted over time with the aim of preventing the commission of heinous acts. On 9 December 1948, the Convention on the Prevention and Punishment of the Crime of Genocide[4] was adopted under the auspices of the recently established United Nations Organization (UN). It came into force on 12 January 1951 and is now binding for 152 States, which is more than two thirds of the international community of states.

---

1 Professor Emerita, Universidad de Buenos Aires; Member of the Institut de Droit International.
2 Todorov, *Les abus de la mémoire*, Arléa, [1995].
3 Nino, *Etica y Derechos Humanos*, 2ª ed. [1989], p.1.
4 78 UNTS 277.

Three years later, the International Court of Justice (ICJ) referred to the Genocide Convention while dealing with a technical issue related to reservations. In its Advisory Opinion, requested by the UN General Assembly, the Court explained that the principles underlying the Convention are principles which are recognized by civilized nations as binding on States, even without any conventional obligation; and that the Convention was intended to be definitely universal in scope[5]. The intention of the United Nations was to condemn and punish genocide as *a crime under international law* involving a denial of the right of existence of entire human groups, a denial which shocks the conscience of mankind and results in great losses to humanity, and which is contrary to moral law and to the spirit and aims of the United Nations (Resolution 96 (1) of the General Assembly, December 11th 1946)[6].

The (International Court of Justice) Court, which is the principal judicial organ of the United Nations, designed a peremptory norm of general international law, a rule *d'ordre public* or *jus cogens*. In fact, a norm of *jus cogens* is a norm of general international law that is accepted and recognized by the international community of States as a whole as one from which no derogation is permitted.[7] Peremptory norms of general international law protect certain overriding interests and values of the international community. They are recognized as being universally applicable.

In my view, in this Advisory Opinion, the ICJ proposes a moral reading – I am borrowing the notion from Ronald Dworkin's *Freedom's Law: The*

5 *Reservations to the Convention on the Prevention and Punishment of the Crime of Genocide*, Advisory Opinion, 28 May 1951, 1951 ICJ 15, p. 15.

6 *Reservations to the Convention on the Prevention and Punishment of the Crime of Genocide*, Advisory Opinion, 28 May1951, 1951 ICJ 15, p. 23: "The solution of these problems must be found in the special characteristics of the Genocide Convention. The origins and character of that Convention, the objects pursued by the General Assembly and the contracting parties, the relations which exist between the provisions of the Convention, *inter se*, and between those provisions and these objects, furnish elements of interpretation of the will of the General Assembly and the parties. The origins of the Convention show that it was the intention of the United Nations to condemn and punish genocide as 'a crime under international law' involving a denial of the right of existence of entire human groups, a denial which shocks the conscience of mankind and results in great losses to humanity, and which is contrary to moral law and to the spirit and aims of the United Nations (Resolution 96 (I) of the General Assembly, December 11th 1946)."

7 *Vienna Convention on the Law of Treaties*, 23 May 1969, 1155 UNTS 331, in force in general on 27 January 1980, 116 States Parties, article 53.

Moral Reading of American Constitution[8] – of the Charter of the United Nations and of the Genocide Convention itself, which were established in the aftermath of the Holocaust.

When the dictatorships of the 1970s in Latin America reached the maximum threshold of systematic violation of human rights, only a few rules of international human rights law were in force, namely, the Universal Declaration of Human Rights[9], the American Declaration of the Rights and Duties of Man[10] as well as the International Covenants on Civil and Political Rights[11] and on Economic, Social and Cultural Rights[12], which entered into force in January and March 1976. Western Europe had already adopted and put into force the first human rights treaty, the Rome Convention on Human Rights[13].

In the field of procedures, since 1970 it was possible to lodge complaints with the Inter-American Commission on Human Rights (IACHR) regarding violations of rights protected in the American Declaration[14]. At the universal level, the United Nations (UN) adopted a procedure to deal with situations that appear to reveal a consistent pattern of gross and reliable attested violations of human rights in all countries[15]. Victims benefited from these procedures.

Even when in some countries domestic law permitted the prosecution of those responsible for human rights violations when their conduct amounted to an offence, no one ever tried to enforce those rules, neither in Argentina nor in any other Latin American country.

On 10 December 1983, a democratic government took office in Argentina. In the following thirty days, the three branches of government adopted important measures regarding the past: the Executive established an inquiry commission to get to the truth, the Judiciary instituted criminal proceedings against those *prima facie* responsible for massive human rights violations and Parliament repealed the self-amnesty act that had been passed

8 Dworkin, *Freedoms's Law. The Moral Reading of the American Constitution*, [1996], pp. 1–37.

9 A/RES/217(III) of 10 December 1948.

10 Adopted by the Ninth International American Conference Bogotá, Colombia, [1948].

11 999 UNTS 171 y 1057 UNTS 407.

12 993 UNTS 3.

13 213 UNTS 221.

14 O.E.A., *Comisión Interamericana de Derechos Humanos. Diez años de actividades 1971–1981*, Washington, 1982, Statute of the IACHR adopted in 1960, as amended on 24 April 1968, Art. 2, p.41.

15 E/RES/1503(XLVIII) of 27 May 1970.

by the former military government. Given the circumstances, and the advances and retreats of his policy, President Alfonsín's investigation and prosecution of human rights abuses held up miraculously well[16] and set the building blocks for dealing with the past.

The way in which each society decides to settle its accounts with its past is illustrative of its intentions and also of the limitations of each transition. Truth, justice and democracy appear to be the universal goals that every society aims to reach, although each progresses in a different context.

Memory, truth and justice should involve the whole of society. Brazil's experience is telling in this regard. The avant-garde position of Cardinal Arns with *Brasil Nunca Mais*[17] and the time elapsed until Brazil decided to move forward, reveal the problems of dealing with this type of process when the government is not onboard.

In the early 1980s, a panorama of open options led several countries in the region to adjust their transitions to what seemed to be closer to a feasible and more accurate view of each democracy's consolidation. Some governments read their reality as a *unicum* and, in that understanding, they decided the courses of action.

Later on, at the regional level, a series of political and legal decisions marked a single path of transition: to repeal the amnesties, to investigate the facts, to prosecute and to punish those *prima facie* responsible, to make reparations to the victims and to adopt measures of non-repetition.

I will now elaborate on some of these elements and their contribution to memory, truth and justice.

II. Inquiry Commissions

An inquiry commission is set by an official act of government, vested with certain authority, to paint an overall picture of human rights violations which have occurred over a pre-determined period of time in the past, and ceases to exist when its mandate ends, usually with the submission of a report of its findings[18].

Essentially, an inquiry commission is a truth-telling tool; it allows us special access to the truth, to examine the facts, to acknowledge the past, to

16 Nino, *Radical Evil on Trial*, [1996], p.186.

17 *Brasil, Nunca Mais*, [1991].

18 Hayner, *Fifteen Truth Commissions – 1974 to 1994: A Comparative Study*, [1994], p.227 – 228.

achieve a precise accounting of the past. An inquiry commission offers an official acknowledgement of long-silenced facts. As Juan Méndez wrote, "knowledge that is officially sanctioned, and thereby made part of the public cognitive scene ... acquires a mysterious quality that is not there when it is merely 'truth'. Official acknowledgement at least begins to heal the wounds"[19]

A honest account of violence prevents history from being lost, prevents a rewriting of history and allows society to learn from its past. It builds up historical memory. It doesn't always seem to happen, but it's worth the effort.

A witness before the Guatemalan Historical Clarification Commission pointed out "that the history we suffered should be taught in schools, it should not be forgotten, so that our children become aware of it".[20]

The Inter-American Court of Human Rights (I/A Court HR) has pointed out at various times that truth commissions contribute to the construction and preservation of historical memory, the clarification of the facts, and the determination of institutional, social, and political responsibilities but that they do not replace the State's obligation to ensure the judicial determination of individual and State responsibilities. They both involve determinations of the truth that complement each other, because each has its own meaning and scope, as well as particular potentials and constraints[21].

III. The trials

The existence of a positive international law obligation to prosecute those *prima facie* responsible for human rights violations cannot be traced back

19 Hayner, *Unspeakable Truths: Confronting State Terror and Atrocity*, [2001], p.26.

20 *Guatemala Memoria del Silencio, Report of the Comisión de Esclarecimiento Histórico*, volume I, UNOPS, June 1999, p.13.

21 Inter-American Court of Human Rights, *Case Zambrano Vélez y others vs. Ecuador.* Merits, Reparations and Costs. Judgment of 4 July 2007. Series C N° 166, # 128. [This dictum is repeated in the following pronouncements, among others: Inter-American Court of Human Rights, *Case Contreras y others vs. El Salvador.* Merits, Reparations and Costs. Judgment of 31 August 2011. Series C N° 232, # 135; *Case Masacres of El Mozote and surrounding area vs. El Salvador.* Merits, Reparations and Costs. Judgment of 25 October 2012 Series C N° 252, # 298; *Case Gudiel Álvarez (Diario Militar) vs. Guatemala.* Merits, Reparations and Costs. Judgment of 20 November 2012 Series C N° 253, # 298; *Case García and relatives vs. Guatemala.* Merits, Reparations and Costs. Judgment of 29 November 2012 Series C N° 258, # 176].

before 1992, when the IACHR decided the cases of Argentina and Uruguay,[22]. The IACHR found that measures adopted by both governments had denied the victims their right to obtain a judicial investigation in a court of criminal law to determine those responsible for the crimes committed and punish them accordingly.

Early in the 1990s, Diane Orentlicher and Carlos Santiago Nino debated on the eventual obligation of emergent democracies to prosecute former dictators for crimes against humanity.

Orentlicher submitted that the central importance of the rule of law in civilized societies requires, within defined but principled limits, prosecution of especially atrocious crimes. She argued that international law itself helps assure the survival of fragile democracies when its clear pronouncement removes certain atrocious crimes from the provincial realm of a country's internal politics and thereby places those crimes squarely within the scope of universal concern and the conscience of all civilized people. She contended that recently developed principles of international law, both customary and conventional, already impose significant obligations in this regard. She explained that even when neither the International Covenant on Civil and Political Rights, the American Convention nor the European Convention on Human Rights explicitly require States Parties to prosecute violations, they are nonetheless obligated to investigate allegations of torture, extra- legal killings, and forced disappearances, and, subject to evidentiary and other legitimate constraints, to prosecute those who are responsible. A state's complete failure to punish repeated or notorious instances of these offences violates its obligations under customary international law. The measures used to secure human rights are no longer subject to the broad discretion of governments when it comes to a core set of fundamental rights that merit special protection. When torture, disappearances, and illegal killings occur, governments must act in good-faith to bring wrongdoers to justice[23].

Her argument is strictly legal, she plays with time: facts occurred by the mid-1980s and she elaborated some years later but in the meantime international human rights law had quickly evolved. However, in the 1980s the

---

22 Annual Report of the Inter-American Commission of Human Rights 1992–1993, Report 28/92, Argentina, Cases 10.147, 10.181, 10.240, 10.262, 10.309, 10.311, OEA/Ser.L/V/II.83, Doc.14. Annual report of the Inter-American Commission of Human Rights 1992–1993, Report 29/92, Uruguay, Cases 10.029, 10.036,10.145, 10.305, 10.372, 10.373, 10.374, 10.375, OEA/Ser.L/V/II.83, Doc.14.

23 Orentlicher "*Settling Accounts: The Duty to Prosecute Human Rights Violations of a Prior Regime*", 100 *The Yale Law Journal*, 1991, 2537–2615.

duty to prosecute was *de lege ferenda*. Only the Convention on Genocide was in force. The Convention against Torture entered into force in 1987[24]; furthermore, the Committee against Torture declared inadmissible *ratione temporis* claims regarding Argentina.[25] The I/A Court HR decided the Velasquez Rodriguez case[26] in 1988 and explained with detail State's obligations under a human rights treaty.

Nino rejected the duty to punish perpetrators of radical evil and argued instead for a more forward-looking duty, to safeguard democracy. He believed that this is what ultimately justified the Argentine trials and should be the focus of any international action[27].

It is clear that Orentlicher is talking about international law *tout court* while Nino seems to be concerned with what would become transitional justice. At that time, it was accepted that there was no universal formula applicable to all transitions but the state of the art evolved quickly.

The establishment of the *ad hoc* criminal tribunals for former Yugoslavia[28] and for Rwanda[29] and later the adoption of the Rome Statute for the International Criminal Court (ICC)[30] conveyed the message that certain serious crimes should not go unpunished.

The Rome Statute provides for the ICC's jurisdiction over persons for the most serious crimes of international concern; this jurisdiction is complementary to national criminal jurisdictions. In so doing, it contributed to set as a legal standard that States have an obligation to exercise their jurisdiction over those crimes. When the Rome Statute entered into force in

---

24 *Convention Against Torture and Other Cruel, Inhuman or Degrading Treatment or Punishment,* New York, 10 December 1984, 1465 UNTS 85, in force in general on 26 June 1987, binding for 169 States.

25 Renée Epelbaum reached the Committee against Torture for her sons Luis, Claudio and Lila. Her presentations were declared inadmissible because the events took place before the entry into force of the Convention against torture in Argentina.

26 This is the first ruling of the Inter-American Court of Human Rights. The case dealt with an enforced disappearance and the Inter-American Court of Human Rights clarified the obligations of States in the light of the Convention. Inter-American Court of Human Rights, *Velásquez Rodríguez Case*, Judgment of 26 July 1988, Series C N° 4, #181.

27 Nino, *"The Duty to Punish Past Abuses of Human Rights Put Into Context: The Case of Argentina"*, 100 The Yale Law Journal, 1991, 2619–2643. See also Carlos Santiago Nino, *Radical Evil on Trial*, [1996].

28 S/RES/808(1993) of 22 February 1993.

29 S/RES/955(1994) of 8 November 1994.

30 2187 UNTS 3.

2002, the regional inter-American rule became universal. The objective of saying "Basta!" to impunity is clear.

All these important events were manifestations of sensitive changes in international law. In fact, in traditional international law society, the prevalent model was the horizontal Westphalian society where liberty was the criterion for the establishment of jurisdiction[31], notwithstanding the fact that the majority of States chose more or less similar criteria in their domestic legislation: the territoriality and nationality principles, among others. Only when collective interests were at stake, any and all could exercise jurisdiction in areas outside national jurisdiction, as it used to be in cases of piracy.

Since the mid-20th century, the model of international society is vertical because, *inter alia*, there is a consolidated notion of public order. The prohibition of genocide as suggested by the ICJ in its Advisory Opinion of 1951; its *dictum* of 1970 regarding "the obligations of a State towards the international community as a whole, ... [which] by their very nature ... are the concern of al1 States. In view of the importance of the rights involved, al1 States can be held to have a legal interest in their protection; they have obligations *erga omnes*. Such obligations derive, for example, in contemporary international law, from the outlawing of acts of aggression, and of genocide, as also from the principles and rules concerning the basic rights of the human person, including protection from slavery and racial discrimination. Some of the corresponding rights of protection have entered into the body of general international law (Reservations to the Convention on the Prevention and Punishment of the Crime of Genocide, Advisory Opinion, I.C.J. Reports 1951, p. 23); others are conferred by international instruments of a universal or quasi-universal character"[32].

The notion of human rights plays a central role in the establishment of the duty to prosecute because all States have an interest in ensuring that these rights are respected. In this sense, the decision of the British House of Lords of 24 March of 1999 to allow the appeal in the file for extradition of General Pinochet to the Audiencia Nacional de España, made clear that a former Head of State is not entitled to immunity from arrest and extradition proceedings in respect of acts alleged to have been committed while

31 *The Case of the S:S. Lotus*, PCIJ Series A No.10, 17 September 1927, p.18 «... Now the first and foremost restriction imposed by international law upon a State is that -failing the existence of a permissive rule to the contrary- it may not exercise its power in any form in the territory of another State.».

32 *Case Concerning the Barcelona Traction, Light & Power Co., Ltd.*, Belgium v Spain, Second Phase, 5/02/1970, 1970 ICJ §. 33–34.

he was Head of State, in the given case the acts of torture were against Chilean nationals[33]. As Christine Chinkin pointed out, "it is now possible to talk of the global enforcement of human rights".[34] Basically it was the confirmation that the consequences of and jurisdiction over serious human rights violations are not limited to the State where they occur or that of the nationality of a majority of the victims. There is an international interest to stop impunity of those more serious crimes of international concern.

As evoked before, the Inter-American Human Rights System (IASHR) provided its own regulation, a regional norm that imposed the duty to prosecute, on the grounds of the decisions taken in reports 28 and 29/92 regarding the cases of Argentina and Uruguay. Later, in 2001, the judgement of the I/A Court HR in the *Barrios Altos case*[35] declared that any legislation granting amnesty or pardon, making room for the statute of limitations or providing an exclusion of responsibility of persons *prima facie* responsible for human rights violations such as torture, extrajudicial executions and enforced disappearances is incompatible with the American Convention on Human Rights. It found those provisions inadmissible and prohibited by international human rights law.

In Argentina, in the *Simón case*[36], a federal judge at first instance decided along the same lines, few days before *Barrios Altos* decision regarding due obedience defences; in 2003, his ruling was confirmed by the Federal Chamber of Appeals and in 2005 by the Supreme Court of Justice[37]. The cases were resumed.

33 House of Lords, *Regina v. Bartle and the Commissioner of Police for the Metropolis and others EX Parte Pinochet (Respondent) (On appeal from a Divisional Court of the Queen's Bench Division); Regina v. Evans and another and the Commissioner of Police for the Metropolis and others (Appellant) EX Parte Pinochet* (Respondent). (On appeal from a Divisional Court of the Queen's Bench Division), Judgment of 25 November 1998; 37 ILM (1998) 1302 (hereinafter Ex Parte Pinochet (HL1)) Lord Lloyd.

34 Chinkin, "*UK House of Lords: Regina v. Bow Street Stipendiary Magistrate, ex parte Pinocher Ugarte. Spanish Request for Extradition*", 93 *American Journal of International Law*, [1999], 703–711.

35 Inter-American Court of Human Rights, *Barrios Altos Case (Chumbipuna Aguirre and others vs. Perú,* Judgment of 14 March 2001, Series C N°75.

36 Argentina, Causa Nro. 8686/2000, "*Simón, Julio, Del Cerro, Juan Antonio s/sustracción de menores de 10 años*" from the registry of the Secretariat No. 7 of the Federal Criminal and Correctional Court No. 4; Judgment of 6 March 2001.

37 Argentina, Supreme Court of Justice of the Nation, Appeal deduced by the defense of Julio Héctor Simon on the cause "*Simón, Julio Héctor s/ privación ilegítima*

The I/A Court HR referred to this obligation in several judgements summarized in the *Gelman case*: "This Court has emphasized the importance of the State's duty to investigate and punish human rights violations, obligation to investigate and, where appropriate, prosecute and punish, is particularly important given the seriousness of the crimes committed and the nature of the infringed rights, particularly because the prohibition of enforced disappearance and its corresponding obligation to investigate and punish those responsible has reached *jus cogens* nature "[38].

In the 21st century vertical model of international society, three different jurisdictions are available to deal with the most serious international crimes: national, foreign and international jurisdictions.

National and foreign jurisdictions are provided for in national legislation and are usually governed by traditional criteria whereas international jurisdiction works on the grounds of binding decisions, as in the case of Security Council decisions under Chapter VII of the UN Charter- Action with Respect to the Peace, Breaches of the Peace, and Acts of Aggression – regarding the *ad hoc* criminal courts, or of an international treaty in force, like the Rome Statute for the ICC.

Universal jurisdiction, which is a form of foreign jurisdiction, seems to have no customary basis, according to the 2002 ICJ judgment in the case of the *Arrest warrant*[39] and the decision of the British House of Lords regarding Pinochet.

International jurisdiction pursues the objective of limiting impunity of the most serious crimes of international concern. It is an exercise of retributive justice in the light of the jurisprudence of the Permanent Court of International Justice in the case of the *Chorzow Factory*[40] in the absence of activity by the involved States. It has the legitimacy of consensus. It takes place in an international, restricted area, far from the society in which the events occurred. It *speaks* a foreign language, although the victims and their representatives are present and have interpreters. International jurisdiction was effective in the context of the Genocide in Rwanda,

de la libertad etc., N°17.768", S 1767 L.XXXVIII, sentence of 14 June 2005 (Opinion of the Attorney General of 5 May 2005).

38 Inter-American Court of Human Rights, *Gelman Vs. Uruguay*. Merits and Reparations. Judgment of 24 February 2011, Serie C No. 221, para. 183.

39 *Case Concerning the Arrest Warrant of 11 April 2000* (Democratic Republic of Congo v Belgium), Judgment of 14 February 2002, ICJ Reports 2002,3.

40 *Case Concerning the Factory at Chorzów*, Merits, Judgment of 13 September 1928, PCIJ, Series A No.17,p.4.

in that of the ethnic cleansing in former Yugoslavia, and in several other trials in which national and international judges worked in mixed courts.

Foreign or universal jurisdiction suffers from the disadvantage of the horizontal notion of the international world of States. It has no choice but to be selective and unequal. In 1996, the *Tribunal de la Grande Instance de Paris* declared in the *Javor case*, that general international law is not explicit in the area of jurisdiction over crimes against humanity and based its decision on the Convention against Torture of 1984. The *Cour d'appel* and the *Cour de cassation* revoked that ruling on the grounds that the Convention was not self-executing. The same situation was repeated in the *Munyeshyaka case* in 1998. In both cases, the requested persons were in France[41].

The Belgian law establishing the universal jurisdiction of its tribunals opened the door to cases from all corners of the world: the case of Hissène Abré, the Chadian dictator convicted of crimes against humanity in Senegal, the cases of the Mayan genocide in Guatemala, complaints against leaders in China, Israel and against the George W. Bush. All of these cases overloaded the courts' dockets and led the Belgian Parliament to limit its capabilities in this regard.

National jurisdiction permits prosecution and also makes room for the social construction of truth. It contributes to the knowledge of truth. A partial truth, a legal truth, a truth supported by evidence on file. A truth that is complementary to that which arises from the commissions of inquiry. It is also an evolving truth, because, for example, in recent years it made room for a gender approach, the notion of violation of human rights of women, crimes committed against women only because they are women.[42]

Legal authorities challenged the decision of the IASHR to reduce all transitions to a single model: the obligation to investigate, to prosecute and to convict all those responsible for crimes against humanity and to award reparations to the victims. The objection does not lie in the content of the obligation, which is practically the normal operation of the law, but

41 In re *Javor*. 1996 Bull, crim., No. 132, at 379. French Cour de cassation, Criminal Chamber, March 26, 1996.
In re *Munyeshyaka*. 1998 Bull, crim., No. 2, at 3. French Cour de cassation, Criminal Chamber, January 6, 1998., 93 *AJIL*, 1999, 525.

42 This begins with the case followed against Gregorio Rafael Molina, Case No. 2086 and 2277, by the Mar del Plata TOF in June 2010.

in its compulsory nature and in the probable consequences for the transition itself as Roberto Gargarella points out.[43]

Certainly, each transition context has its own features; and the way in which each of them handles truth, justice and democracy is different as well. It may be questionable whether all transitions should be treated with a universal recipe but it may also be questionable to entrust bodies such as the IACHR or the I/A Court HR to legally and politically assess the contexts to determine whether certain transition measures could have been enforced because the democratic level of the society allowed them and *vice versa*. Human rights bodies are not competent for such decisions.

We should be fair and acknowledge that the universal recipe of the IASHR has led many Latin American States to devise different ways of complying with it. Moreover, it became a useful tool for sectors of society and those governments that wanted to go further because they felt supported.

On the other hand, whenever society and government do not agree to deal with the past in order to seek the truth, to create memory and to establish justice, democracy is fragile. The present, unfortunately, provides examples.

IV. The right to the truth

Both inquiry commissions and judicial proceedings regarding human rights violations in the past have contributed to the establishment of a right to the truth to which the whole society is entitled.

In 2006, the United Nations High Commissioner for Human Rights, Louise Arbour, proposed to the Commission to recognize the right to the truth as an *inalienable and autonomous* right, which *should be considered as a non-derogable right and not be subject to limitations. The right to the truth implies knowing the full and complete truth as to the events that transpired, their specific circumstances, and who participated in them, including knowing the circumstances in which the violations took place, as well as the reasons for them.* She presented a study on the right to the truth, as requested by Argentina[44], which reaffirms the existence of this right, dispersed in the UN ju-

43 Gargarella, "No place for popular sovereignty. Democracy, rights and punishment in the case Gelman", available https://digitalcommons.law.yale.edu/cgi/viewcontent.cgi?article=1124&context=yls_sela.

44 *Study on the Right to the Truth.* Report of the Office of the United Nations High Commissioner for Human Rights. UN Doc. E/CN.4/2006/91.

risprudence, as reflected in both the Convention against Enforced Disappearance adopted in 2006 by the Human Rights Council of United Nations, as well as in the Organization of American States' practice. On December 21, 2010, the UN General Assembly proclaimed by A/RES/65/196 March 24 as International Day for the Right to Truth with regard to Gross Violations of Human Rights and Dignity of Victims and also commemorates the day of the murder of Monsignor Romero, the Archbishop of El Salvador.

In the mid-1990s, when in Argentina there was no legal possibility of prosecuting and convicting crimes of the past, human rights organizations and the relatives of the victims brought their request to know the fate of victims to the judiciary. They rooted their demand in the existence of a right to know the truth. Judges generally accepted the demands and received various testimonies, which contributed to the construction of the truth. Even some of the wrongdoers declared, persuaded that they had no pending accounts with the society. Fortunately, that was wrong and some of their statements in those trials contributed later as evidence in different proceedings, for instance, to the conviction of Miguel Etchecolatz issued on September 19, 2006[45].

The construction of the truth of what happened found an unprecedented possibility in court. That was possible because the local community was aware of the existence of a criminal plan of repression enforced by state agents, because the judges of the Constitution conducted investigations, because the relatives of the victims never gave up demanding truth and justice, because the NGOs did not stop contributing to the consolidation of democracy and because the Argentine people deserves a better future.

In the case of Argentina, truth first appeared in global terms but it did not make progress in specific terms. Notwithstanding the significant number of cases, still open, already completed or in progress and the efforts made by civil society to keep them active as well as by state powers so that they can continue, justice is done but the truth only advances with the testimony of the victims. No perpetrator felt the need or saw the possibility of giving information. Is it because they were not offered any advantage in the conviction or in the enforcement of the judgement? In any case, the Mothers and Grandmothers of the Plaza de Mayo, as all of us, are getting older and have an obvious desire not to pass away without knowing what

---

45 I dealt with that in: «*Los juicios de la verdad en Argentina*», 42 *Hechos del Callejón*, December 2008, PNUD-Colombia, 17–19.

happened to their children and grandchildren. Sadly, we are still not able to answer all of their questions.

V. Conclusion

Certainly, the last quarter of the 20th century drafted a new chapter regarding how democratic governments should settle their accounts with the recent past. Policy guidelines were adopted and legal rules designed to know what happened, to achieve justice and to strengthen the newly installed democracy. However, every political community and each government gave its reading to these purposes and awarded different levels of importance in accordance with their common interests.

In 1983, Argentina's recovered democracy took off with these policies and became bound by human rights treaties. The *Never Again Report* by the National Commission on the Disappearance of Persons (CONADEP) and the Federal Criminal Court of Appeals' judgement of 9 December 1985 in the Trial of the *Juntas* shed light on human rights violations during the military government. The political situation in the country deteriorated and legislation was passed to close all criminal proceedings regarding the near past. In 1992 the Inter-American System contributed to the development of a regional standard on the obligation to prosecute and to convict, which became universal with the entry into force of the Rome Statute of the International Criminal Court. In 2001, the Argentine judiciary resumed its files.

William Schabas rightly argues that "A priori, it would be best to institute proceedings before the national courts of the State where the crimes were committed. Criminal law has an important declaratory function, which is better fulfilled when the process takes place at the scene of the crime. The public can attend the deliberations, or at least, participates through the local media. Witnesses are more easily available, judges and juries are well aware of the context of violation of human rights and the judgement is better suited to a sanction according to the values prevailing in the country[46]. The Argentine case is paradigmatic in this sense.

46 Schabas, "Réconciliation nationale et poursuites pénales: comment résoudre cette equation dans le respect des droits fondamentaux et de la démocratie?», *Campagne contre l'impunité: portrait et plan d'action. Essais sur les droits humains et le développement démocratique*. [1997], 237–270.